TRAVELLER EDUCATION SERVICE
SOUTH GLAMORGAN
GREENWAY SCHOOL
LLANSTEPHAN ROAD, RUMNEY   TEL 792211

Belfast Studies in Language, Culture and Politics

General Editors
John M. Kirk and Dónall P. Ó Baoill

Other volumes in preparation

www.bslcp.com

Travellers and their Language

Edited by

John M. Kirk and Dónall P. Ó Baoill

Cló Ollscoil na Banríona
Belfast 2002

First published in 2002
Cló Ollscoil na Banríona
Queen's University Belfast
Belfast, BT7 1NN

Belfast Studies in Language, Culture and Politics 4
www.bslcp.com

The publishers gratefully acknowledge the support from the Cultural Diversity
Programme of the Community Relations Council, which aims to encourage
acceptance and understanding of cultural diversity, and from the Equality and Social
Need Division of the Office of the First Minister and Deputy First Minister, Northern
Ireland Executive, which the production of this book has received.

Cover photograph of Traveller as Tinsmith or Tinker by Derek Speirs, reproduced
with kind permission.

British Library Cataloguing-in-Publication Data
A catalogue record for this book is available from the British Library.

ISBN 0 85389 832 4

Typeset by John Kirk in New Times Roman

Printed by Optech, Belfast

Some of the papers in this volume were presented at a Symposium
on Travellers' Language held on 15 August 2000 as part of
Dialect2000: *Language Links*
an International Conference
on the Languages of Scotland and Ireland
9–16 August 2000
Queen's University Belfast
an event of the Irish-Scottish Academic Initiative

CONTENTS

Part 1: New Studies on Travellers and their Language

Part 2: Travellers on Travellers' Language Transcripts and Responses

CONTRIBUTORS

Dr Alice Binchy is a refugee resource worker at the West Tallaght Resource Centre, Dublin and author of a University of Oxford Ph.D. thesis entitled "The Status and Functions of Shelta".

Marian Browne works at the Department of Education and Science in the area of Traveller Education and is currently a doctoral research student at University College Dublin working on Cant syntax.

Mary Burke is a doctoral research student at Queen's University Belfast working on literary representations of Travellers.

Dr Sheila Douglas is one of Scotland's most accomplished traditional singers. A former teacher of English at Perth Academy and currently Tutor in Scots and Folklore at the Royal Scottish Academy of Music and Drama, Glasgow, she completed a University of Stirling Ph.D. thesis on Scottish Traveller folk narratives.

Dr Ricca Edmondson is Lecturer in Sociology at the National University of Ireland, Galway.

Gavin Falconer is a doctoral research student at Queen's University Belfast working on Scots.

Dr John M. Kirk is Senior Lecturer in English at Queen's University Belfast and has published widely on linguistic topics pertaining to Scotland and Ireland.

Ellen McDonagh is an Irish Traveller who lives in Navan.

Sinéad ní Shuinéar is an anthropologist specialising in Traveller issues, currently completing a doctorate on Travellers for the University of Greenwich.

Dr Dónall P. Ó Baoill is Professor of Irish at Queen's University Belfast and has published on all aspects of language pertaining to Ireland, including Travellers' language.

Mícheál Ó hAodha has an M.A. in Irish from the National University of Ireland, Galway. He is a librarian working in Limerick, who also works as a literacy tutor and part-time development worker with Limerick Traveller Development Group and the Travelling community.

Níall Ó Murchadha is a retired primary school headmaster from Co. Galway who has made extensive recordings of Traveller speech not just in Ireland and Scotland but worldwide.

Jimmy Power is an Irish Traveller who lives in Navan.

Len Smith is an English Traveller who lives in the New Forest, England, and is Secretary General of the European Committee on Romani Emancipation (ECRE).

Sheila Stewart is a Scottish Traveller who lives in Blairgowrie and is one of Scotland's finest traditional singers and storytellers.

Richard J. Waters is an Irish-American Traveller who lives in New Jersey.

The anonymous contributor is a Gammon-speaking Irish Traveller who may be contacted through the Editors.

ACKNOWLEDGEMENTS

We are grateful to the many people who willingly helped with the preparation of, or participated in, the original symposium on Travellers' language in 2000, or who have kindly answered our queries or assisted during the preparation of this volume over a long and at times rather fraught period. Further details are provided in the Introduction to Part 2.

The Editors are grateful to Derek Speirs for permission to use his photograph of Tinkers which appears on the front cover, to the Belfast Travellers Support Group for permission to reproduce the photograph of Michael Mongan which appears on p. 151, and to John Doherty, Nigel Craig and Colin Young of Optech for their help with these reproductions and the production of the volume.

For financial support for the publication of this volume, the Editors wish gratefully to acknowledge the Cultural Diversity Programme of the Northern Ireland Community Relations Council and the Equality and Social Need Division of the Office of the First Minister and Deputy First Minister, Northern Ireland Executive.

In particular, we wish to acknowledge their indebtedness to Margaret McNulty and Brian Walker whose initial encouragement and advice confirmed our desire for this publication, to Sinéad ní Shuinéar for her many constructive suggestions with regard to the content of this volume and for her practical help at every stage, to Mary Burke for her valuable comments on an early draft of the entire text, to Hilary Bell and especially to Gavin Falconer for assistance with the production of the volume and their many constructive editorial comments, and to Maire Ó Baoill and Colin Neilands for their constant support and affection.

John M. Kirk and Dónall P. Ó Baoill
Belfast, November 2002

Introduction: Travellers and their Language

John M. Kirk and Dónall P. Ó Baoill

The ultimate context for this volume arose form the growing political desire at the millennium for rapprochement and reappraisal of the relationships between Ireland and Scotland. The peace process in Northern Ireland, which culminated in the Belfast Agreement signed on Good Friday 1998, had come to recognise that the East-West relationship was as important as that North-South, that in Northern Ireland Scottish identity based on immigrant ancestry was as important as Irish identity, and that each relationship was culturally underpinned through language: Irish Gaelic and Scots. In academia, these political developments were being paralleled through the establishment of the Irish-Scottish Academic Initiative, involving the Universities of Aberdeen and Strathclyde as well as Trinity College Dublin and Queen's University Belfast, and being led through the University of Aberdeen's Research Institute for Irish and Scottish Studies, which in 2001 begot an Arts and Humanities Research Board Research Centre for Irish and Scottish Studies. Scottish-Irish academic links were not entirely new, for since the early 1980s, for instance, there has existed a Forum for Research on the Languages of Scotland and Ulster. It was on behalf of the Forum that we originally undertook to organize its Sixth Triennial International Conference on the Languages of Scotland and Ulster at Queen's University Belfast from 9-16 August 2000, which came, in turn, to be recognized as an official event of the Irish-Scottish Academic Initiative, and which became known as the **Dialect2000: *Language Links*** Conference.

As we began to plan the conference programme in this wider developing context, the issue of Traveller language began to emerge as a theme which embraced many of the current political and linguistic tensions in both Ireland and Scotland. In countries, many Travellers refer to their language as "Cant", yet in Scotland Cant is a form of Scots whereas in Ireland Cant is a form of Irish, neatly subverting the relationship of opposites between Irish and Scots upon which the new political order has primarily focused its language policy. Scottish Travellers possess a rich and varying mythology about their ancestry, believing that they were the original inhabitants of the place, that they are descendants of royalty, and that the land belongs to them. Kings and queens regularly feature in the traditional ballads and songs which Scottish Travellers sing. On the other hand, historical evidence clearly suggests that Travellers have never been favoured socially nor accepted as equals or understood by the rest of society. With the passing of the Race Relations Order (1997), Northern Ireland became the first jurisdiction to recognise Irish Traveller ethnicity and to offer them protection from discrimination. The Republic of Ireland followed suit with the Employment Equality Act (1998) and the Equal Status Act (2000), and, in 2000, Great Britain amended the Race Relations Act to include Irish Travellers. Despite these legislative developments, the issues surrounding Traveller ethnicity may remain controversial if not proven, or if denied by Travellers themselves, and some further refinements in the definition may be necessary.

As Travellers' affairs become more politicised and appear in the public eye, society has become more tolerant, interested and responsible about the Traveller community, placing particular emphasis on the provision of a sound basic education for all Travellers as well as instruction for teachers, health workers and all those others who come into close contact with Traveller language. In such contact situations, it is to be expected that educationalists, linguists and sociolinguists will begin to study and analyse the linguistic behaviour of Travellers vis-à-vis the so-called "settled community" with whom they interact daily. Travellers' use of language impinges to such an extent on their success within the educational system that the need for effective communicative interaction cannot possibly be ignored. Description of current Traveller language is the first step on the road to understanding and tolerance of its use and the link to successful participation on an equal footing in interactive social communication with the rest of society.

It is very obvious, from a perusal of the papers published in this volume, that a great deal of linguistic research still needs to be done to demonstrate in an unambiguous way what constitutes linguistic competence among the many and varied linguistic repertoires found in the speech of Travellers in both Ireland and Scotland. As shown by Mícheál Ó hAodha and Sheila Douglas in this volume, it is highly probable that Travellers in both Ireland and Scotland, and perhaps elsewhere, spoke Irish or Scottish Gaelic as their mother tongue. In due course, as the sociolinguistic situation changed in both countries over time, Travellers adjusted to the new linguistic situation, passing through an unstable bilingual stage and eventually evolving more and more towards a monolingual English-speaking community, heavily influenced by the Irish or Scottish Gaelic substratum. Marian Browne's research on Hiberno-English syntax as well as the wordlist compiled by Sheila Douglas and analysed by John Kirk and Gavin Falconer show clearly that the common language of most Travellers is a "broad" variety of either rural Hiberno-English or rural Scots. We can reasonably conclude that these Irish and Scottish varieties of Cant reflect local dialect usage as the superstrate but contain substratal Irish or Gaelic borrowing as well as retentions from Romany, and that these substratal influences have likely affected all linguistic levels – phonological, morphological, syntactic as well as lexical.

The general variety of Traveller language used in Ireland and Scotland is referred to by different labels and names. The most common name is *Cant,* but in Ireland it is also known among native-speakers as *Gammon* or among scholars as *Shelta.* The traditional belief is that all varieties have been shaped by extensive historical lexical borrowing from Irish and/or Scottish Gaelic. This borrowed vocabulary has been adapted and changed according to well-formed linguistic rules common to many so-called "secret languages". Secretion processes are phonological and include syllable inversion, phonological substitution, addition of initial consonant clusters etc. These changes have been discussed by different commentators over the years, beginning with Macalister (1937), and reiterated to various degrees in this volume in Ó hAodha's and Douglas's contributions. Their origin and use, however, has not gone unchallenged as shown by the contribution by Binchy and ní Shuinéar, as well as those given by all four Irish Travellers, Ellen McDonagh (referred to in the transcripts as Nell), Jimmy Power, Richard J. Waters and the anonymous Traveller.

We are extremely pleased that the publication of the present volume has opened up the debate about the origin and formation of Cant and subjected it to fresh and critical reappraisal. Such reappraisal must, however, be based on sound linguistic principles, backed up by genuinely phonetically transcribed Cant data. It must also show an equally confident understanding of the linguistic features of all "contact" languages and dialects. We are confident that the challenges presented by the arguments outlined in many of the papers included in this volume will be taken up in the near future by linguists and sociolinguists familiar with the contact languages and dialects which have contributed to the formation of the Cant as we know it today. This is a prerequisite to healthy and informed objective debate about the origins and development of this important variety of language, which forms an integral part of Traveller identity.

In their contributions, Ellen McDonagh and Jimmy Power report that Cant and Gammon are two variants of the same language spoken by Irish Travellers. The relationship of one or both varieties to Scottish Traveller language has never been investigated, despite the shared name Cant, which has been shown to derive from a simple anglicisation of *caint* 'talk' or 'speech'. A shared name does not always imply that they are one and the same but, considering the sociolinguistic environments in which the Cant varieties have flourished and continue to flourish, there is a need for closer linguistic investigation before the majority dialect/language takes over in those domains which have hitherto been the preserve of Cant. Power shows that he did not feel threatened by the word list presented by Sheila Douglas in her contribution because there was little overlap between it and his Irish Cant.

Our original aspiration had been the exploration of common themes within the framework of the symposium held on 15 August 2000. Although it proved difficult to find speakers willing to talk about Travellers in both countries, the discussion certainly established many links and comparisons. For that reason alone, the transcripts of the ensuing discussions are worth publishing, as they signal possible fruitful lines of exploration in the future. Besides, Travellers have been a conference focus for anthropologists, ethnologists and folklorists (e.g. McCann et al. 1994, Acton and Mundy 1997) but, to our knowledge, their language has never been the sole focus of a symposium for linguists – certainly not in Ireland and Scotland.

The symposium succeeded in bringing together not only interested academics from all over the world who were participating in the overall conference, but also local Traveller welfare and support activists and especially Irish Travellers

themselves who are speakers of Cant. Although it was not unprecedented that
Travellers should agree to participate in an academic event which was essentially
about them, it was unprecedented that they should talk about their language – all the
more pleasing for us in pursuit of our original aims.[1]

The present volume builds on the symposium in two ways. It reproduces revised
versions of each of the five academic papers which were presented that day in the
following order: Mary Burke, Sheila Douglas, Mícheál Ó hAodha, Alice Binchy, and
Sinéad ní Shuinéar, and also, as a transcript, the discussion following the papers by
Binchy and ní Shuinéar, reflecting the international composition and interests of the
participants.[2] At the same time, it reproduces as transcripts the spontaneous and
unscripted presentations made that day by Ellen and Jimmy and the ensuing
discussion. In addition, the volume extends the symposium by including three new
commissioned scholarly papers: by Marian Browne, Ricca Edmondson and Níall Ó
Murchadha, and a second contribution by Mícheál Ó hAodha, thus rounding out and
enriching our understanding of Traveller language both in Ireland and elsewhere.
What is more, it extends the section of Traveller presentations by adding two further
commissioned presentations, by Richard J. Waters and Sheila Stewart, each with a
response to tape-recordings and transcripts of the original symposium session
presented by Ellen and Jimmy. The set is completed by a personal written statement
by Len Smith, an English Romanichal Traveller. As a result, the second part of the
volume contains a set of six unprecedented and unique statements by Travellers on
the use of their language, its nature and characteristics, and their attitudes to it.
Academic papers can readily find publication outlets, but the publication of
transcripts of personal experience is rare. We are privileged to have earned the
respect and trust of Ellen McDonagh, Jimmy Power, Richard J. Waters, Sheila
Stewart, Len Smith and the anonymous Traveller which have let us proceed.

---

[1] As organizers, we are deeply grateful to Ellen McDonagh and Jimmy Power for
their participation and feel gratified that we created a sensitive and respectful context
which made them feel that they could participate. We are also just as indebted to
Michael McDonagh and Sally Flynn who had originally accepted the invitation, but
who were later prevented from attending.

[2] In this connection, we wish to point out that we had not set out to record the
symposium; serendipitously, one participant, Eliza Schneider of the Henry Higgins
Foundation, made her own recording, but only began with Alice Binchy's paper.
Had it not been for Eliza's presence with her hi-tech tape recorder and the pure luck
that she taped anything at all, these discussions, as well as Ellen McDonagh's and
Jimmy Power's spontaneous presentations and the ensuing discussions would have
been lost forever. With hindsight, we regret that so much of the earlier debate was
lost, for what was not recorded was just as fascinating and relevant as that which was.

Each of the academic papers takes a fresh critical eye over the existing scholarly literature, particularly that of Shelta, from its inception through Leland's earliest study of 1880 and 1882 to the culmination of several scholars' work in Macalister's magnum opus of 1937. The juxtaposition of this criticism is very stimulating, and the academic deconstruction of Macalister becomes even more strongly reinforced by Ellen and Jimmy and especially Richard. Caution, however, is needed in any efforts to debunk Macalister's contribution to the debate. It is certain that he may have overstepped the mark at times in his efforts to find Irish-language "cognates" for Cant words. Nevertheless, much of what he has stated in his book is founded on solid linguistic comparisons and cannot be easily, if at all, dislodged. It is therefore crucial that any study of Cant be carefully transcribed in detailed phonetics, including sociolinguistic variation, in order to allow linguists to compare like with like. The biggest stumbling block facing anyone undertaking the study of Cant – and this also pertains to many previous studies – is the interpretation of written transcriptions. Most of these transcriptions are in written English, which is scarcely suitable to capture the different nuances reflected in Cant. Even those important contributions transcribed in written Irish must also be scrutinised with extreme care. The reasons are many: the transcribers, while competent in Irish, were not trained linguists; they were subject to the vagaries presented by the Irish written code; the differentiation between dialect and a "standard" written code is not clear-cut; the background information on informants may not always be as complete as we would wish in this day of large and detailed sociolinguistic studies; and so on. Neither is it clear how pervasive an "Irish language type" pronunciation of Cant was in relation to those speakers who had little or no contact with Irish speaking areas. We are, therefore, heartened by the phonetic indications given in Edmondson and Ó Murchadha's contribution in this volume, not least because of the breadth and scope of their investigative study.

Alice Binchy presents a very accessible account of the nature and function of Traveller language based on her extensive fieldwork and from the perspective of a non-Traveller. Sinéad ní Shuinéar deconstructs academic treatment of Traveller language to date and proposes a radical reassessment in accordance with contemporary thinking in anthropology and linguistics. Mícheál Ó hAodha presents an analysis of Gammon vocabulary by categorizing its word-formation (or word-concealment) processes. Mary Burke takes readers on a comprehensive tour of the portrayal of Traveller language and Traveller life in general in recent Irish literature.[3] Sheila Douglas introduces readers to the Scottish Traveller as a transmitter of traditional Scottish and specifically Highland culture; she provides a wordlist of

---

[3] Her original presentation included some English literature as well, e.g. the character of Heathcliff in *Wuthering Heights*.

Scottish Cant which is lexicologically analysed in an appendix by John Kirk and Gavin Falconer.

In the three commissioned papers, Marian Browne shows how Traveller language has all the main syntactic characteristics of spoken Hiberno-English, proving beyond doubt that Irish Cant is a variety of English, no matter how much the influence of Irish Gaelic can still be traced in its vocabulary. This is probably the end product of a long period of bilingualism and language contact with a majority language/dialect. It is the inevitable result of extensive language contact and the adaptation of sociolinguistic norms for communication with the 'majority' community. Mícheál Ó hAodha revisits the period in which the first interest in Cant arose and, with considerable insight, considers the cultural motivations behind the early collectors – in Ireland as elsewhere. Ricca Edmondson and Niall Ó Murchadha have written a wide-ranging paper on Cant and its uses among Travellers in North America, Ireland, England and Scotland and their efforts to collect it. It is fair to claim that, on the whole, the paper is more sociologically rather than linguistically oriented, but the use of Cant vocabulary is discussed and phonetic transcriptions given where appropriate. We look forward with anticipation to the publication of their entire study into the life, education, identity and language use of Travellers with original roots in Ireland, but who are now to be found on several continents. It is important to place such studies in their proper context by attending to language attitudes and to the ideas of class language, sociological norms and sociolinguistic attitudes.

From these eight papers, we gain a rich and renewed understanding of Traveller language especially in Ireland but also of its nature elsewhere and the deficiencies and desires in academic scholarship past and present. Each paper has been written out of respect and admiration for the long-enduring, orally-transmitted cultural phenomenon that is Traveller language. No Traveller has ever before spoken so candidly about their own language, what it means to them, when and why they use it, how they feel about academic and other non-Traveller treatment of it.

In preparing the transcripts of the oral presentations by Ellen, Jimmy, Sheila and the anonymous Traveller for publication, the editors have had to face up to the contentious issue of whether to reproduce speakers' actual Cant or Gammon words, recognizing that a willingness to utter them in front of non-Travellers is not tantamount to agreeing to their reproduction in print. In their written contributions, Richard avoids giving examples of the language, whereas Len replaces them with [glosses]. In each case, we simply reproduce what was submitted to us and subsequently checked and agreed by the contributor.

Although we recognize scholars' demand for illustrative material, we are aware that the transcripts in this volume are testimonies of a highly personal nature. We have therefore opted for what we believe is the proper moral position: we consulted with Ellen, Jimmy, Sheila and the anonymous Traveller and have respected their wishes. Where Traveller-specific vocabulary is reproduced in the transcripts, it is with the written consent of the contributor; otherwise, it has been replaced by [glosses] or Xs. Besides, we feel that we do not need to give away actual words. The testimonies by Ellen, Jimmy, Sheila and the anonymous Traveller which include anecdotal and contextual illustrations of how the language is used, including, for instance, the fantastic in-family incident of the child being "bold" in the shop and his little sister expressing dismay are fine as they stand. The contributions by Richard and Len were, however, written by themselves, who controlled their own presentations including such vocabulary or [glosses] as each felt appropriate. We also let each Traveller contributor inspect the final proofs and obtained their written permission to publish. What we have assembled here is first-person, inside-track material, which we believe is both historically and globally unprecedented. It has been given to us for dissemination with goodwill; we wish to reciprocate that goodwill. Besides, some of the academic papers contain word lists and sentences, so that some Traveller language is presented in linguistic form, either written or transcribed phonetically.

Where does the scholarly and especially the linguistic study of Traveller language go from here? The criticisms of Macalister stress the need for accurate phonetic transcriptions of Cant/Gammon/Shelta. Orthographic transcriptions, such as Macalister's, however well-informed by philology, are no guide to the manner or quality of any realisation. The few transcriptions of sometimes "broad", sometimes "slender" qualities of consonantal articulation included in the volume (especially by Edmondson and Ó Murchadha) show not only how productive phonological processes such as palatalisation and velarisation in Traveller speech are, but also that those are central phonetic bases on which Traveller speech is differentiated from that of non-Travellers. For present and future scholars to know what Travellers are saying, phoneticians or linguists trained in phonetic transcription need to become involved. Whereas Ó Baoill has provided transcriptions for the Shelta words selected by ní Shuinéar from various lists, they too have their limitations for they were inevitably undertaken without reference to the actual pronunciation of those words by present-day Travellers. Douglas's word list for Scottish Travellers begs the same question whether Travellers would have the same normative realisation as suggested by these spellings for a typical speaker of Scots.

The solution to this task depends of course on the attitude of Travellers to whether they wish their speech to be preserved as phonetic transcriptions capable of reproduction. It is clear that opinion is varied among Travellers and scholars as evidenced through the various styles of reproduction in this volume. Xs and [glosses] (either no form and no meaning, or meaning but no form) may be what the present Travellers want, but from them no pronunciations can be reconstructed. We have attempted to facilitate the moving forward of Traveller-language scholarship, but until the phonetic investment is both approved and undertaken, no advance in knowledge or understanding can be made, nor can Macalister's spellings, about which different presuppositions have led to a range of views, be properly and critically evaluated.

If it is accepted that what underlies Traveller language in Ireland is the general societal shift from Irish to English, then its study is essentially that of contact linguistics. The evidence from detailed fine-meshed phonetic analysis needs to be co-related with that from syntax (clearly Hiberno-English) and lexis (modified Irish) on the one hand and universals of language-contact behaviour on the other. This is a further area where all work has yet to start, although there is much of real interest at every level of structure or in situations or domains of use, and for sociolinguistics and pragmatics.

But none of this strikes us as relevant until the Travellers as a whole are prepared to express a desire for the enterprise and co-operate with it. The issue is doubtless bound up with the ways in which Travellers wish to see their society develop – with the mainstream, and part of its multi-cultural diversity, or separate from it, as if marginalised or ghettoised. Study of their language would surely strengthen their identity, through wider informed understanding, not dilute or threaten it. In fact, Travellers could aid the investigation of their own speech immensely by recording their speech themselves, for it is they who have best access to the most informal of speech situations where Cant is likeliest to occur. We can envisage a productive partnership between Travellers and academic researchers. We would be prepared to host a further symposium in due course if we were satisfied that this necessary fieldwork and analysis of consenting Travellers and by qualified contributors had been undertaken. It is striking that all contributors of papers to this volume – however valuable their insights are otherwise (and we mean no disrespect here) – are not themselves trained linguists, as needed for the task of reproduction and evidence creation. The way forward, as we see it, starts with a change of attitude among Travellers with regard to their language being studied, and carries on with that study being carried out by academic linguists capable of analysing and connecting the actual utterances with the big linguistic-interpretive issues. No amount of politicisation, recognition or legislation will answer those questions or address those challenges.

Buri talosc to your dhíls ('Good luck to ye!')

References

Acton, Thomas, and Mundy, Gary eds. 1997. *Romani Culture and Gypsy Identity.* Hatfield: University of Hertfordshire Press

Macalister, R.A. Stewart. 1937. *The Secret Languages of Ireland. With special reference to the origin and nature of THE SHELTA LANGUAGE, partly based upon the Collections and Manuscripts of the late JOHN SAMPSON.* Cambridge: Cambridge University Press

McCann, May, Ó Síocháin, Séamus, and Ruane, Joseph eds. 1994. *Irish Travellers: Culture and Ethnicity.* Belfast: Institute of Irish Studies, Queen's University Belfast (for the Anthropological Association of Ireland)

PART 1

NEW ACADEMIC STUDIES ON TRAVELLERS AND THEIR LANGUAGE

The papers by Alice Binchy, Mary Burke, Sheila Douglas ('Travellers' Cant in Scotland'), Sinéad ní Shuinéar and Mícheál Ó hAodha ('Travellers' Language: Some Irish Language Perspectives') were originally presented at the Symposium on Travellers' Language on 15 August 2000. We include an edited transcript of the discussion following the papers by Alice Binchy and Sinéad ní Shuinéar. The papers by Marian Browne, Mícheál Ó hAodha ('Exoticising the Gypsies: The Case of Scott Macfie and the Gypsylorists') and Ricca Edmondson and Niall Ó Murchadha were commissioned for this volume.

Travellers' Use of Shelta

Alice Binchy

The Concept of Shelta

When discussing the language Shelta, I should first of all make it clear that I am referring to an academic version of what Travellers speak. No Traveller refers to the language as *Shelta*, but I consider it nonetheless quite a useful term, in that it is established academically as a term for the language and is also a convenient cover term for *Cant* and *Gammon*, which are the varieties spoken by Travellers in Ireland. It is useful to make a distinction between the academic version of the language and what Travellers actually speak, because it is important that Travellers do not feel that settled people are taking over their language and describing it in terms that they would not be comfortable with. It is good to have a kind of distance between what Travellers speak and how it is perceived by settled people because, when I was doing fieldwork on the language, I was always conscious that I was getting a version that a settled person would get. I could never write about the language as it actually is spoken because I am not a Traveller: I was always hearing the language as an outsider.

When Shelta was first written about in the 1880s, it was described as the "secret language" of Travellers, or "Tinkers", as they were then called. That description came about because, at that time, Travellers were considered to be an occupational group consisting of people who followed a number of different trades, including tinsmiths, horse-dealers, chimney sweeps, musicians and pipers: a group of tradespeople who lived, worked and travelled together. It was thought at that time that the only purpose of the language was as a secret code to exclude outsiders, as other occupational groups, for example doctors and lawyers, have medical, legal or other jargons which exclude lay people. There was a perception that the "Tinkers" needed a secret jargon in the same way – to exclude outsiders. They were considered an occupational grouping rather than a group with an ethnic identity of its own. That has obviously changed now. We now know a good deal more about Traveller society than people did in the 1880s. We know now that you cannot become a Traveller by buying a trailer and taking to the road. We know that Travellers are born, not made, and that you have to have at least one Traveller parent to be considered a Traveller. Even if you marry into the community, you do not become a Traveller, but your children will be considered Travellers. They are not a group that you can opt into on the basis of lifestyle or occupation. They are a natural social group bound by a complex system of blood and marriage links. We know now that Travellers prefer to marry among their close relatives as a way of strengthening their ties within the group, and we know too that not one trade but rather the ability to adapt to new economic opportunities and a preference for self-employment are the trademarks of Travellers. And we also know that nomadism is not a passing fad with Travellers, but a tradition passed down for generations which is integral to the whole Traveller way of life and seems to have a very deep influence on their language. In short, we now know that Travellers are a distinct ethnic group within Irish society. We as settled people know this now, but Travellers have always known that they were different, and it has always been important for Travellers to mark that difference and to keep a barrier between that Traveller world and the settled world. That is the context of Shelta – maintaining the barrier between the Traveller world and the settled world.

Contexts of Shelta Use

Groups living as linguistic minorities in larger societies tend to divide the world into "them" and "us", the "us" group obviously being those who share their linguistic background, and the "them" group being the majority. Travellers reflect that "them/us" divide in their language use. Broadly speaking, the "us" language is Shelta and the "them" language is English, but it is not as simple as that. Travellers do not speak Shelta all the time in their own community. But while Shelta is never spoken to non-Travellers and English is the everyday language of the Traveller community, Shelta is spoken within the community in specific contexts. On the basis of the fieldwork I conducted over the past fifteen years, I can say from an outsider's perspective that contexts for speaking Shelta include three in particular. The first is when Travellers are together in the presence of settled people, the second is when Travellers are making a living among settled people, and the third is within the Traveller community when talking about sensitive subjects and in other specific situations.

In the first of those, the presence of settled people is a trigger for Shelta to be spoken. The function is to protect the privacy of the Traveller world from settled people. So, for example, in years past, Travellers sitting around the fire at a roadside camp might interrupt their chat or storytelling and say *Krawdji a minute there's a byohr krushing* ('Wait a minute, there's a woman coming'). So they would actually interrupt their talk, which would be in English, until the person passed, so that nothing was heard which would threaten their privacy. And in the same context Traveller mothers say that the language is useful for controlling their children when settled people are around: one woman told me that it is "very hard to talk to Traveller kids, like when someone comes in to talk to you. It's very hard to shout at them to be quiet, so you can tell them in your own language with a nice tone of voice without anybody knowing what you're saying to them". The settled person therefore does not realise that the Traveller children needed to be corrected. Another woman said the language was useful to disguise public arguments among Travellers from settled people who might hear. She said that if another Traveller woman was getting on her nerves and she wanted to tell her to shut up, she could say *Krush away and stop torying* without anyone knowing that they were arguing. Speaking Shelta in situations of this type is not for secrecy as such. Travellers are not necessarily commenting on the settled people present: it is the Traveller world that they are protecting by using the language. Another context in this category is when Travellers are in public places and feel uneasy in the presence of settled people. They can use the language to draw solidarity from their own community. For instance, if a couple of Traveller women found themselves in a doctor's waiting room full of settled people, one might say to the other *Galyune the needjas are all sunyin at me, I'm aneishif* ('The [settled] people are all looking at me, I'm embarrassed'). In saying that, she would not be using the language against the settled people but as a way of drawing solidarity from her own community in an alien place. In all those contexts, there is nothing particularly secret that needs to be protected. As one woman said to me, the language "is spoken out of pride, because you wouldn't want settled people knowing your business".

There are circumstances, however, where Shelta is used for secrecy. Those mainly concern the police. For example, if the Gardaí (police) come to a camp looking for a particular person, a child might be dispatched with the message *Sheids anawsha, krush and lobi* ('The police are here, go and hide'). Similarly, when Travellers are in custody they often communicate in Shelta for fear that something incriminating might be overheard. In the context of making a living, Shelta is spoken among Travellers when dealing at fairs or markets, buying or selling scrap, or trying to get a best price from settled customers. Buying at a horse fair, for example, one Traveller might say *Gami kuri, bug the feen less greid* ('It's a bad horse, offer the man less money'). Until quite recently Traveller women used to go around the houses in suburban areas asking for food or cast-off clothing. When she had been given food at a door, a Traveller mother might say to one of her children as she turned away from the door *Geig a few nyuks* ('Ask for a few pennies'). The money would be more likely to be given if the person in the house thought it was a spontaneous request from the child.

The third context is not surprisingly the most difficult for a settled person to penetrate, because when you ask Travellers about situations where Shelta is used they invariably tell you that it is spoken only in the presence of settled people. But the same informants then give you examples of Shelta being spoken when there is no possibility of settled people being present, and the fact that they also tell you that children pick up the language in infancy indicates that it actually is spoken within the community, since small children are obviously brought up mainly within the Traveller community rather than in the presence of settled people. This would seem to suggest that Shelta is spoken unselfconsciously within the community, without the switch from English to Shelta being noted either by speaker or listener. As far as my fieldwork went, I came across a number of contexts where Shelta was clearly spoken within the Traveller community. One was when discussing subjects which according to Traveller norms cannot be spoken about openly, such as women's health and matters relating to childbirth. There seem to be euphemisms used which involve the use of Shelta. For example, I was told that you might hear somebody saying about another woman *she has an inokh in the nyuk*, which literally means 'she has a pain in the head', but is in fact a euphemism for 'she's pregnant'. Another area where Shelta is undoubtedly spoken within the community is by parents giving coded instructions in the presence of younger children or babies, such as *bug the golya to lee* ('Put the child to bed') in the same way as a settled person might spell out the word *bedtime*. Obviously, that usage has a built-in limitation: one Traveller said to me "When my little sister was young, my mammy used to say to me *Krush the golya up to lee anawsha and bug her to greep,* and we used to know she was saying 'Bring the child up to bed and put her to sleep'; one night, the child went 'No you won't bring me up and put me to sleep at all.'"

Travellers and Society

It could be said that Travellers participate selectively in the mainstream culture in Ireland while maintaining their own culture as far as possible, especially in areas where the settled world does not intrude. In this regard, they are similar to ethnic or minority groups in bilingual or multilingual communities who divide their language functions in such ways. The danger for groups in that situation is that they will eventually be swallowed up – that the majority language will with the passage of time intrude more and more into their internal community life, and that group members will come to be equally at home in the mainstream environment and will gradually be assimilated and lose their ethnic identity. The only way that such groups can maintain their own language over a period of generations is if they are able to keep their two worlds separate. For Travellers, this has been possible partly because of their position in society, since even if they wanted to – and most of them do not – it is very hard for Travellers to become part of the settled world as Travellers and be accepted as equals. If they were willing to break ties with the Traveller community, and if they thought that the benefits of the settled world were worth it, then it might be possible, but very few Travellers wish to do so. The vast majority of Travellers are proud of their identity and intend to remain Travellers and to bring up their children as Travellers. It seems to me that this is why Shelta continues to survive, though it is under greater pressure now than it ever has been. If we compare Travellers' lives today with their forebears even 50 years ago, we see that there have been huge changes. Fifty years ago Travellers were still overwhelmingly a rural phenomenon, moving around the country in family groups, having social contact only with their own group, and having only business contacts with the settled community. At that time the Traveller world was a bigger part of Traveller lives than it is now although, even today, Travellers still mix almost exclusively with their own group, their contacts with the settled community not having broadened significantly beyond the context of business transactions. Because of urbanisation they now live closer to their settled neighbours, and radio, television and videos all play a major part in Travellers' as well as in settled people's lives. All those factors together have the effect of shrinking the Traveller world and expanding the world which Travellers share with settled people. This means that in some ways the contexts for speaking Shelta are shrinking, and those for speaking English are growing. But while that change is taking place, there is also a change in attitudes towards Shelta. When one talks to older Travellers, one finds an almost deprecating attitude to the language. They do not speak about it with much respect, even if they would like to see it being maintained. This may be what they say to a settled person: I have been told that "it's only rubbish talk and nobody's interested in it now". That attitude is very common among older people who seem to see the language as harking back to the bad old days when Travellers lived lives of near destitution. Younger Travellers, and especially those with some education, are more likely to see the language as something to be proud of. This is clearly linked to the growth in Traveller pride generally. It is interesting how many young Travellers say that they will ensure that their children speak it. One young woman, not then married, said to me, "I feel that if I have any children I'm going to teach them the language. I really feel strongly that if everyone seems to be getting to know it I'll just make up ways that I can talk to them, some secret ways and things like that. But I will make sure that they'll have their own language. They'd want to feel that they could say something to me without no one knowing." I found that a recurrent attitude among younger Travellers: they feel it is important to maintain the barrier between the Traveller world and the settled world and to protect their Traveller identity from being encroached on by the latter.

Shelta and English

Travellers refer to Shelta as a language. In their view they have a language of their own which they distinguish from English. They do not consider it to be a variety of English. It will probably be clear from the examples I have given that Shelta shares its grammar and syntax with English. Shelta words take English plurals, possessives, verb endings and auxiliaries. So one can say *comra* is 'dog' and *comras* is 'dogs', *sunying* is 'seeing', *losped* is 'married', *I will chelp* 'I will cook'. Most of the early commentators on Shelta called it a jargon or slang, partly, as I have already suggested, because they were mistaken as to the nature of the group, but also because they believed that Shelta bore the same relationship to English as slang does. At a superficial level, that appears to be so, since Shelta replaces only the lexical items in a sentence, as slang does. For example, compare a slang sentence *the kid nicked the dosh* to a Shelta sentence *the gawlya beeged the greid*. The lexical items are replaced, but the syntax is English.

So are Travellers wrong to believe that they have a language of their own? The definition of what is and what is not a language has as much to do with social, historical and political factors as it has with linguistic ones. Some languages which share grammar are still considered to be separate entities, for example, Hindi and Urdu are accepted as distinct languages even though they share the same grammar, because they are spoken by groups which are distinct socially and historically. Although they are clearly distinct socially, Travellers have not been recognised as distinct historically or culturally, so it is not surprising that their language is not considered a distinct language.

The question of why there is no surviving Shelta syntax is interesting. If we suppose that at some stage Shelta had a distinct syntax, it is possible that that syntax disappeared because of the way Travellers lived. All of the evidence suggests that Travellers were traditionally service-providers, so they would have to speak at least the rudiments of the language of their customers and clients. Travellers would have had dealings with the Irish-speaking peasants and probably also with the English-speaking gentry, for example through horse-dealing. It may be that at some point in history Travellers were trilingual, speaking what we might term Old Shelta (with a grammatical system of its own) and also Irish and English. Each of those three languages would then have had a distinct role in Traveller life. In similar circumstances in other parts of the world this has led to several distinct systems converging, in the sense that grammatical differences are evened out and disappear, leaving only lexical differences. The sociolinguist Suzanne Romaine has said of this phenomenon:

> When a situation exists where all the speakers are constantly using
> all the languages available to them, they lessen the psychological
> load of having separate systems by allowing them to merge.[1]

It seems possible that this is what happened with Shelta: constantly changing from the "us" language to the "them" languages eroded grammatical differences. It is interesting that the same pattern exists in modern Anglo-Romany as spoken by the British Romany population. Add an Anglo-Romany sentence to the example I used earlier:

slang	*the kid nicked the dosh*
Shelta	*the gawlya beeged the greid*
Anglo-Romany	*the chavvi chored the luvva*
Standard English	*the child stole the money*

The British Romany community share many aspects of their lifestyle with Irish Travellers, and their relations with their settled neighbours are very similar. They have the advantage over Travellers that in their case there is documentary evidence that their language once had an independent grammatical system. Its decline and the encroachment of English on the language are attested by examples of the Romany language collected and published over the past 300 years, from the time they first arrived in Britain in the 1600s.

At present, I estimate the average vocabulary of Shelta spoken by adult Travellers at about 300 words. I have collected about 500, but some of those are known only by older people. It is not a large vocabulary, but one has to remember that it is a language spoken by a very close-knit community where blood relationships are underpinned by marriage alliances between certain families. It is a face-to-face language whose speakers are in intimate contact with one another for much of their daily lives. A language spoken by such a group need not be as complex as one spoken by a more disparate group where no assumptions can be made on the basis of shared background knowledge. There is a good deal that can go unsaid in Shelta.

---

[1] Suzanne Romaine, *Bilingualism* (Oxford: Blackwell, 1989) 163

Discussion of "Travellers' Use of Shelta"

Manfred Görlach: Two small questions. How many people speak Shelta? And the second is: in your reconstruction of Shelta ... Old Shelta, let's say ... you spoke about a possible Shelta syntax. Does this include inflection? Because normally, of course, it would be inflected language which survived into the nineteenth century in Wales.

Alice Binchy: Right! No, there's very little. In Macalister there are just a couple of tiny fragments.

Sinéad ní Shuinéar: I'm going to be talking about this and giving an overview.

Manfred Görlach: Right, fine.

Sinéad ní Shuinéar: Macalister mentions these *en passant*, but he rejects them immediately because, obviously, this is just a made-up jargon, so how could it possibly have these traits? So we don't take them seriously.

Alice Binchy: In terms of numbers of speakers, I think Nell or Jimmy would be the ones to give you information on that but, when I was doing my fieldwork in the 80s and 90s, I was surprised by the number of people who still know the language. Even though when you asked them casually did they speak it, they would say "no", but when you started asking them "what does this mean?" it would come back. There is an awful lot there. Travellers are not reflecting on their language use. I think that's an important point. There is a lot of the language there, just beneath the surface in an awful lot of people, and it's interesting that a lot of young parents think it's important to pass it on to their children.

Raymond Hickey: Two questions. First of all, what do we know about any possible Romany input into the language?

Alice Binchy: There's very little. There isn't as much as there would be in the Scottish Cant, because the Romanies really didn't come to Ireland, and the only bits were brought by people who went to England, and shared sites with Romanies there. But the two groups do not get on very well. There are certainly some words in it. When I was collecting, I didn't come across very many. Occasionally people had a Romany word as a variant, but they would usually have the Shelta word as well.

Raymond Hickey: The other question concerns present-day Shelta. You were saying that Shelta obviously went through the same language shift from Irish to English as the general community did in the early modern period. So, do they have the same sorts of typical features of Irish English which we expect settled speakers to have?

Alice Binchy: Do you mean Hiberno-English constructions? Yes, you would.

Raymond Hickey: And do they create new words – is it an active language in that sense?

Alice Binchy: That doesn't seem to be a big feature now, but a couple of replacement words are used quite frequently, like the word *inokh* which is similar to 'thingamajig'. And that would be a spur-of-the-moment usage of it: *Get that thing ... innock ... out of the way* or something like that. But the construction of words from Irish, I think Sinéad would agree, is much, much less than Macalister thought. He worked out rules for transforming Irish words into Shelta, and most of those are really spurious ... but the construction of words certainly continued in the English-speaking period, for a lot of words still being used actually came from English. There are many words which, interestingly, are given an Irish consonant cluster when they are transformed. For instance, there's a word for 'dish' which is *srish*, which is that Irish consonant cluster. It's a fairly effective disguise among English-speaking people.

Sheila Douglas: Alice Binchy reminded me of something that I didn't say, but maybe should have: that the Perths, the Stewarts and the Northern Travellers would have originally been Gaelic-speakers, and when they were Gaelic-speakers they actually had a place in Highland society. They had a function. I don't know what that would say about whether they used Cant in those days. I don't know much about Gaelic but I know it's got a different word order from Scots or English, and there are all sorts of things to be explored there. And, talk about making up words, I know Sheila made up a word for her brother, from the Cant word *greinm* for 'grain', 'corn', and she said he had *greinm trousers*!

Alice Binchy: I came across *grapple* when I was talking to a child once, when I asked her the word for 'apple'. And the word that I had written down from Macalister was *grulla*, which is the *gr* put in front of the Irish *ull*. But the child couldn't think of the word, so she said, *grapple*, which was exactly the same thing. That was in the 80s. I didn't actually investigate that, in particular; it would have been interesting. But you don't think of those things at the time.

Ellen McDonagh: What word did you say was for 'apple', Alice?

Alice Binchy: Apple? Well, there's one in Macalister which is *grull, grulla*.

Ellen McDonagh: We would use [apple].

Alice Binchy: I don't think that's in Macalister, but I've heard that one too. That's one that you hear more often. But I was checking the words from Macalister, seeing whether people knew them.

Raymond Hickey: Just on that, very briefly, are there other instances of kids doing that sort of thing, where they'd realise what the processes are and apply them to new words such as 'computer'? It would be an example of a productive process.

Alice Binchy: Absolutely. And adults do that to some extent, but I only had one example of a child doing it. And that must have been spontaneous. She hadn't been taught to do it.

Raymond Hickey: How old was the child?

Alice Binchy: She was about eight.

Sinéad ní Shuinéar: Could I just comment that we're going on the assumption that this is deliberate obfuscation, and I don't think that's fair. There are different sound systems, and you can't say that Irish deliberately changed the /j/ sound in borrowed words to /s/ in order to hide them. It did so simply because it made more sense to Irish. And you can think of lots and lots of examples: for example, when I speak English, I don't say [with an Italian accent], *spaghetti*, I say [with a Hiberno-English accent] *spaghetti*, because that makes sense in English. It's not obfuscation at all.

Alice Binchy: I take what you say about it not being deliberate obfuscation. But one possible reason would be that, in such a language, like that which was in danger of being swamped by the dominant language around it, perhaps that was how people actually built up the word store: by taking in words and making them their own.

Sinéad ní Shuinéar: That's called "borrowing".

Alice Binchy: Of course it is. But borrowed words aren't transformed in quite the same way, usually. They are given a native pronunciation rather than actually tampered with structurally.

Sinéad ní Shuinéar: I think *oráiste* is a fairly good example, don't you?

Alice Binchy: Yes. But that's just giving an Irish flavour ...

Sinéad ní Shuinéar: Oh, no, it's not. There's no /t/ in *orange*.

Alice Binchy: No. But it makes it sound like an Irish word.

Sinéad ní Shuinéar: Yes, it does. That's exactly my point.

Fionnuala Williams: So, one last comment ... ?

Sheila Douglas: Do Irish Travellers use personal nicknames?

Jimmy Porter: Yes.

Alice Binchy: Yes. Very much so.

Sheila Douglas: I mean this is something, in the north of Scotland, you know if you go to a part of the Highlands and everybody's called MacDonald, they all need to have nicknames ... The Travellers, in many ways, are very like Highland people – they attach a great importance to kinship, hospitality, songs and stories, all the things that Highland people care about.

The Curious Case of *Shelta*

Sinéad ní Shuinéar

The Concept of *Shelta*

As will emerge, this is a not a paper about Irish Traveller languages.[1] It is a paper about *Shelta*, a term and a concept constructed by Victorian Gypsylorists, and its preservation and continued use to the present day in defiance of developments in linguistic science generally presents a very curious case.

For the term *Shelta*, Macalister (1937, and see below) hypothesises a convoluted etymology from the Irish word *béarla*, which once meant "language" generally, but there is a far simpler explanation. The most common Irish language terms for "Traveller" are variations on the verb *siúil* [ʃuːlʲ] 'to walk': *an lucht siúil* [ənˠ ɫuxt̪ˠ ʃuːlʲ], literally, "the people of walking", has recently been updated to *an lucht taistil*, [ənˠ ɫuxt̪ˠ tʲaʃʲtʲɪːlʲ] literally, "the people of travelling", in Irish government publications such as the 1995 report. One such term is *siúltóir*, literally, "a walker". Whether or not Travellers ever used this name for themselves, they would have been aware that it was what most non-Travellers in Ireland called them, and it seems likely that this is how they would have replied to non-Travellers, including the English tramps from whom this term was collected, asking who they were. An English speaker pronouncing this word would characteristically drop the final *r*, transforming *Siúltóir* [ʃuːɫt̪ˠoːrʲ], to *Siúl-ta* [ʃuːɫt̪ˠə], an anglicised version of a term for the people – known in England as *tinkers* – extended to their language. Hence, the term *Shelta*.[2]

Insisting on *Shelta* as the "real" name of the language (despite the fact that only two, nineteenth-century, sources, both of them English, appear to have been familiar with it and virtually all commentators with first-hand acquaintance with speakers explicitly state that is unknown to Irish Travellers[3]) is analogous to British scholars' former insistence on the callipygous *Erse* over and above anglicised versions of

---

[1] A previous version of this paper was presented at the Annual Conference of the Gypsy Lore Society, Florence, on 29 June 1999.

[2] Editorial note: However, *siúlta* is a genuine Irish word: the past participle or verbal adjective from *siúil*.

[3] Binchy 1994: 134; Cash, 1977: 179; Court, 1985: 18; ffrench, 1890: 127; Hancock 1984: 385; Douglas Hyde ("the eminent Erse scholar" and subsequently first President of Ireland) quoted under the heading "Irish Gypsies", *Journal of the Gypsy Lore Society* series 2, vol. 2 (October 1908): 130; MacRitchie 1901: 23; Norwood, 1887: 13; ní Shuinéar 1996: 1.

speakers' own term *Gaeilge* as "Gaelic" or "Irish"; it is essentially a statement of contempt. If one does not respect the speaker, to the extent of insisting that one knows better than he or she what the language he or she is speaking is called, then one is hardly likely to respect anything else the speaker has to say. It is precisely this withering contempt for Irish Travellers themselves which has characterised virtually everything written to date about Irish Traveller language.

Since *Shelta* studies equate lexis with language and (arbitrary) orthography with etymology, this paper must address that paradigm, despite the fact that the paradigm itself is the problem. Traveller *language* has never been studied, whereas selected elements of *exotic vocabulary* unique to Travellers have. In this paper, I will outline the methods and assumptions of this approach to date; it will be up to others more qualified than the present writer to break this mould and provide more accurate descriptions of the language. I hope that the points raised here convince them that this task remains to be addressed.

Shelta and the Gypsylorists 1882–1908

Reviewing scholarly treatment of Irish Traveller language, there is a clear watershed in the 1937 publication of R.A. Stewart Macalister's *The Secret Languages of Ireland*, a synthesis of all the work which had gone before; virtually everything since has comprised minor reinterpretations of this text. As Macalister, like the overwhelming majority of those who have commented on the language in the ensuing half century, carried out no original research, the database on which the entire *Shelta* edifice is constructed dates from the period of the *Shelta* craze: 1882–1908. We must therefore examine its methodology with particular care in order to assess the reliability of its findings.

The earliest mention of *Shelta* is in Charles Leland's *The Gypsies* published in 1882, which concluded with a chapter (pp. 354–72) outlining his "discovery" of *Shelta*, a "fifth British Celtic tongue". In 1889, the *Journal of the Gypsy Lore Society* began coverage of *Shelta*, in the form of additional word lists collected in England and Scotland, and one, comprising 17 items, in Ireland itself. At the editor's request, John Sampson took up the pursuit of *Shelta*; the *Journal of the Gypsy Lore Society* published his findings in 1890, and Kuno Meyer, the first Celtic scholar to approach the language, built on them. These three men planned a joint work on the subject, but with Leland's death the project was shelved, to be completed by Macalister in 1937. The *Journal of the Gypsy Lore Society* published nothing on *Shelta* from 1908 until it reviewed Macalister's book, and it has published very little since.

For all its brevity, the *Shelta* vogue was phenomenal while it lasted; Leland, reviewing his tenure as President of the Gypsy Lore Society on his retirement, unequivocally names the investigation of *Shelta* as its greatest achievement (1892: 195). Yet attitudes to language are inseparable from attitudes towards speakers, and conventional academic wisdom on Irish Travellers and their language is very much a product of Victorian England, with its characteristic attitudes to both the Irish in general and to the "Orient", of which "Romany Gypsies" were supposedly the local branch. From its inception in 1888, the *Journal of the Gypsy Lore Society* frequently asserted the Sanskrit-based legitimacy of the Romani language and the folly of popular dismissal of it as mere slang. The inclusion of tinkers – as Irish Travellers are consistently termed – was so problematic that the editor felt a need to justify it in the following, characteristically lepidopterist, terms: "He who catches a tinker has got hold of half a Gypsy" (MacRitchie 1889: 350). Tinkers could not be conceded as the equals of Romanies in any sphere and therefore could not have a proper language. Cultural and linguistic legitimacy are openly conflated and denied in tandem; consider Sampson's remark: "[the tinker's] moral and social code, like his language, is certainly of the backslang order" (1890: 220). The very first publication on *Shelta* muses "The question which I cannot solve is this: on which of the Celtic *languages* is this *jargon* based?" (Leland 1882: 370). This dual assumption: that *Shelta* is a jargon, not a language, and that it is a scrambled version of somebody else's, has persisted to the present day.[4] Kuno Meyer's 1891 proclamation (p. 257) that "Mr Sampson has succeeded in reading the *riddle* of *Shelta*, which had baffled *all* who had approached it before him. He has *conclusively proved* that the jargon spoken by travelling Irish tinkers ... is a deliberate and systematic modification of Irish Gaelic" [my italics] has achieved the status of conventional wisdom. Those assertions beg a number of questions. First, why is *Shelta* a "riddle"? Second, since Leland was Sampson's only predecessor in the field, who were the "all" who had approached "solving" it before him? Third: what, exactly, is the "conclusive proof"?

Irish and *Shelta*: Nineteenth-Century Theories

The Irish language, from which *Shelta* purportedly derives, with which it has undoubtedly coexisted over the centuries, and whose basic sound system it shares, is an Indo-European language of the Celtic group, radically different from the Germanic language spoken by our dominant neighbours, the English. Since Irish (and indeed *Shelta*) and English have very different sound systems, with little overlap, the former cannot be conveyed by the orthography of the latter; conversely, Irish orthography conveys little to the Anglophone. Compare, for example, some of the anglicised transcriptions employed by the bilingual nineteenth-century novelist William Carleton

---

[4] Leland, the first collector, offered among his etymological speculations that the *Shelta* word *lakeen* ('girl') is an anagram of the Romani *rakli* (1882: 359); subsequent theorists (cf. Macalister 1937: 199), having replaced the "scrambled Romani" hypothesis with "scrambled Irish", make it an anagram of the Irish word *cailín*.

with standard Irish orthography and with transcriptions of the latter in the International Phonetic Alphabet (IPA), as presented in Figure 1.[5]

Figure 1: Comparative Orthographies of some Irish Terms

Carleton's Anglicised Orthography	Standard Irish Orthography	IPA of Irish
acushla machree (voc.)	*a chuisle mo chroí*	[ə xuʃlʲə mˠə xɾˠiː]
musha	*muise*	[mˠöʃə]
a chiernah (voc.)	*a thiarna*	[ə çɪəɾˠn̪ˠə]
a cholleen dhas (voc.)	*a chailín deas*	[ə xalʲinʲ dʲasˠ]
achora (voc.)	*a chara*	[ə xaɾə]
banath latht	*beannacht leat*[6]	[bʲan̪ˠatˠ lʲatˠ]
ma chorp an diaoul	*mo chorp an diabhal*	[mˠə xoɾˠpˠɔnˠ dʲauət]
pishthrogue	*pisreog*	[pʲɪʃɾˠog]
seanachie	*seanchaí*	[ʃanˠəxi]

As we see from the IPA, the Irish language employs a great many sounds which simply do not occur in English and cannot therefore be conveyed in anglicised spellings. We also note that standard Irish orthography employs entirely different conventions from those of English. In Carleton's orthography, *ch* represents both [x] and [ç] – both sounds which do not occur in English – and *th* can either represent [xtˠ] or silently indicate that the preceding vowel is lengthened.

   Unlike Carleton, the collectors of *Shelta* were neither well qualified nor sympathetic. Sampson, sent into the slums of Liverpool to gather vocabulary from "uncleanly and evil-looking men", lamented that "*Shelta* is a language which no gentleman should be asked to collect" (Macalister 1937: 134). Only one of these nineteenth-century collectors, Kuno Meyer, had *book* knowledge of "ancient"[7] Irish;

---

[5] I am extremely grateful to Dónall Ó Baoill for providing the IPA transcriptions for Figures 1–4 and elsewhere in this article and for providing comments by way of editorial notes.

[6] Editorial note: in the IPA transcription, the sound [x] represented orthographically as *ch* is elided because the sound has been lost in Tyrone and South-east Ulster, as indicated by Carleton's spelling *banath*.

[7] Victorian scholars appear to have used this to mean both "Old" Irish – technically, that dating from the seventh to the ninth centuries A.D. – and the indigenous Irish language generally, to differentiate it from the more "modern" language, English.

all admit that transcribing *Shelta* is a challenge they have met but poorly. "As the pronunciation is very soft and liquid, I am not sure that I always succeeded in rendering them all quite correctly" cautions one scholar (ffrench 1890: 127), while Leland admits that "I ... have not succeeded in writing a *single word* according to his pronunciation of it" (Leland 1882: 369,[8] my italics). Sampson, in turn, notes his informant's visible sympathy as he struggles to transcribe "some *peculiarly* Celtic sound" (Sampson 1890: 209); that he is working purely from a written base, with no first-hand knowledge, is clear from the fact that his proposed compound etymologies are ungrammatical.[9]

These early collectors have provided a double Rosetta Stone by which to measure the competence of their transcriptions. Their unfamiliarity with Irish led them to copy down as Traveller-specific many common Irish terms: Leland, for example, gives us the numbers in Irish under the illusion that they are *Shelta*. The IPA, indicating how the Irish words are actually pronounced, reveals the inadequacy of Leland's orthography. We must assume that his *Shelta* orthography is equally inadequate.

Moreover, insofar as the direct speech of "tinkers" is transcribed for exotic or comic effect, there is a record of the collectors' sensitivity to their informants' speech. A typical instance is Leland's opening dialogue with his sole "tinker" informant. Challenging him, in *Shelta*, "Can you speak *Shelta, boy*?" Leland receives the reply, "An' begorra! I think it's very remarkable, sorr, that ye should know there *is* such a language" (Leland 1907–08: 175) – a stage-Irish "begorra", a deferential "sorr", and "ye" (the second person plural purportedly used in the singular)[12] all in this single utterance. Another instance comes from John Barlow, a Liverpool-based Ulster tinker, who was Sampson's main and Meyer's sole informant; the only sample of Barlow's Hiberno-English is an anecdote wherein, noting Sampson's difficulty in transcribing "peculiarly Celtic sound", he innocently recommends a spelling book that "lades ye on from the alphabet up to anti-titterumtairums ... (a long pause of admiration)" (Sampson 1890: 209).

---

[8] This was expunged on republication in the *Journal of the Gypsy Lore Society*, a fact highlighted by Macalister when he quotes it, p. 131

[9] For example, despite disparaging comments on the tendency of the Irish language to aspirate consonants out of existence Sampson (1890: 206), had no grasp of even the most basic systematic rules governing this process. For example, he hypothesises (ibid., 212) that the *Shelta limpath* is an inversion of the Irish *mo plaid* [*sic*] despite the fact that [p] preceded by *mo must* be aspirated; and the orthographic *i* preceding *d* shows that the pronunciation of /d/ is palatalised, giving *mo flaj* [mˠə ˈfˈlˠadʲ].

[12] Editorial note: since this was transcribed by an American, it could just be an attempt to reproduce the unstressed Hiberno-English form of *you* as [jə].

We have seen that even a sympathetic bilingual, such as Carleton, can fail to convey the speech sounds with which he was intimately familiar. How much more misleading, then, must be the orthography of English and American collectors who found Hiberno-English rollickingly comical and Gaelic sounds "peculiar"? Yet it is this orthography on which theorising as to the origins of the language and its speakers rests unchallenged.

Figure 2: The Numbers 1–5 in Irish[10]

Leland's Orthography	Standard Irish Orthography	IPA of Irish
1. *hain*	*a haon*	[ə heːnʸ]
2. *do*	*dó*	[d̪ˠoː]
3. *tri*	*trí*	[tʲɾʲiː]
4. *k'hair*	*ceathair*	[cɛhəɾʲ ~ cɛːɾʲ][11]
5. *cood*	*cúig*	[kuːɟ]

A person who cannot count to 5 in a language clearly has no knowledge of it – or, as Leland himself put it, "I am not proficient in Celtic but, like the lady who had never seen Niagara, I 'have heard it highly spoken of'" (Leland 1891: 321). This did not stop him, or his equally un-"proficient" successor Sampson, from comparing the vocabulary they collected to lists of "ancient Irish" (i.e. Gaelic, not "modern" English) words; Sampson suggests 27 different ways in which these were "perverted" by "methods of disguise ... frequently too complex to be self-evident" (Sampson 1890: 209) to become *Shelta*. The far-fetchedness of the alleged connections is itself cited as proof of tinker deviousness: "like one of their own stolen asses, it is so docked and disguised as to be barely recognisable" (ibid.) – in other words, "tinkers steal donkeys = tinkers steal language", an equation noted by Bernard Leblon (1995: 82) in relation to popular denial of Gypsy input into flamenco as "Gypsies steal chickens = Gypsies steal music". And these, of course, are not Gypsies, but tinkers, an inferior breed altogether; note, for example, that Sampson rejects Leland's interpretation of a set of verb endings as conveying the infinitive on the grounds that "the infinitive is too abstract a conception for the tinker mind to apprehend" (Sampson 1890: 219).

---

[10] In Figures 2–4, all *Shelta* and Irish spellings are reproduced from the originals: i.e. Leland (1882), Sampson (1890) and Macalister (1937).

[11] Editorial note: in the second transcription, intervocalic [h] has been deleted. What Leland heard cannot be reconstructed. The variant without /h/ is probably what Leland heard, as indicated by his spelling *k'hair*. If so, it was probably a South-east Ulster speaker of Irish that Leland heard.

Meyer, agreeing with "Mr Sampson's conclusions as to the Irish origin of Shelta", sets out "to show that Shelta is a secret language of great antiquity", and that "its knowledge was once possessed by Irish poets and scholars, *who, probably, were its original framers*" concluding "that Shelta was invented at an early period of the Irish language", "certainly anterior to the eleventh century" (Meyer 1891: 258, 260).

Macalister's *Secret Languages* (1937)

There followed 30 years of silence before the publication of *The Secret Languages of Ireland. With special reference to the origin and nature of THE SHELTA LANGUAGE, partly based upon the Collections and Manuscripts of the late JOHN SAMPSON*. Its author, R.A. Stewart Macalister, occupied the Chair of Celtic Archaeology at University College Dublin from 1909 until his retirement in 1950. Half a century later, in 1996, Damian McManus, Professor of Early and Modern Irish at Trinity College, assessed his overall contribution thus: "Macalister's forte was epigraphy rather than philology ... Had he been a little more circumspect, and more willing to consult expert advice, he could have avoided the criticism made by the linguistically oriented reviewers of his work ..." (McManus 1996: g). In fact there were murmurs of dissent on *The Secret Languages* even at the time of publication: the review published in *Irish Historical Studies* bewails the fact that "there is nowhere any explanation of the symbols employed nor any indication of the dialect from which the particular word with its pronunciation is taken" (O'Brien 1938: 97). This is a major problem, in that even today, after 70 years of concerted government effort to standardise the Irish language, the dialect groups remain quite distinct in both sounds and vocabulary, though Irish-language broadcasting has increased intercomprehensibility. The *Journal of the Gypsy Lore Society* reviewed it too, of course, in a tone of general enthusiasm, yet dared to whisper criticism: "A full bibliography would have been a welcome addition, especially when so many of the references are unaccountably vague" (Foster 1937: 143). In short, Macalister builds his case on sweeping historical speculations, *inter alia* about the "vagabonds" of pre-Christian Ireland, with almost no backing references whatever.[13]

---

[13] The chapter entitled "The Vagrants of Ireland" has a single reference – *Lives of Saints from the Book of Lismore* – in support of a single assertion about encounters between "'troublesome' or 'greedy'" persons (no reference to their being "vagrants") and the procurators of monasteries (Macalister 1937: 124). Bearing in mind that Macalister was a member of the academic establishment, and should therefore have respected current conventions governing academic writing, it is instructive to compare *The Secret Languages* with Daniel Corkery's reconstruction of eighteenth-century Gaelic society, *The Hidden Ireland*, published in 1924 and meticulously referenced with lengthy quotations from primary and corroborative sources.

Macalister set out to write the synthesis which Leland, Sampson and Meyer had planned but never completed. In so doing, Macalister undertook no original research – in fact he admits (1937: 154) that, despite living in Dublin, he had *never heard the language spoken*, but confined himself to the above-mentioned sources (including their unpublished notes) and to a second set of word lists collected in Ireland, in the early 1930s, by Pádraig Mac Gréine.[14]

Macalister's source materials were gathered over a wide range of time and space, the majority outside of Ireland, and thus from persons distanced from the linguistic matrix and subject to "foreign" influences, by collectors of varying scholarly ability and credibility, whose criteria for including or excluding items are no clearer than Macalister's in selectively compiling his own list from theirs. I have already pointed out the attitudes of collectors towards their informants, and the difficulties they faced in transcribing "peculiarly Celtic" sounds – in fact, each uses a system of his own devising, without providing keys to pronunciation. This did not prevent Macalister – whom we recall had never heard the language spoken, and so had no baseline against which to measure this material – from commenting on *Shelta*'s sound system in minute detail, having first spelled *Shelta* words to show their putative Irish origins, or, as he puts it himself, "It is possible to form a fair idea of how the words are pronounced, by taking the average of all the varied spellings used by different observers ... The usually obvious etymology of the words helps to determine their phonetic form" (Macalister 1937: 154).[15]

Meyer attributes the language's characteristically unaspirated consonants to its antiquity. "This being incredible," says Macalister, "we must find some simpler explanation, and the explanation surely is that the inventors of the language [English-speakers, within the past two centuries] worked it out from *written* forms of Irish"

---

[14] A propos, it is very instructive to note that Macalister gratuitously anglicises the name Pádraig Mac Gréine to "Patrick Greene", thereby revealing his predilection for imposing his own order on others' realities and simultaneously providing yet another Rosetta Stone: subsequent commentators who cite "Greene" clearly do so via Macalister.

[15] Further insights into Macalister's circular logic include the following. On etymology: "For example, the word given as *jumik* 'to swear' must [*sic*] be derived from the Irish *moidighim*, 'I swear' ... the Shelta *jum* is a reversal of the Irish *móid* (*mód*) and the *j* is therefore not *dž* but *d'* (*dy*)." (Macalister 1937: 154-5); on pronunciation: "Leland seems to have been very deaf to this letter (*r*), and he often drops it where it *must* have been present on the lips of his informants." (ibid.: 155, italics in original) and "The sound *č* (*ch* as in 'church') ... is not really a Shelta sound ... the sound written *ch* by collectors should really be regarded as *t'*. In some cases, however, it seems to mean χ ..." (ibid.: 156). [Editorial note: a palatal *t* sound without affrication is probably what Macalister means.]

(Macalister 1937: 162–6). Obvious questions, such as *how* a geographically dispersed, internally fragmented, non-literate nomadic people would appropriate neologisms devised by scholars, or *why* such people should suddenly have felt the urge to do so, are not addressed. The mechanisms of alleged lexical distortion, by contrast, are covered in great detail, on the understanding that tinker language is "essentially of a random nature, not governed by any phonic principle" (Macalister 1937: 169). Macalister lists a total of 137 different methods of alleged "deformation", no less than 67 of which are illustrated by a single example. Without going into the plausibility of same, that is 50% of all the methods, and 28% of all the words, examined. Even so, he is unable to propose etymologies for over half his *Shelta* vocabulary. How can language X, over half of whose vocabulary – supposedly the crucial indicator – admittedly bears no resemblance to language Y, be dismissed as a deliberate obfuscation of the latter?

Macalister skates over other aspects of language: "There are […] some traces of a native plural", "traces of a few native inflections", and "some native prepositions" (Macalister 1937: 158–63), he admits, but "[i]n general, it must be said that in the verbal construction of Shelta we can see the same helplessness as in the Broken-English of Negroes or Polynesians" (ibid.:161). I don't know how kosher this sort of verdict was in linguistic circles when these words were published, in 1937[16] – a full decade after the death of Hugo Schuhardt, the father of creole studies and the man who explained that "Broken-English" is systematic, not "helpless" – but it appears to be acceptable in the twenty-first century, because Macalister is still being recycled by purportedly serious academics.

American Scholarship

It was not until the early 1970s that *Shelta* again came under academic scrutiny, this time in the Southern US where Harper and Hudson published three short papers. Before discussing Harper's original fieldwork, these papers give an historic overview, assuring us that Macalister "summarised all previous work, correcting the interpretations of his predecessors and putting all their Shelta ... into a reasonably consistent and accurate [!] orthography. ... Although Macalister never heard Shelta spoken, he had a better understanding of its sound system than did any of his predecessors" (Harper and Hudson 1971: 80). For Harper and Hudson, Irish Travellers speak "an argot, a mode of disguised linguistic communication ... not a language in the conventional sense, but a jargon akin to pig-latin" which "began as a systematic modification of Irish Gaelic ... now ... frozen into a set of variant words" (Harper 1971: 20, 22). Since it is "akin to pig-latin", word formation techniques are simple: "Macalister was wrong when he concluded that the devices by means of

---

[16] Scientific racism, formulated and promoted by the academy, was espoused by millions of Europeans in 1937, the eve of its murderous implementation.

which Shelta was formed were so intricate they could not have been invented by illiterate people" (Harper and Hudson 1971: 82).

Questions of etymology pale into insignificance next to the unaddressed but remarkable fact of the persistence of even the limited vocabulary they collected among the descendants of pre-famine Traveller immigrants to the US – most of it still recognisable to Travellers here in Ireland, a century and a half on. This survival proves that the language, and its speakers, predate the famine: both had to exist in Ireland before the split, and language is just one of many distinctive cultural traits, including high mobility and an ethos of self-employment, shared by people on both sides of the Atlantic who call themselves "Irish Travellers". If the main purpose of the language were (as is commonly believed) to conceal communication from outsiders, why did Travellers based in the American Deep South keep a handful of jargon terms and jettison the all-purpose, bona fide language, Irish – the vernacular of the majority of Irish people at that time and utterly incomprehensible to the population in which they moved?

Harper and Hudson also comment that southern Travellers have "lost the 'Irish brogue'" (1971: 82). The conflation of dozens of Hiberno-English dialects into a sort of stage Oirish – which neither Travellers nor anybody else speaks – is a pervasive problem among English and American commentators, as the nineteenth-century transcripts of Travellers' direct speech, cited above, demonstrate. Moreover, when I heard on video members of the same South Carolina-based Irish Traveller community with whom Harper did his fieldwork, I was stunned to note that, beneath the Good Ole Boys' drawl (these *are* the descendants of Travellers who immigrated in the 1840s!) their pronunciation does indeed preserve the uniquely Traveller markers which make their speech strikingly distinct from any dialect of non-Traveller Hiberno-English.

The next scholar to turn his attention to the language is also North American based: Ian Hancock, a professor of linguistics and specialist in creole studies, himself a native speaker of Romani who mixes, and can speak, with Irish Travellers – as I can confirm from having heard him in dialogue with them. Hancock sees Traveller language as "a problem of classification". He considers – and rejects – the possibility of *Shelta* as an ethnic mother tongue, despite prefacing his remarks to this effect by noting that "For some families, Shelta is a first language" (Hancock 1973: 131) (what is an ethnic mother tongue if not one's first language?). Hancock notes the need for a new linguistic classification covering "codes whose purpose is in making messages inaccessible to outgroups" (ibid.: 132) – an umbrella under which he reconciles Anglo-Romani and *Shelta*. Whereas this dismissal of *Shelta* as a cryptolect is simply conventional wisdom, Hancock's dismissal of Anglo-Romani is a defiance of it – particularly astonishing coming from a native speaker.

Hancock (1984) significantly pairs *Shelta* with "Polari", "a lexicon of 80 to 100 words" mostly employed by homosexuals, but which "unlike Shelta ... was probably not consciously created ..." (ibid.: 391). Hancock summarises Macalister's work on the former as "the most complete to date, despite its subjectivity and a certain lack of linguistic sophistication" (ibid.: 386) – a remarkably charitable assessment, particularly coming from a professional creolist. When we recall that the professional creolist is also a native speaker of Romani, with a vested interest in perpetuating the great divide between Sanskrit-based legitimacy and scrambled Irish bogusness, the charity becomes more understandable; he also notes that "With the exception of one or two of the processes listed by Macalister, such as reversal, the distribution of these supposed modifications is quite random" (ibid.: 387). Hancock makes no comment on the plausibility of this claim, but goes on to give illustrations of the techniques of alleged disguise listed by Macalister.

Finally, two years later, in a comparative overview of the ethnolects of three American Traveller groups of British Isles origin, Hancock states that Irish Travellers' Cant includes "features from Shelta, a [Romani-] related cryptolect based largely on Irish" (Hancock 1986: 207).

Scholarship 1987–2000

Published academic work between 1987 and 2000 is, apart from passing references, limited to three conference papers, two of them originally given at the 1991 Anthropological Association of Ireland Conference on Traveller issues. One of these, by an editor of the present volume (Ó Baoill 1994), was a brief overview of existing work from the perspective of Celtic studies; the other, by Alice Binchy (1994), summarised her trojan labours dealt with below. The third and longest, by Anthony Grant, was given at the University of Leiden Workshop on Mixed Languages in May 1993 and subsequently published, along with 14 other conference papers, in *Mixed Languages: 15 Case Studies in Language Intertwining*. Grant uncritically re-creates Macalister's assumptions and methodology: "The material in this paper derives principally from Macalister (1937), the chief published source on the language, but also from Harper and Hudson (1971) and Hancock (1973; 1984; 1986) and from the materials upon which they have drawn," he explains (Grant 1994: 124). Bearing in mind that Harper and Hudson provide no more than three pages of original material, in American Cant, not *Shelta*, while Hancock (1973) gives 64 terms also collected in North America, followed in 1984 by a single page of *Shelta*, Grant's material comes not "principally" but overwhelmingly from Macalister's word lists, up to 140 years old, now fourth-hand and still uncorroborated by original research. "My own opportunities to hear *Shelta* spoken have been few, and mostly of a casual nature," he admits (Grant 1994: 124). With source materials as impeccable as this, why bother?

"I have adopted an orthography for Shelta which is based on the American Phonemic system, using doubled vowels to represent vowel length" (Grant 1994: 126). Now it is Grant's turn to impose an orthography on a language he has never heard, based ("principally") on the standardisations of a man who had also never heard it and who cheerfully admits (as we saw above) that he ignores the phonic systems employed by the second-hand sources he consults when these do not gel with his theories. Like Macalister 60 years before him, Grant meets the challenge of *Shelta* in the privacy and comfort of the ivory tower, without clouding the issue by comparing the written word with the "utterances" of even one native speaker, boldly venturing opinions on impressively esoteric issues such as "morphosyntactic framework", "derivational morphology", "postvocalic and word final /r/, and dental rather than alveolar /t~d/", "phonotactics", etc., concluding with general assertions about its speakers in his final section, "Towards the Genesis of Shelta".

I suggest that such methodology is not acceptable in mainstream linguistics and that the only reason Grant appears to have got away with it is that the subject of his musings is spoken by mere tinkers. I would also point out that the apparently unproblematic omission of original fieldwork is incomprehensible, given that speakers of this language are both numerous and geographically accessible.

It was not until the 1980s, nearly a century after the *Shelta* craze peaked, that the first ever systematic work on the language in Ireland itself was undertaken by sociolinguist Alice Binchy. Her M.A. and Ph.D. theses, though unpublished, are invaluable resources, filled with verbatim transcripts and contemporary word lists, with observations on the methodology and ethics of researching a language whose speakers see it as a form of protection against the researcher's own group. Among her major innovations is a reassessment of the "secrecy" aspect of *Shelta* in terms of group boundary maintenance rather than nefarious plotting against decent settled folk (Binchy 1993: 200–12, 299). She likewise demonstrates how the fact that *Shelta* grammar is currently essentially that of Hiberno-English is not, as Macalister insisted, proof that the language has had an English grammar from its inception (and cannot, therefore, predate the dominance of English). Rather, she shows that grammatical convergence can and does occur where code-switching is common (ibid.: 174, 312) and that in this context – the desire to keep the very existence of ethnolect secret – there are compelling reasons for *Shelta*'s exhibiting such convergence, pointing out that Anglo-Romani has undergone similar metamorphosis for similar reasons. Moreover, noting (ibid.: 183) that many of the instances of alleged "disguisal" are risibly transparent to anyone with the slightest familiarity with the Irish language, Binchy suggests that this type of modification points to the workings of unconscious mechanisms rather than deliberate obfuscation.

Irish and *Shelta*: A Reconsideration

Binchy is, astonishingly, the only scholar besides the present writer (ní Shuinéar 1979, 1984, 1996) to reject the "deliberate, random scrambling" hypothesis by which one can "prove" that *any* language is a "perverted" form of *any* other. Binchy does not develop her objections, perhaps because the flaws in the theory are so pervasive and glaring. Its formulators and perpetuators fail to recognise the possibility of cognate words from a common historical root, the mechanisms of borrowing, or the very existence of structural regularities. Applying these methods and assumptions by way of illustration, Irish – already old when first committed to writing in the sixth century – can easily be dismissed as an exotic form of English, its vocabulary ranging from direct parasitism (*carr, fón, forc*), to minor modifications (*lampa, tae, caife*), to inept scrambling (*box* inverted to *bosca*, 'spoon' + arbitrary suffix = *spúnóg* [sp̯ʸuːn̯ʸoːg], or *James*, by modifying the initial consonant and adding a second syllable, becomes *Séamus* [ʃeːmʸəs̯ʸ]. What has happened is the unremarkable universal process of linguistic borrowing, by which loanwords are not passively accumulated, but appropriated. The Anglophone pronounces *tagliatelle, sauna* and *biscuit* to fit in with existing sound patterns, and in so doing may render them incomprehensible to speakers of the languages in which they originated – a consequence of, not the reason for, making the word one's own. Loanwords that have been around for a long while may not even be commonly recognised as such – how many Anglophones know that *admiral* derives from the Arabic and *mutton* from French?

The Irish language, which has been influencing *Shelta* for longer than any other, functions quite differently from English – a fact lamented but not grasped by the Anglophone Gypsylorists. Consider the following characteristics of Irish:

1. Irish is an inflected language: the nominative singular noun form given in the dictionary tells you no more about how the word functions in practice than the infinitive of a verb does about how it conjugates. For example, the man's name, *Tomás* [t̯ʸömʸaːs̯ʸ] in the nominative, becomes *a Thomáis* [ə hömʸaːʃ] in the vocative: two of the three consonants changing.
2. Irish consonants mutate: each can be realised by up to six different sounds. For example **b** [bʸ] or [bʲ] (e.g. *bád* 'a boat'), **bh** [w] or [vʲ] (e.g. *mo bhád* 'my boat'), **mb** [mʸ] or [mʲ] (e.g. *a mbád* 'their boat') are simply points on a continuum represented by the letter *b*, while **d** [d̯ʸ] or [dʲ] (e.g. *dán* 'a poem') **dh** [ɣ] or [j] (e.g. *mo dhán* 'my poem'), or **nd** [n̯ʸ] or [nʲ] (e.g. *a ndán* 'their poem') are aspects of *d*. In Irish, the *s* at the beginning of a word can sound like it does in English – for example the [s] of *súil* 'eye' – or, depending on context, [h] of *mo shúil* ('my eye'), [t] of *an tsúil* 'the eye', or, as we saw earlier, [ʃ] as in *siúil* 'to walk'. It is therefore unsurprising that Irish is full of alternative versions of words in which consonants chop and change: *minseach* and *binseach,* for example, *túr* and *súr, scioblach* and *gioblach*.
3. Irish unselfconsciously changes the order of consonants[17] both internally (*milseán* and *misleán,* for example, are synonyms, as are *cairéal* and *cailéar, urchóid* and *dochar)* and in loanwords (*box* becomes *bosca*).

---

[17] Editorial note: metathesis.

4. These characteristics, in combination, often profoundly transform loanwords, as the IPA transcriptions of the following examples show:[18]

'encyclopaedia'	» *ciclipéid*	[ˈcɪclʲɪpʲeːdʲ]
'orange' –	» *oráiste*	[ˈöɾˠaːʃtˠə]
'mayonnaise' –	» *maonáis*	[mˠeːnˠaːʃ]
'philosophy' –	» *fealsúnacht*	[fʲəlˠsˠuːnˠəxt̪ˠ].

No one has ever suggested that, by altering pronunciation values, or switching consonants, or switching syllables, as Irish habitually does even with its own vocabulary, speakers were attempting to "disguise" words. Every language has its own attitude to pronunciation. English treats the nominative singular form of the noun (and its accompanying adjective) as a word's canonical form. Not so in Irish, nor apparently so in *Shelta*.

Languages that rub up against one another rub off on each other. English has influenced Irish, and Irish has influenced not only Hiberno-English but the vocabulary of Anglophones everywhere (loanwords from Irish include *Tory*, *galore*, *whiskey*, a *slug* [of liquid], etc.). It is therefore unremarkable that Irish – its words and spoken characteristics – has influenced Traveller language, just as Travellers' language has impacted on the speech of those around them (*viz.* the lyrics of The Saw Doctors, whose home town Tuam has a 30% Traveller population). The "scrambled Irish" hypothesis, however, is essentially different because it places Travellers outside otherwise universal linguistic rules: simple borrowing becomes nefariously motivated obfuscation, and structure of every kind is replaced with a presumption of chaos. By applying Macalister's methodology to Irish as scrambled English, it is possible to explain

srón [sˠɹˠoːnˠ] ('nose' reversed + arbitrary *r*)

sráid [sˠɹˠaːdʲ] ('road' + arbitrary *s*)

úll [uːl̩ʲ] and *bláth* [bˠlˠaː] ('apple' and 'blossom' respectively, each minus a syllable)

urlár [öɾˠlˠaːrˠ] ('floor', replace initial *f* with arbitrary *ur-* and modify final vowel sound)

gloine [glˠɪnʲə] ('glass', vowel replaced with diphthong and the final consonant *-s* with *-ne*)[19]

bó [bˠoː] ('cow', initial consonant arbitrarily switched from *c-* to *b-*)

---

[18] The astute reader will have noticed that these are all loanwords in English, too. Note that the forms given are nominative singular – they undergo further transformation in context.

[19] Editorial note: the vowel remains a monophthong because no dialect of Irish has a diphthongal pronunciation in this word.

Figure 3: Some hypothetical Irish etymologies of *Shelta* words (Sampson)

Shelta	Irish[20]	IPA of Irish
chinnoχ	*nidh*	[nʲɪː]
stēsh	*seadh*	[ʃa]
limpath	*mo plaid*	[mˠə pˠlˠadʲ] ~ [mˠə fˠlˠadʲ]
thalosk	*latha*	[lˠaː]
dorra	*aran*	[aɾˠa(ː)nˠ]
lai-imon	*bliadhain*	[bʲlʲiənʲ]
grīsh	*croidhe*	[kɾˠɪː]
chimma	*maide*	[mˠadʲə] ~ [mˠɪdʲə]
gâth	*óg*	[ɔːg]
grīnlesk	*líon*	[ʌɪːnˠ]
shlīūχ	*leugh*[21]	[lʲuːx]
shīka	*tri*	[tʲɾʲɪː]

Figure 4: Some hypothetical Irish etymologies of *Shelta* words (Macalister[22])

Shelta	Irish	IPA of Irish
šeldrū	*Bēarla*	[bʲeːɾˠlˠˠə]
graisk	*snath*	[sˠnˠaː]
g'et'a	*fiche*	[fʲɪhə]
atómier	*mōr*	[mˠoːɾˠ]
brauen	*arbhar*	[aɾˠəwəɾˠ]
glūtug	*olann*	[olˠˠ̥ənˠ]
got'a	*dath*	[d̪ˠah]
elum	*baile*	[bˠalʲə]
mantri	*anbruth*	[anˠbˠɾˠu(h)]
m'aunes	*deagh-nōs*	[dʲaː nˠoːsˠ̥]
grādni	sathairn	[sˠahə̯ˠɾˠnʲ]
getūl	*eagla*	[ag(ə)lˠə]
bl'antaχ	*lēine*	[lʲeːnʲə]
n'urt	*anois*	[ə'nɪʃ]

---

[20] Editorial note: the Irish in Figures 3 and 4 is based on unreformed spellings.

[21] Editorial note: although Sampson gives this word, there is no such word in Irish.

[22] Editorial note: with few exceptions, such as *atómier*, Macalister uses macrons instead of fadas in both Shelta and Irish.

and so on. It takes very little effort to get *inis* [ɪnʲɪʃ] from *island* by reordering the letters **i**, **s**, **n**. The fact that the Irish word includes a letter which is no longer pronounced in English appears to prove that the "perversion" was carried out on written, not spoken, vocabulary, or else (perhaps more charitably) that the process occurred a very long time ago. (Note that the fact that Irish *-is* is pronounced like English *-ish* is going to sail right over the scholar's head because he or she has never heard the language spoken.) Bearing this in mind, consider the sample etymologies for Traveller vocabulary in Figures 3 and 4, which go much further, showing the far-fetchedness of some of Sampson's and Macalister's hypothetical etymologies of *Shelta* words from Irish equivalents. Those become even more fantastic when we compare the *Shelta* – deliberately spelt to maximise similarity with written Irish – with the IPA indicating how the Irish *sounds* as opposed to *looks*. Such hypothetical etymologies tell us more about their proponents than they do about Traveller language. Derived from written, not spoken, Irish – by and large the nominative singular form, with no indication of geographical distribution and rarely of pronunciation, and pervasive orthographical errors despite orthography being the core of the hypothesis – they embody untenable assumptions about speakers, *viz.* that, although too primitive to cope with abstracts or infinitives, they have "docked", "disguised", and "perverted" language in a "random" manner, "not governed by any phonological principle". Insofar as linguistics no longer recognises the validity of such assumptions, the etymology of Traveller vocabulary requires a radical reassessment, this time within a holistic approach including phonetics, syntax and so on.

Traveller Language: The Way Forward

From the very outset of scholarly interest in it, *Shelta* has been assumed to be a deliberately scrambled version of somebody else's language; subsequent consensus identifies some proportion of this as "ancient" Irish on the grounds that *Shelta* "preserves" certain of its characteristics, albeit in "perverted" form. While Irish itself has, along with every other language on the planet, evolved over the centuries, Traveller language, like Travellers themselves, is deemed to be in some sort of time warp, immune from otherwise universal processes – except, tellingly, decay (*every* commentator tells us that the language is on the way out).

Traveller language continues to be treated as a shopping list of individual exotic words to be assigned an origin in somebody else's language, with little attention as to how they are combined, and none at all on how the structures and phonetics of Travellers' own language shape their use of English. Traveller language, like Travellers themselves, has never been taken seriously, on its own terms. This is, of course, what it all boils down to: what Irish Travellers *speak* is, as far as academia and non-Travellers in general are concerned, what Irish Travellers *are*. And vice versa: what Irish Travellers *are* – a "backslang" sort of people, dropouts, bogus

Romanies or peasants in a time warp – predetermines how academia interprets what Irish Travellers *speak*.

Traveller English has never been systematically investigated. Scholars – most of them outsiders who could not differentiate the multitude of dialect trees within the Hiberno-English forest – simply dismiss Traveller English as "the same" as that of "the settled population" – a clear nonsense as it implies that a single dialect is spoken by all Irish people, geography and class (not to mention ethnicity) notwithstanding. *Any* speaker of Hiberno-English can identify a speaker of Traveller English, even without visual clues – for example, on the radio. Traveller English, while not entirely outside the Hiberno-English forest, is pervasively different from *any* variety of Hiberno-English. It must, therefore, have at least in part a separate and distinct linguistic substratum.

Let us examine assertions indicating the existence of a fuller substrate language. John Barlow, born in 1811, when Irish was still the vernacular of over half the population of Ireland, was Sampson's main and Meyer's sole informant. His, and other Irish informants', insistence that *Shelta* was their first language is corroborated by outside observers. Sampson, for example, quotes an "old Connaught tradesman" as stating that "the ould tinkers could spake naythur English nor Irish corrictly" (Sampson 1890: 206). An English visitor to Kerry in 1907 was struck by the fact that "[tinkers] speak no Irish among a Gaelic population" and are instead to be found "standing apart and talking in jarring, unlovely, un-Irish voices" (Curtis 1907: 132). The two Irish Travellers who had, prior to the present groundbreaking volume of papers, written about their language, stress its expressive potential and use in intimate contexts [see Cash 1977 and Maher 1984][23]. Traveller Hiberno-English is to this day as distinctive as Black American English and, I would suggest, for the same reason: an iceberg of linguistic substratum, of which exotic lexicon – the only aspect to have been studied to date – is but the merest tip.

A skilled linguist could reconstruct a great deal of Travellers' own language, or languages, on the basis of how Travellers speak English today, in precisely the same way as the structures of Irish could be partially reconstructed on the basis of, say, the speech of Dubliners who have not one conscious word of the language: for example, the constructions *I'm after* [*seeing her at the bus stop*] and *I do be* [*in town of a Saturday*] reflect the absorption into Hiberno-English of syntactic constructions from Irish; similarly, the bi-syllabic pronunciation of *film* as *filum* [fɪləm] provides an

---

[23] Very similar points are made by Betsy Whyte, a native speaker of Scottish Traveller Cant, in her two-volume autobiography *The Yellow on the Broom* and *Red Rowans and Wild Honey*, passim. See, in particular, p. 178 of the former, under the heading "Traveller cant [*sic*] and Scots words used in my story", reproduced verbatim in the latter, p. 213.

illustration of how pronunciation features from Irish were also absorbed, and so on. Add to this the fact that the average Dubliner uses – whether they know it or not – dozens of words and phrases taken directly from Irish, *and* that a considerable number of words shared by Standard English and Hiberno-English were borrowed by the former, and we begin to realise that living speakers have a great deal to offer.

Breaking out of the Nineteenth-Century Mould

Active collection of, and theorising about, Traveller language had its heyday in the years 1882–1908; three decades later, this original material was systematised, copperfastening a conventional wisdom gradually entrenched as timeless truth. What little has been done since has been carried out upon the foundations, and within the confines, traced in this paper. The methodology on which the edifice was built – analysing individual, out-of-context words in an orthography reflecting not how words actually sound but their alleged etymology, while ignoring syntax, pronunciation, etc. and doing so (usually) comparing third- and fourth-hand transcriptions to dictionary entries in a language (usually) unknown to the researcher – has long been rejected by linguistic science, as have the assumptions which pervade it (e.g. the human capacity for linguistic randomness, the view that regards creoles as "Broken-English", the existence of human groups so psycholinguistically primitive that they cannot grasp the notion of the infinitive, the assigning of nefarious motives to the transformations accompanying linguistic borrowing, etc.). Moreover, and unique to the *Shelta* paradigm, are fundamental premises that are both preposterous (that a fragmented, nomadic people would universally adopt random modifications devised by scholars, and retain these rather than the more complete and equally "cryptic" system, Irish, in the New World) and demonstrably inaccurate (the alleged influx of dislocated scholars onto the roadsides of Ireland following the dissolution of the monasteries under Henry VIII is a projection of English realities which simply did not apply here [Bradshaw 1974]). The purpose of this paper is to deconstruct the scholarly edifice, thereby discrediting it and, hopefully, instigating a radical reassessment of Traveller language in accordance with twenty-first century academic standards.

This paper began with the caveat that it is about *Shelta* – a term and a concept constructed by Victorian Gypsylorists – rather than Irish Traveller languages, which remain a virgin field for serious research. Far from being satisfactorily answered, the relevant questions have not even been asked yet. How Travellers talk must, at long last, be analysed in accordance with the assumptions and methodology currently applied to all speech communities, and extended beyond Traveller-exclusive lexicon to include the syntax, pronunciation, etc. of Traveller talk generally so as to comprehensively compare this to other varieties of Hiberno-English; identifying differences will give a fuller picture of the substrate system.

There are compelling practical reasons for undertaking such an exercise. For example, so long as Victorian assumptions about "Broken-English" continue to be applied to Travellers, the "education" system will continue to treat their linguistic difference as deprivation to be redressed rather than as the distinct system it is. We are beginning to see the downstream practical effects of academic reassessment (and grassroots assertion) of Black English Vernacular as Ebonics: the legitimacy of *what* people say is filtered through perceptions of the legitimacy of *how* they say it. It is high time that we began to take Travellers as seriously, and as respectfully, as we – theoretically – do "Negroes and Polynesians". Academia, and specifically linguistics as a branch of anthropology, started off by rubber stamping popular notions of a primitive "them" versus an evolved "us", but in time came to play a crucial role in promoting popular understanding that "different" is not the same as "inferior"; applying those lessons closer to home is long overdue. This paper is offered as simply the first stage in righting a deeply entrenched wrong. I hope it inspires others more qualified than the present writer to pursue all the issues which together make the case of *Shelta* so curious.

References

Binchy, Alice. 1985. "Shelta: An Historical and Contemporary Analysis". Unpublished M.A. thesis, National Institute of Higher Education, Dublin

Binchy, Alice. 1993. "The Status and Functions of Shelta". Unpublished Ph.D. thesis, Somerville College, University of Oxford

Binchy, Alice. 1994. "Travellers' Language: A Sociolinguistic Perspective". In eds. McCann et al.,134–54

Bradshaw, Brendan. 1974. *Dissolution of the Religious Orders in Ireland under Henry VIII*. Cambridge: Cambridge University Press

Carleton, William. 1972. *The Black Prophet. A Tale of Irish Famine*. Shannon: Irish University Press [facsimile of original 1847 ed.]

Cash, Anthony. 1977. "The Language of the Maguires". *Journal of the Gypsy Lore Society* 4th ser. 1.3: 177–80

Corkery, Daniel. 1924. *The Hidden Ireland. A Study of Gaelic Munster in the Eighteenth Century*. Dublin: Gill and Macmillan

Court, Artelia. 1985. *Puck of the Droms: The Lives and Literature of the Irish Tinkers*. Berkeley, CA: University of California Press

Curtis, Edward. 1907. "The People of Kerry; Iberians and Tinkers at Killorglin". *Manchester Guardian*, 28 October 1907, reprinted as "Irish Gypsies". *Journal of the Gypsy Lore Society* 2nd ser. 2 (October 1908): 130–2

ffrench, Canon J. 1890. "Additional Notes on the Irish Tinkers and their Language". *Journal of the Gypsy Lore Society* 2.2: 127–8

Foster, Idris L. 1937. "Obscure and Mystical Languages: being a review of R.A. Stewart Macalister's Secret Languages [...]". *Journal of the Gypsy Lore Society* 16: 138–44

Grant, Anthony P. 1994. "Shelta: The Secret Language of Irish Travellers viewed as a Mixed Language". In eds. Peter Bakker and Martin Mous. *Mixed Languages: 15 Case Studies in Language Intertwining.* Amsterdam: Uitgave IFOTT. 123–50

Hancock, Ian F. 1973. "Shelta: A Problem of Classification". *Journal of the Gypsy Lore Society* 3rd ser. 51: 79–87

Hancock, Ian F. 1984. "Shelta and Polari". In ed. Peter Trudgill. *Language in the British Isles.* Cambridge: Cambridge University Press. 384–403

Hancock, Ian F. 1986. "The Cryptolectal Speech of the American Roads: Traveller Cant and American Angloromani". *American Speech* 61.3: 206–20

Harper, Jared. 1971. "'Gypsy' Research in the South". In ed. K. Moreland. *The Not so Solid South: Anthropological Studies in Regional Subculture.* Southern Anthropological Society Proceedings No. 4. Athens, GA: University of Georgia Press Press. 16–24

Harper, Jared and Hudson, Charles. 1971 "Irish Traveler Cant". *Journal of English Linguistics* 15: 78–86

Harper, Jared and Hudson, Charles. 1973. "Irish Traveler Cant in its Social Setting". *Southern Folklore Quarterly* 37: 101–14.

l'Amie, Aileen (ed.) No Date. The Irish Travelling People. A Resource Collection. "*Shelta*, the Secret Language" (set 6, 4 vols, total 542 pp; a 5th volume in the *Shelta* set is currently being compiled)

Leblon, Bernard. 1995. *Gypsies and Flamenco.*Hatfield: University of Hertfordshire Press

Leland, Charles G. 1882. "Shelta, the Tinkers' Talk". In *The Gypsies.* Boston: Houghton, Mifflin and Co. 354–72; reprinted as "The Tinkers' Talk". *Journal of the Gypsy Lore Society* 2nd ser. 1 (1907–8): 168–80

Leland, Charles G. 1891. "Shelta". *Journal of the Gypsy Lore Society* 2.4: 321–3

Leland, Charles G. 1892. [on his retirement as president of the GLS], *Journal of the Gypsy Lore Society* 3: 195

Macalister, R. A. Stewart. 1937. *The Secret Languages of Ireland. With special reference to the origin and nature of THE SHELTA LANGUAGE, partly based upon the Collections and Manuscripts of the late JOHN SAMPSON.* Cambridge: Cambridge University Press; facsimile ed., Armagh: Craobh Rua Books, 1996

McCann, May, Ó Síocháin, Séamus, Ruane, Joseph (eds.). 1994. *Irish Travellers: Culture and Ethnicity.* Belfast: Institute of Irish Studies, Queen's University Belfast (for the Anthropological Association of Ireland)

McManus, Damian. 1996. Preface to Macalister's *Corpus Inscriptionum Insularum Celticarum.* Dublin: Four Courts Press. pp. e–h. First published 1945

MacRitchie, David. 1889. "Irish Tinkers and their Language". *Journal of the Gypsy Lore Society* 1.6: 350–7

MacRitchie, David. 1901. "Shelta: The Cairds' Language". *Transactions of the Gaelic Society at Inverness* 24 (1899–1901): 429–68; reproduced as a separate volume later that year

Maher, Seán. 1984. Introduction to Irish Traveller Resource Collection volumes on "Shelta, the Secret Language"

Meyer, Kuno. 1891. "On the Irish Origin and Age of Shelta". *Journal of the Gypsy Lore Society* 2.5: 257–66

Meyer, Kuno, 1909. "The Secret Languages of Ireland". *Journal of the Gypsy Lore Society* 2.3: 241–6

ní Shuinéar, Sinéad. 1979. "Commentary on Macalister". Revised 1984, privately circulated

ní Shuinéar, Sinéad. 1984. "Macalister Debunked. The Case for Critical Assessment of Macalister's Assertions re. the Origins of the Shelta Language and of its Speakers, the Irish Travellers". Unpublished manuscript, privately circulated

ní Shuinéar, Sinéad. 1996. "On Anthony Grant's Preliminaries". Privately circulated

Norwood, T.W. 1887. "Tramps' Language". *The Academy* 765 (1 January 1887): 12–13

Ó Baoill, Dónall P. 1994. "Travellers' Cant: Language or Register?". In eds. McCann et al., 155–69

O'Brien, M.A. 1938. Review of *The Secret Languages of Ireland* by R.A. Stewart Macalister. *Irish Historical Studies* 1: 95–7

Purdon, Edward. 1999. *The Story of the Irish Language*. Cork: Mercier Press

Sampson, John. 1890. "Tinkers and their Talk". *Journal of the Gypsy Lore Society* 2.4: 204–21

Whyte, Betsy. 1979. *The Yellow on the Broom*. Edinburgh: W. and R. Chambers

Whyte, Betsy. 1992. *Red Rowans and Wild Honey*. London: Corgi

Discussion of "The Curious Case of *Shelta*"

Terence Odlin: Are you claiming that you can reconstruct a substrate language from the existence of a language today?

Sinéad ní Shuinéar: I'm claiming that there is certainly something to be looked at there, and it hasn't been, yet. Hiberno-English, certainly: if you wanted to reconstruct Irish if there were no native speakers of Irish left, if there were no written texts, you would still have some idea of what Irish syntax and phonics and so on are, just from looking at Hiberno-English.

Terence Odlin: The problem there is that, if we didn't have Irish to go on, we could reconstruct Irish in any number of possible ways. The fact is that we do have Irish to go on, and that gives us some reason to claim that there is substrate influence. I just don't think the methodology you're proposing here will work.

Sinéad ní Shuinéar: I take it from your accent that you're an American?

Terence Odlin: Could be Canadian.

Sinéad ní Shuinéar: Could be Canadian, all right, fine. North American, excuse me.

Terence Odlin: But, excuse me, I don't think ethnicity really matters much when you're talking about linguistic reconstruction.

Sinéad ní Shuinéar: Oh, no, it doesn't. But it does matter as to sensitivity of ear. To me, there is such a thing as "an American accent", which is a clear nonsense for people who live there. For me, there is such a thing as "a New Zealand accent", which is clearly nonsense. For me, there is such a thing as "a general New Zealand / Australian accent", which is clearly a nonsense if you live there. And for people who live on this particular island, we all know, whether we're Traveller or country, when we hear a Traveller speaker. This is pervasive. It's as pervasive as Black English is in North America. And I cannot think of any logical explanation for it except that there's a separate linguistic substrate.

Terence Odlin: I certainly can! And there are a lot of people here who can. And I'm not disputing the claim that you're making. Maybe others would, but I'm not disputing the claim that there might be an identifiable Traveller accent. But what do you make of that in terms of historical source? My point, once again, is that you have a range of possible options, and unless you have the substrate language, you can't really be sure that there was a substrate language to begin with, or that you can say what the substrate language was like. Lots of people have tried to do this in different historical contexts, and I don't know of any case yet of where they've succeeded in giving a persuasive reconstruction.

Sinéad ní Shuinéar: I'm only saying it's worth looking at. I'm not a linguist. I'm an anthropologist.

Raymond Hickey: All of us here share your criticism of people like Macalister, who are full of all sorts of racial prejudice, of course, which I hope none of us would dream of associating themselves with nowadays. But the problem for us, if we're coming with open eyes to something like this – and that's the reason, I presume, why most of us are here – is: what's the alternative? Are there alternative sources? Are there alternative descriptions? If someone is genuinely interested in looking at Shelta, what can you offer him or her assuming that the sources we have from Meyer down to Macalister are unacceptable for the reasons you've outlined?

Sinéad ní Shuinéar: There are no other sources. Full stop.

Raymond Hickey: Well, that's the crux for people who are interested in the language as such ...

Sinéad ní Shuinéar: That's why living speakers have to be looked at.

Manfred Görlach: There were modest attempts at making Anglo-Romani teachable. Have there been any for Shelta?

Ellen McDonagh: There are a number of Travellers themselves who have attempted to teach Cant in training centres, but there are very few because unfortunately the circumstances have made it so.

Manfred Görlach: Are there any written materials for it?

Ellen McDonagh: I know one Traveller in particular has attempted to write it down and tried to ... But I think it only comes from Travellers themselves.

Manfred Görlach: Are you going to increase this?

Ellen McDonagh: It's an attempt that's being made, and we're trying to do that, and we're trying to encourage more and more Travellers to show an interest in it, However, again, due to the wider circumstances in society, a number of Travellers, and many of the younger ones, would feel ashamed of the language because it identifies them in a negative way. And that's why. So we have to get over all those barriers, and the [educators?].

Aileen l'Amie: Can you remember the two little publications by Acton?

Sinéad ní Shuinéar: *Have You the Feen's Grade Nyocked?* was one of them, and the other was *Mike's Book*. They were two very small books.

Manfred Görlach: For Romani yes, but ...

Sinéad ní Shuinéar: No. These are in Gammon.

Alice Binchy: In Shelta.

Manfred Görlach: In Shelta.

Mícheál Ó hAodha: We're trying to use them in Limerick.

Fionnuala Williams: For primary school children?

Mícheál Ó hAodha: Yes.

Mary Burke: I was going to ask about that. Is Shelta being encouraged in creative writing if you're teaching literacy or anything like that?

Ellen McDonagh: Maybe by teachers who are specifically trained to work with Travellers, but I'm not aware of it within the educational system.

Sinéad ní Shuinéar: Are you aware of any teachers specifically trained to work with Travellers?

Ellen McDonagh: No, I'm not.

Sinéad ní Shuinéar: No. So, in other words, they don't use it.

Mary Burke: Right. I've just noticed collections, for example, the Tullamore Travellers' Women's Travellers' Collective have produced a book of poetry, but it was all in English. Was there any resistance to that? Do you know if there are people who wanted to write in Shelta? Were they happy in English?

Ellen McDonagh: They may want to, but the educational ability of many of the Travellers in that age group which would have the knowledge of Cant is very limited. With the ability to write on paper, what you can say is that there are very few. I've heard songs entirely in Cant, and I've heard prayers entirely in Cant, but I've never seen them written down.

Alice Binchy: Isn't it true that there isn't really a tradition of storytelling in Cant? Would you agree with that?

Ellen McDonagh: Yes, I would agree with that. There isn't.

Alice Binchy: So writing in Cant would be artificial?

Ellen McDonagh: It would.

Sheila Douglas: On that subject, one of the greatest Traveller storytellers is Stanley Robertson, who has done several books. The first, the one I mentioned when I was talking, *Malcolm's Windows*, is a glorious mixture of Aberdeenshire Scots, which is very distinctive, Cant, and English. And most people apparently find it quite difficult to read. I didn't find it difficult because I understand the Cant and I understand Aberdeenshire Scots. But it's very, very vivid writing. Of his other books, some are in Scots, and one is entirely in English. But it's full of great stories. And the storytelling has become very strong in Scotland. We've a network of storytellers, and we have named as our patrons of our storytelling centre Traveller storytellers such as Stanley, Duncan Williamson, Belle Stewart, Willie MacPhee, and so on.

Travellers' Language: Some Irish Language Perspectives

Mícheál Ó hAodha

In this paper, I would like to provide a brief survey of the academic study to date on the language of the Travellers and then look at some of the ways in which the Irish language has influenced the lexicon of Shelta. I would like to take as an example a list of Shelta words which were recorded from a West of Ireland Travelling woman in the 1950s[1] and look at a few of the ways in which the Irish language influenced the formation of much of her vocabulary.

Shelta was first "discovered" in the 1880s. Charles Leland, an amateur historian and gypsiologist, and author of the book *The Gypsies*, told of coming across an Irish Traveller in Britain who mentioned another language that was allegedly far older than Romany and was habitually spoken by Irish tinkers, as they were then called. The language was called *Shelta* or *Sheldru*, which Leland in his excitement described as a fifth Celtic language, maybe even the lost language of the Picts. When Leland published news of his discovery, which came at the time of a great upsurge of interest in the Gypsy/Traveller way of life, many amateur folklore collectors were galvanised into action, and before long the pages of the *Journal of the Gypsy Lore Society* (a society which included artists like Augustus John and poets like Yeats) were filled with sightings of Irish Travellers and a few specimens of their language. Although it was accepted that the language belonged to Irish Travellers and was not related to Romany, most of the interest in Shelta was evidenced outside Ireland itself. The greatest part of the early material collected consisted of word lists, and since few of the collectors had any knowledge of Irish, Irish words were frequently included mistakenly. One of the early collectors, Crofton, who published an article entitled "Shelta, the Tinkers' Language" in 1886, however, knew enough Irish to be able to recognise that some Shelta words were formed by the application of disguise rules to Irish words, e.g.

Shelta	Irish
rodas	*doras*
laicín	*cailín*
tobar	*bóthar*

---

[1] The list in question was recorded by a contributor to the archives of Roinn Béaloideasa Éireann (The Irish Folklore Commission) whose central archive is located in University College Dublin. His name was P. Ó Caomhánaigh, who was from Cluain Máire, in Inishowen, Co. Donegal. The list is referenced at RBÉ Iml. 1255: 171. The acronym "RBÉ" refers to the archives of Roinn Béaloideasa Éireann (The Irish Folklore Commission). References including this acronym are succeeded by the acronym "Iml." which refers to the exact volume and page number within the archive at which the material is located.

Academic interest in the language began when John Sampson of the University of Liverpool, and the German Celtic scholar Kuno Meyer,[2] took up the study of the language. Both of these believed that the language was very old and they based their theory on three main facts:

1. One or two archaic words were allegedly preserved in Shelta, sometimes in disguised form, words which had previously been known only from old texts.
2. Some of the methods of disguising words in Shelta were identical to those employed in monastic manuscripts in ancient times, by monks who wanted to preserve some material in secrecy.
3. Some words seemed to have been formed from pre-aspirated or lenited Irish.

Although Sampson and Meyer both published papers on Shelta, the definitive work on the language was written by R.A. Stewart Macalister, as a chapter of *The Secret Languages of Ireland*, published in 1937. This was published after Sampson's death and was a compilation of all previously published work on Shelta. Macalister, unlike Sampson and Meyer, believed that the language was of recent origin and that it had been formed by people who were predominantly English-speaking, who had been aided in its construction by educated people: this explained (to his satisfaction) the inclusion of material from early manuscript sources. Macalister may be criticised on a number of fronts (e.g. that he was working from word lists which were not terribly reliable, or that he had heard very little Shelta, if any, spoken), but one of the main flaws in his work is that he saw the Travellers ("Tinkers") as an occupational group even though earlier collectors had described the language as spoken by chimney-sweeps, knife-grinders, sieve-makers, flower-sellers, hawkers, pedlars and other "wandering" people.

In this short article, I intend only briefly to review the actual linguistic research undertaken by Irish academics on Shelta.[3] Alice Binchy (1994: 140) says that the language is an ethnic marker for the Irish Travellers, and that it is part of the proof that the Irish Travellers have a separate ethnicity from the settled Irish population. To bolster her argument Binchy refers to the Shelta which is still spoken by the descendants of Irish Travellers in the southern United States – in states such as Georgia and North Carolina – and which is very similar to the Shelta still spoken in Ireland. The ancestors of these Travellers left Ireland between 1848 and 1850 and were probably Irish-speaking. The question Binchy asks is why those Travellers retained Shelta? If all they needed was a secret code, to use in the presence of settled Americans, they could have used Irish. After all, many other Irish emigrants who left

---

[2] It is worth noting that the study of Shelta was only a very minor interest of Meyer's. He wrote just two brief articles for the Gypsy Lore Society about Shelta.

[3] Other articles on Shelta have been written by English scholars such as Ian Hancock and Anthony Grant.

Ireland around the time of the famine were Irish-speaking, and the Irish language was retained for some time in America where there were Irish-speaking ghettoes in some of the larger cities. Binchy also argues that the fact that Shelta seems to have no independent grammar does not mean that it cannot be described as a language. She says that definitions of what is or is not a language are based on social and political, rather than purely linguistic factors – and it is Shelta's unfortunate position to find itself in close proximity to two languages whose prestige has been established linguistically for centuries, namely Irish and English. It is her contention that the small scale of Travellers' daily interaction with their own group was not enough to maintain Shelta grammar and that the present system is one whereby lexicon is the ethnic marker, and the grammar represents those parts of life shared with the settled society.

Dónall P. Ó Baoill (1994: 157) does not examine the question of Traveller ethnicity, but concentrates his research primarily on the syntax and structure of Shelta. He finds that Shelta is a form of speech which has an identical grammar and structure as well as a large amount of shared vocabulary with another language (in this case English) with which it has close ties and continuous contact. He emphasises the English-language linguistic structure of Shelta, i.e. the fact that the word order of Shelta is English – the means by which one asks questions is English – the grammatical endings used even on the non-English words are from English grammar (e.g. the verb endings -*ed*, -*ing* and the plurals -*(e)s*. Consider such phrases as:

> *ód niucs* 'two pennies' (Irish: *dó + ceann*)
> *lósped* 'married' (Irish: *pós + -ed*)

Since Shelta is a different form of language used for specific purposes, Ó Baoill considers that it would not be inappropriate to define it as a "register". Shelta is thus a special type of language used on well-defined occasions, a special type of language with a relatively large number of words of non-English origin, but being held together as a linguistic system by elements of English syntax and grammar. The overall structure of Shelta therefore is formed outside of the structure of Irish, and Irish words are "borrowed" in order to replace the content words (nouns, verbs, adjectives, adverbs). Ó Baoill hypothesises that Shelta must have been created at a time when its original speakers were bilingual, having a knowledge of both Irish and English, i.e. some time within the last 350 years or so.

As an Irish-speaker, I am particularly interested in those words which appear to have been derived from the Irish language. The question of the origin of the non-Irish element of the Traveller vocabulary is contentious and complex. It is an area of study which should be explored by scholars – preferably Travellers themselves – in the future.

The Vocabulary of Mrs. Stokes

The words to be examined here come from a brief list[4] of words taken down from a Traveller woman (or 'tinker' as she described herself) named Mrs. Stokes (née Mongan) in 1952 as she travelled through Donegal. I would like to look at some examples of the disguise process and how it took place in the case of some words in her vocabulary derived from the Irish language. Mrs. Stokes told her interviewer, a man from Cluain Máire in Inishowen, Co. Donegal, that she was born in Roscommon and that she was then 60 years of age. Mrs. Stokes's maiden name was Mongan and the Mongans are west-of-Ireland Travellers who travel through counties Mayo, Galway, Sligo and Roscommon. Her married name Stokes was associated with Travellers who, during the 1950s, travelled around Meath, Westmeath, Offaly, Longford, Cavan and further up towards the border with Northern Ireland.

When speaking of Travellers and their use of Irish, it is worth noting that a significant majority of Travellers today have very little knowledge of the Irish language, partly through their being (often unfairly) segregated or put into special classes in national school, and for this reason many are unaware of the Irish words that underlie some of their vocabulary. This was not always the case, however. It is possible that Mrs. Stokes was an Irish-speaker, as there were Travellers in Galway, Mayo, Donegal, Waterford and Kerry who were native speakers right up until the 1950s.

A few words in her list are taken directly from the Irish language[5] and are not subject to any form of word disguise but there are Shelta words that would have been known by non-Irish-speaking Travellers. Amongst them are:

> (S) *brovan* 'straw', oats (Ir. *breothan* 'oats')
> (S) *blaineog* 'cow'(Ir. *bleánach* 'a cow with a large quantity of milk')
> (S) *armuch/alamuch* 'milk' (Ir. *leamhnacht* 'new milk')
> (S) *laprog* 'duck' (Ir. *lapóg/lapróg* 'a fat low-sized woman, little waddling toddler').
> (S) *séineóg* 'six pence' (Ir. *sé* and Shelta *neóg/niuc* from the [inverted] Irish word *ceann* 'head' or 'penny')
> (S) *malay/molly* 'camping place' (Ir. *mallaigh/moilligh* 'to slow down, stop, on one's journey')
> (S) *shaideog* 'policeman' (Ir. *séideog* 'the one who blows, whistles, squeals, gives out')

---

[4] I have placed the capital letter S in brackets before any words that were given in Mrs. Stokes's list to indicate that the form given is the exact spelling as given by the man who transcribed the word list from Mrs. Stokes.
[5] The dictionary definitions of the Irish words in this article are taken from Ó Dónaill (1977).

Three interesting words on Mrs. Stokes' list with probable Irish-language derivations are:

> (S) *tearachar* 'knife' (Ir. *tearcaigh* 'to make scarce, decrease, diminish, make thin')
> (S) *sponch* 'tobacco' (Ir. *sponc* 'coltsfoot' or 'tinder'. The herb known as *sponc* was smoked as a tobacco and used to alleviate coughs, bronchitis and asthma)[6]
> (S) *moisín* 'goose' (Ir. *oisín* 'little goose', cf. *níl inti ach oisín* 'she's just a little goose')

Another word which has appeared in a few previous word lists is:

> (S) *lew-og* 'meal' (Ir. *luadh lamhail* 'abundance' or 'engagement [meal]')'

Three other words are interesting because they look like they come from Irish but their derivation is not immediately obvious:

> (S) *guiseop* 'pint tin'
> (S) *rumóg* 'egg'[7]
> (S) *maoltóg* 'shirt'

There are traces of dialectal variation in the Shelta forms taken down at various times, and if the recorder of Mrs. Stokes was transcribing her pronunciation correctly (and there is a reasonable chance that he was, since he was an Irish-speaker and able to write the Irish language) then her Shelta word list too may show traces of dialectal variation.[8] The fact that the vowel is marked long in the second syllable of the following words from Mrs. Stokes' list indicates that they are of Connacht or Munster

---

[6] The leaves of this herb, when boiled, were also used as a cure for sores, insect stings and ulcers.

[7] The archives of the Irish Folklore Commission record this as an Irish word in use in the Hiberno-English of country people in Co. Armagh in the 1940s and 1950s. It meant the round congealed globs of cream that often appeared on the top of a bucket of unpasteurised milk.

[8] This is an interesting point in itself because most of the people who recorded Shelta were not Irish-speakers, apart from two folklore collectors who worked for the Irish Folklore Commission, Pádraig Mac Gréine who recorded from 1931–34 in Co. Longford, and Mícheál Mac Éinrí, who recorded in 1939 in Co. Mayo. In fact, the recording of Shelta proved to be a very difficult task for those unfamiliar with the Irish language. The majority of scholars who recorded Shelta word lists during the nineteenth century was English – as most of the interest in the Travellers' language came from outside Ireland itself, and few of the collectors had any knowledge of Irish. Irish words were frequently included mistakenly in the lists.

Irish origin rather than Ulster Irish which tends to shorten the long vowels in the second syllables of words. These words may be of Munster origin since the Munster dialects tend to put the stress on the second syllable where there is a long vowel or before a voiceless velar fricative.

(S) *séineóg* 'sixpence'
(S) *maoltóg* 'shirt'
(S) *mincíoch* 'tinsmith'
(S) *pincín* 'vermin'
(S) *taineóg* 'halfpence'
(S) *rumóg* ' 'egg'

We cannot be certain of course that the transcriber was always correct in his inclusion or omission of length marks. If the transcription is accurate it could indicate a Munster influence on Mrs. Stokes's speech. This is not impossible since the Stokes' like the McDonaghs and Wards were a very well-travelled family and references to them appear not just in the west and north but also further south in counties such as Limerick and even Kerry.

Another interesting aspect of the transcriptions from Mrs. Stokes is the way the transcriber spells certain words. The endings *–óg* and *-íoch* appear at the end of a number of words which are not pronounced in this way today. This may have been the way that Mrs. Stokes pronounced these particular words.

(S) *cíneach   / cena / cēn* (Ir. *teach* 'house')
(S) *mincíoch / mincéir* (Ir. *tincéir* 'tinsmith')
(S) *moileach / máille* (Ir. *lámh* 'hand')
(S) *rudasc / rodus* (Ir. *doras* 'door')

The word *chera/chini* 'fire' also appears in Mrs. Stokes' list. This seems to originate from the Irish word *t(e)ine/tinidh* meaning 'fire'. This alteration can also be heard in the Shelta word *rodus/rorus* door from the Irish word *doras*.[9]

Types of Linguistic Alteration

In his book *The Secret Languages of Ireland* Macalister gave an in-depth account of how he considered Shelta words were formed. His work was an amalgam of his own theories and the work of Sampson and Meyer before him. Macalister's theories on the

---

[9] Interestingly the interchange of *r* and *d* is a common consonant substitution in certain dialects of English. Cf. also the well-known Dublin pronunciation of *delighted* as *delira* with interchange of *r* and *t*.

etymology of Shelta included a very complex[10] list of rules,[11] some of which should almost certainly be treated with caution[12] as it may be that he was straining himself unnecessarily in an attempt to derive as large a proportion of the Shelta lexicon as possible from Irish base forms through the application of several rules per syllable. Although it is clear that some sound substitutions on the part of Irish words have taken place in Shelta, it may well be the case that some of the more abstruse etymologies proposed by Macalister are false, insofar as they concern words which did not derive from Irish in the first place. Macalister's reputation has suffered because of his tendency, in certain cases, to analyse a Shelta word and an Irish word of similar meaning and to try to devise a way of forcing or bringing the two words together. Macalister's eagerness to find an Irish origin for many words fitted in of course with the "literate help" theory, i.e. his theory that Shelta had been formed by people who were predominantly English-speaking but who had been aided in its construction by educated people. This may be the reason why he did not pay so much attention to those Shelta words which do not seem to have been derived from Irish or to those whose origin is unclear. Of course, the study of the large non-Irish language portion of Shelta is something that still remains to be undertaken.

What is clear to all the linguists who have studied Shelta to date e.g. Meyer (1891, 1909); Macalister (1937), Hancock (1973, 1984), Grant (1994), Binchy (1994), Ó Baoill (1994) is that a very substantial portion of the Shelta lexicon is Irish in origin, and, rather than being directly borrowed from Irish, it has been subject to a number of modifications including the prefixing and suffixing of syllables, the substitution of consonants and vowels and reversal. The Celtic scholar, Kuno Meyer, laid down

---

[10] While these rules appear complex, it should be noted that when compared with the incredibly complex rules of rhyme and alliteration employed by the nomadic bards (discussed below), they are relatively simple.

[11] Macalister lists eight methods of word formation or word disguise. These are:
    (a) deaspiration
    (b) denasalisation
    (c) substitution
    (d) apocope
    (e) prefixes
    (f) metathesis
    (g) reversal of syllables
    (h) complete reversal

[12] It has become fashionable in certain circles to dismiss Macalister's work out of hand because of the alleged bias with which Macalister approached the compilation of his Shelta lexicon. It is not correct, however, to dismiss all of Macalister's work because of possible bias in his methodology. The Irish-American Traveller Richard Waters has pointed out in another contribution to this volume that the Cant words he knows tend to validate enough of Macalister's lexicon for him to take the rest of it on faith as regards the general accuracy of its inclusions, despite probable transcription errors.

fairly simple rules for what he considered the main processes of word disguise operating in Shelta. Those were:

1. reversal of the Irish word, especially words of one syllable
2. prefixing an arbitrary letter or letters to the word
3. substituting another letter or letters for the initial
4. transpositions of letters or anagrams

Similar methods of word transformation were in operation in the other "secret" "cants" that were spoken in Ireland in the nineteenth century, including the only other "secret" language which survived into the twentieth century, the *Béarlagair na Saor* 'Language of the Stonemasons'.[13]

Shelta's Methods of Disguise

Let us consider a few examples of the disguise methods described by Meyer (and subsequently Macalister, Grant, Binchy, etc.) and how they apply to some of the words recorded from Mrs. Stokes.

Substitution/prefixes
This is by far the most frequent method of word formation in Shelta. Substitution is used when the source word begins with a consonant, prefixing when it begins with a vowel. Substitutes are *gr-*, *sr-* or *s-*. Most of the words formed by this method are based on Irish, e.g. the word *grool* for 'apple' (from Irish *úll*), and *grubble* 'public house', 'pub', probably from the Irish *pobal* ('public', 'people'). As a substitute/prefix, *gr-* seems to have been used as a method of constructing *ad hoc* words from English by some Travellers until very recently. Examples include *grandy* ('sweets' or 'candy') as used by Irish American Travellers and *groilet* 'toilet' as used by some Irish Travellers in England. Examples from Mrs. Stokes's list include:

---

[13] Although the name given to this language indicates that it was the cant used by stonemasons, it seems clear that it was spoken by a much wider range of Travelling people, including pedlars, knife-grinders, and horse-trainers. It consists largely of innovated words or modified Irish words used in an Irish grammatical framework. The question of "monastic" influence on these "secret" languages was mooted by scholars like Meyer and Macalister. In fact Macalister (1937: 257) maintains that the language of today's Irish Travellers (formerly known as 'Tinkers'), Shelta, is just one of a number of "secret" languages apparently devised or inspired by medieval Irish Travelling monks and poets and compromising vocabularies formed from the engineered interaction of Irish Gaelic with other languages including Latin, Greek, Hebrew and English.

> *srideal* 'bottle' (Ir. *buidéal*)
> *grithíun* 'onion' (Ir. *oinniún*)
> *sreata* 'gate' (Ir. *geata*)
> *sarc* 'field' (Ir. *páirc*)
> *griúcra*[14] 'sugar' (Ir. *siúcra*).

Reversal

Reversal or "backslang" was a linguistic process common to many Travelling/Gypsy groups it appears. It is probable that the same process operated in other languages, including Irish at one stage. In Shelta the reversal of the first syllable is common.

> *laicín* (S. *leáicín*) 'girl' (Ir. *cailín*)
> *rodas* (S. *rudasc*) 'door' (Ir. *doras*)
> *gópa* (S. *gópa*) 'pocket' (Ir. *póca*)
> *nnaca* (S. *neaca*) 'tin can' (Ir. *canna*)

Reversal is applied only to words from Irish, and those words formed in this way are considered by some older Travellers to be more genuine old Shelta words, or the "real" Gammon. Some of the Rathkeale Travellers, for instance, consider *rodas* (or its variants *rudus* and *rodus*) from Irish *doras* to be a more authentic Shelta word for door than *jigger*, a word from English Cant.

The usage and pronunciation of certain words varies from dialect to dialect and from family to family. In the introduction to a children's picture book (with Gammon phrases) written by Michael Connors (a London-based Irish Traveller) and the Romany scholar Thomas Acton in the mid-1970s, the authors stated that they could identify at least five different dialects of Shelta while at the same time recognising that even within those dialects different families pronounced words differently. These were a Southern Irish dialect, a 'deeper' Ulster dialect, a northern Scottish dialect and more Romany-influenced mid-Scottish and south Welsh dialects.[15] It is noteworthy that one of the words for 'policeman' which Mrs. Stokes gave to her recorder as *musco*, from the Romany word *muskero / musker / muskra / musca* 'policeman', she said was used more by Scottish tinkers. Travelling in Donegal would of course have

---

[14] It is interesting that Mrs. Stokes gave two words for 'sugar'. She also gave the word *powder*. The word *limis/libis* from the Irish *milis* meaning 'sweet' is another Shelta word for 'sugar'.

[15] Certain Travelling families also had their own "private" Shelta lexicons incorporating different vocabulary, word reversal (including reversal of Shelta words) and backslang. These lexicons functioned as a vehicle for private communication when in the presence not only of "settled" people but also of "stranger" or unrelated Travellers. It is my own belief that, in the past, there were a more differentiated range of lexicons or "cants" in Shelta which varied according to the primary occupation of the Travelling families in question, i.e. whether they were traditionally associated with tinkering, musicianship, poetry, tailoring, herbalism or other trades, etc.

brought her into contact with Scottish influences. The other word which she used for policeman was *gleocot*[16] which may be an extension of *gleoch* 'man'. In this context it may be more likely to mean 'the one who looks or watches', the verb *gleoch* coming from the Irish *gliúc* ('look', 'peep', 'peer').[17]

Other examples of reversal may be *scemeisc* 'drunk' from Irish (*ar*) *meisce* (by developing a double final consonant represented by *sc*) and (S) *sarc* 'field' from the Irish loanword *páirc* or older Irish *riasc*.

Metathesis

Metathesis happens with words from the Irish language only, and so it is a process no longer happening in Shelta. Why the formation of new words (including the borrowing of English forms) into Shelta has not taken place to a much greater degree is an interesting question.[18] One would think that the creation or incorporation of new words into Shelta would (as in Irish) be an ongoing process, but that does not seem to be the case.[19] In the Shelta spoken today, some words seem to have shortened variants, e.g.

sheideog	shade – 'garda, policeman'	(Ir *séideog*)
garead	grade 'money'	(Ir. *airgead*)

Others, such as the Shelta words for 'yes' and 'no', *stéis* and *ní déis,* seem to have a wider range of meaning than previously – something that one could pessimistically attribute to language decline or shrinking vocabulary. Interestingly, the process of metathesis still happens in Irish in certain instances. The people in the Aran Islands sometimes say *Gaeigle* instead of *Gaeilge*. In Shelta words of more than one syllable, the second is usually left intact, e.g.

(S) *goréad* 'money' (Ir. *airgead*)
(S) *niukal* 'candle' (Ir. *coinneal*)

---

[16] The word *gleoch* has two different meanings in Shelta. There is a noun *gleoch* 'man' (probably from the Irish *óglach* meaning 'young man, warrior, vassal' and a verb *gleoch* 'look, see' from the Irish *gliúc* 'look, peer'.

[17] Cleeve (1983: 260) suggests that *gleocot* [glox gut] is a play on meaning and derives from the words *gleoch* ('man') and *gut* ('black') –literally 'black man' or by extension 'man in a black uniform'.

[18] One hears older people in the Irish-speaking areas bemoaning the fact that their children and grandchildren speak a creole of Irish and English. i.e. Irish with many borrowed English words.

[19] There is evidence that a few new Shelta words have been created by Irish-American Travellers but only a few.

Metathesis is often combined with other elements, either suffixed or prefixed, e.g.

      (S) *lohsped* 'married' (Ir. *pós* 'marry' + English *-ed*)
      (S) *krolusk* 'hungry' (Ir. *okras*)

or a word which has not appeared in previous word lists:

      (S) *loscan* 'salt' (Ir. *salann*)

Travellers and Shelta

In this paper, I have briefly focused on a few aspects of the influence of Irish on Shelta. What was most surprising at the symposium upon which some of the papers in this book are based was the fact that there was a body of opinion which appeared to doubt that these well-documented linguistic "disguise" processes existed at all. It was as if the existence of these "disguise" processes was in some way a source of embarrassment or "took away" from Travellers' Shelta when the opposite is clearly the case. The existence of "disguise" processes in Shelta actually reflects the richness and antiquity of Shelta rather than the opposite. This latter-mentioned body of opinion would appear to echo an older view of Traveller language as proposed by some of the early gypsylorists of the British Gypsy Lore Society. The gypsylorist view of Traveller language implied that all Travellers were "illiterate" tinkers and that, if these "disguise" mechanisms existed in Shelta, then it must have been the case that the Travellers were "helped" by literate people to "disguise" their language. The question that I would ask is why it was or still is so commonly assumed that all Travellers were (a) tinkers and (b) illiterate in the past? Travellers themselves have never defined themselves as "just" tinkers but have generally preferred to refer to themselves as Travellers. There is also overwhelming evidence, particularly in Irish-language literary sources, that many Travelling people were highly literate in the past. What of those Travelling people known as "*scoláirí bochta*" ('poor scholars') or "*báird-dochtúirí*" ('bard-doctors' or 'healers'), many of whom relied on literacy as one of the central tools of their trade? That many Travellers were highly literate was even acknowledged by some of the extremely prejudiced "settled" community respondents who answered the 1950 Questionnaire on Tinkers that was issued by the Irish Folklore Commission. Witness the following statement from a man in County Galway when asked what term the "settled" community used to refer to Travellers:

      Tincéaraí anois. Fadó théadh "lucht siúil" thart. Ní tincéaraí (lucht
      stán) a bhíodh i gcuid mhór aca sin.........Scoláirí is aos léanta eile
      ina measc. Eolas aca ar luibh-leigheasa, galair duine is ainmhí &rl.[20]

---

[20] RBÉ, Iml. 1255: 15

(They are called tinkers nowadays. Long ago "Travelling people" used
to go around. Many of these people were not tinsmiths. [...] Scholars
and the lettered class were amongst them. They had knowledge of
herbalism and diseases that affected both humans and animals etc.)

And what of the rich literary tradition of those nomadic Travellers known as the
bards, poets who specialised in extremely complex formulaic praise poetry and satires
and amongst whom (strangely enough!) such names as Sweeney, O'Donnell,
McDonagh, Ward and Leary occur again and again? The fact that this literary or
bardic or "written" aspect of Travelling culture is glossed over today ignores a
significant aspect of Traveller history and is a denial of their significant role in the
reproduction of Irish culture generally. Michael McDonagh (2000: 31) is the first
Traveller activist to have pointed out the connection between the nomadic bards and
the ancestors of today's Travelling people. As he points out, this connection is made
manifest in one of the most common surnames found amongst the Travelling
community, *Ward*. The surname *Ward* comes from the Irish *Mac an Bháird* meaning
'son of the bard'. Irish texts make reference over many centuries to a "private"
language, known as *Béarla na bhFilí* ('the language of the Bards'), in which the
highly literate bards communicated "private" messages to one another or made in-
jokes, a language which used many of the same "disguise" processes found in Shelta
today. And what of the incredible body of poetry left behind by the eighteenth-
century Traveller stonemason Eoghan Rua Ó Súilleabháin, who, it was said,
composed satires in a number of different "cants"? The role of Irish Travellers as
bards who both praised and satirised the community survived well into the twentieth
century, particularly in the rural Irish-speaking regions of Ireland, as evidenced by the
following description recorded in the Donegal Gaeltacht in the 1940s:

*Bhí fear eile ag 'ul thart annseo a dtabharadh siad Féidhlimidh na fidle
air. Féidhlimidh Ó Baoighill an t-ainm ceart a bhí air. Shiubhaileadh sé
seo leis thart ó áit go h-áit* [...] *Bhí aithne agus eolas ag an fhear seo ar
gach duine agus argach áit ins a' chonndae go h-uile* [...] *Ní tháinic
seisean ariamh go doras toigh óstais nach dtabharfadh sé amach an
fhideal agus le cois seinm, dhéanfadh sé fhéin abhrán a chumadh mar
bhuailfeá do dhá bhois ar a chéile. Dhéanfadh sé abhrán molta do fhear
an toighe sin* [...] *Thíos annseo i nGort a Choirce ins na laethibh sin bhí
fear siopa ann a raibh Séarlaí Ó Gallachubhair air* [...] *nuair a thiocfadh
Féidhlimidh ós coinne an toighe sin, bhéarfadh sé amach an fhideal agus
thoiseochad sé a sheinm, agus a dhul cheóil ins an am chéadna. Bhí
Féidhlimidh ábalta ceól binn a bhaint as an fhideal* [...] *Rachadh sé soir
'un Fhál Charraigh annsin go doras Seán Mhic Fhionnlaoich agus
chumfadh sé abhrán eile annsin a d'fhóirfeadh do Sheán. Bhí sé ábalta
abhrán a dhéanamh ag an doras a d'fhóirfeadh do achan fhear, dó Ghall
nó do Ghaedheal nó do thighearna, nó do dhuine ar bith. Bhí abhrán ag
Feidhlimidh a d'fhoirfeadh do gach aoinneach, agus leóga an t-é nach*

sásochadh é, bhí sé ábalta abhrán a dhéanamh dó a cháinfeadh go maith é.[121]

[There was another man travelling here who was called Féidhlimidh the Fiddler. Féidhlimidh Ó Baoighill (Phelim O'Boyle) was his proper name. He would walk from place to place. He knew everybody and every place in the entire county. [...] He never came to a hospitable door that he did not take out the fiddle and while he was playing he would compose a song as quickly as you could clap your two hands together. He would compose a praise poem for the man of the house. In those days in Gortahork there was a shopowner named Charlie Gallagher [...] when Féidhlimidh would come to his place he would take out the fiddle and start playing and singing at the same time. Féidhlimidh was able to make sweet music with his fiddle. He would go over then to Falcarragh to Seán McGinley's door, and he would compose another song there, a song that was appropriate for Seán. He was able to compose a song on the doorstep that would suit every man, be he local or stranger, landlord or other. Féidhlimidh had a song that would satisfy everybody, but God help the person that displeased him, he was able to compose a very sharp satire for that person.] (my translation).

Richard Waters's assertion (cf. his paper 'The Trivialization of the Cant' in this volume) that the Irish-American Travellers have been very successful at preserving their language *from*, rather than *for*, the younger generations of Travellers is unfortunately also true in an Irish context. He also makes an invaluable point when he says that he hopes that attitudes towards the writing down of Shelta will change soon enough to save or even restore Shelta "rather than see it disappear". This is all the more pertinent when one considers that many Irish Travellers in the past were clearly very literate, and some of them obviously wrote significant elements of their language down in the first place. It is pretty unlikely that the highly literate Travellers who first 'invented' a word like *acháram* (*ach-ár-am*) 'tomorrow' from Irish *amárach* would have had a problem about writing down their language – or at least those aspects of their language they did not use for protective purposes – particularly if by so doing it might help to 'save' their language and preserve their culture. Acton (1994: 44) points out that, in the century following the Gypsies' first arrival in Europe in the fifteenth century, they had a sophisticated political leadership which negotiated with kings, popes and emperors so that they were known for entertaining and practising medicine at European royal courts. Two significant Romany vocabularies were recorded from Gypsies at this juncture, a fact which indicates that they did not keep their language a secret at that time. Within a generation, however, everything had changed. The end of the feudal way of life meant huge economic changes in the agricultural sector, including a switch from arable farming and an attendant minimalisation of labour

---

[21] RBÉ, Iml. 818: 123–4

costs. A huge new population of newly redundant labourers were transformed into migrants and perceived as "vagrants".

This new "vagrancy", rather than being seen as the by-product of economic crisis, was deemed to be its cause and was consequently demonised. The contribution of the Gypsies to scientific, medical and cultural progress was dispersed as though it had never been, and prejudice against all Travelling groups, including those Irish Travellers then travelling in European countries, became widespread. Taking the case of the Gypsies as an example, might it not also be the case that other Travelling groups, including the Irish Travellers, became more 'secretive' about their language at this juncture in an effort to survive in an increasingly hostile environment? This might explain differing present-day attitudes amongst Travellers themselves regarding the writing down or development of their own language. When the centuries of prejudice and persecution inflicted against Travellers are taken into account it is hardly surprising that some older Travellers say that their language should never be written down. Their attitude should be respected because it is based both on the cultural formation which they received in their own community and the widespread prejudice they encountered from the "settled" community. However, as with many marginalised groups, it is probably the case that some older Travellers internalised the prejudice directed at them and were made to feel embarrassed about aspects of their culture which they should have been very proud of, including their language.[22]

Since Shelta is often classified today as a "secret" language it is often assumed that Travellers have *always* been very "secretive" about it. The historical evidence regarding the ethnogenesis of the Irish Travellers and the strong evidence for "written" or "poetic" influence in the evolution of Shelta makes this proposition very unlikely in my view. Binchy (2000: 130) has pointed out that, just because the context in which Shelta is used today is often that of "privacy" or "secrecy", that does not mean that that was always the case. There are many documentary sources which indicate that relations between Travellers and the settled community were much better in previous generations. In such an environment, the usage of Shelta for "secrecy" would not have hugely important, and it may be that is only relatively recently, in the context of the increased oppression of Travellers, that the "secrecy" function has assumed more importance. One wonders, in fact, whether the designation of Shelta as "secret" owes more of its genesis to the "projections" of the "settled" community and the way Travellers have been defined by "settled" scholars than it does to Travellers themselves? It may be the case that the "settled" community including those scholars who have defined Travellers to date have actually been culpable in distorting the image of what Shelta is and how it functions. Binchy (2000: 131) argues that the perception of Shelta has been put out of focus by its designation as a "secret" language. This designation as "secret" can of course be linked to the "exoticist"

---

[22] This feeling of 'embarrassment' amongst certain minority-language speakers is not confined to Travellers, of course. Until recently, many elderly fluent Irish-speakers from the Gaeltacht ('Irish-speaking area') preferred to speak broken English to one another when visiting Galway City on a Saturday rather than be heard speaking Irish.

discourse of the gypsylorists of yesteryear. Even the very title of Macalister's 1937 work on Shelta, *The* **Secret** (my emphases) *Languages of Ireland* hints at this "exoticist" discourse. Would it not be a terrible loss to Traveller culture if the gypsylorist emphasis on "secrecy" and their legacy of "exoticism" as applied to Travelling culture functioned to inhibit younger Travellers from developing and preserving their language through all the media that are available?

Culture and its transference to the next generation is not something static. If it is to survive and develop, it needs to be able to adapt to changing societal circumstances. The cultural experience of the older generation of Travellers was different in many ways from that of younger Travellers today. Younger Travellers now are prouder of their heritage and more assertive about their identity.

Many younger Travellers are also well aware that a substantial proportion of the Shelta vocabulary already exists in printed sources, some of which have been produced by Travellers themselves, e.g. Maher (1972), Cash (1977), Connors (1974) or by non-Travellers (Binchy (1993, 2000), Grant (1994), Macalister (1937), Harper (1966), Cleeve (1983), Brady (2001), etc. Some Shelta vocabularies are even available at the touch of a button on the Internet. As a literacy worker dealing with Travellers, an increasing number of whom are now accessing third-level education, it is my experience that many younger literate Travellers would echo Richard Waters's sentiments regarding the writing down of those aspects of their language which are not used for protective purposes. There is much evidence to indicate that Shelta, like all minority languages, is presently under great pressure from the twinned forces of globalisation and assimilation, and that this situation is not confined to Irish-based Travellers. Literate Travellers know that a greater awareness of Traveller language amongst settled people can only be beneficial to the recognition of their distinct culture and can only enhance their ongoing attempt to achieve ethnic status in an increasingly multicultural Ireland. The only proviso they make is that their language should ideally be defined and developed by themselves, the speakers of Shelta, rather than by outsiders, as has hitherto been the case with so many other aspects of their culture. The future of Shelta is in the hands of the Travellers themselves. They must decide how they want Shelta developed or passed on so that it can continue to be a part of their identity. Perhaps the time is now right for Travellers to engage in a more comprehensive debate on the future of their language.[23]

---

[23] Virtually all the Shelta words cited in this paper have already appeared in the many previously published word lists and are thus *blown* (an English Cant term meaning 'made the subject of general knowledge') by being available to whomever is interested in the subject. I am thus not betraying any confidences by drawing upon this body of data for illustrative purposes. It is also the case that many Shelta words which appear in this article are no longer used. Their publication therefore does not negate the protective function of Shelta for those Travellers who still use the language today. Some words currently in use which I have cited in this article are *shade*, *grade*, *laicín* (*lac*), *gleoch* and *sarc*, etc. These words no longer have a protective function for Travellers because they have also become part of the vocabulary of the 'settled'

References

Acton, Thomas. 1994. "Categorising Irish Travellers". In eds. McCann et al.. 36-53
Binchy, Alice. 1993. "The Status and Functions of Shelta". Unpublished Ph.D. thesis, Somerville College, University of Oxford
Binchy, Alice. 1994. "Travellers' Language: A Sociolinguistic Perspective". In eds. McCann et al., 134–54
Binchy, Alice. 2000. "Shelta/Gammon in Dublin". In eds. Thomas A. Acton and Morgan Dalphinis *Language, Blacks and Gypsies*. London: Whiting and Birch. 128-32
Brady, Peter. 2001. *Paveewhack*. Dublin: New Island Press
Cash, Anthony. 1977. "The Language of the Maguires". *Journal of the Gypsy Lore Society* 4th ser. 1.3: 177–80
Cleeve, Brian. 1983. "The Secret Language". *Studies* 72: 252–63
Connors, Michael and Acton, Thomas (eds.). 1974. *Have You the Feen's Grade Nyocked?* London: Romanestan Publications
Crofton, Henry T. 1886. "Shelta, the Tinkers' Language". *The Academy*, 18 December 1886
Grant, Anthony P. 1994. "Shelta: The Secret Language of Irish Travellers viewed as a Mixed Language". In eds. Peter Bakker and Martin Mous. *Mixed Languages: 15 Case Studies in Language Intertwining*. Amsterdam: Uitgave IFOTT. 123–50
Hancock, Ian F. 1974. "Shelta: A Problem of Classification". In eds. David de Camp and I. Hancock. *Pidgins and Creoles: Current Trends and Prospects*. Washington: Georgetown University Press. 130-37
Hancock, Ian F. 1984. "Shelta and Polari". In ed. Peter Trudgill. *Language in the British Isles*. Cambridge: Cambridge University Press. 384–403
Harper, Jared. 1966. "Irish Traveller Cant: An Historical, Structural, and Sociolinguistic Study of an Argot". Unpublished M.A. thesis, University of Georgia
Macalister, R.A. Stewart. 1937. *The Secret Languages of Ireland. With special reference to the origins and nature of THE SHELTA LANGUAGE, partly based upon the Collections and Manuscripts of the late JOHN SAMPSON,* 8 vols. Cambridge: Cambridge University Press
McCann, May, Ó Síocháin, Séamus, and Ruane, Jospeh eds. 1994. *Irish Travellers: Culture and Ethnicity*. Belfast: Institute of Irish Studies, Queen's University Belfast (for the Anthropological Association of Ireland)
McCormick, A. 1907. *The Tinkler Gypsies*. Dumfries: Maxwell

---

community in larger urban centres like Galway and Limerick. I would like to thank the people who helped me with this essay, in particular those Travellers who were always generous with their insights and their time. I would like to thank the staff of the Folklore Department, University College Dublin for allowing me access to their archives and for their generous help in researching this topic.

McDonagh, Michael. 2000. "Ethnicity and Culture". In ed. E. Sheehan. *Travellers – Citizens of Ireland.* Dublin: The Parish of the Travelling People. 26-31
Maher, Seán. 1972. *The Road to God Knows Where.* Dublin: Talbot Press
Meyer, Kuno. 1891. "On the Irish Origin and Age of Shelta". *Journal of the Gypsy Lore Society* 2: 257–66
Meyer, Kuno. 1909. "The Secret Languages of Ireland". *Journal of the Gypsy Lore Society*, new ser. 2.3: 241–6
Ó Baoill, Dónall P. 1994. "Travellers' Cant: Language or Register?". In eds. McCann et al., 155–69
Ó Dónaill, Niall. 1977. *Foclóir Gaeilge-Béarla.* Baile Átha Cliath: Oifig an tSoláthair
Sampson, John. 1891. "Tinkers and their Talk". *Journal of the Gypsy Lore Society* 2: 204–21

The Syntactic Structure of Present-day Cant: A Case of Convergence with Hiberno-English Syntax

Marian Browne

Travellers in Irish Society

Travellers are Irish people. They attach great importance to their status as a distinct ethnic group in wider Irish society. McDonagh (1993: 13–14) states that Travellers' ethnic identity means that they have a shared birthright, history, language and religion. Central to Traveller identity is the concept of nomadism. Travellers are considered one of the most marginalised and disadvantaged groups in Irish society. "Irish Travellers are still seen and treated as a 'lower caste' in society" (Mac Gréil 1996). Ó Connell (1997: 2) quotes from a report by the Economic and Social Research Institute, which describes Irish Travellers thus:

> ... a uniquely disadvantaged group: impoverished, under-educated, often despised and ostracised, they live on the margins of Irish society.

According to Ó Connell (1994: 114), Ireland has always presented an image of itself to the world as a monocultural society. With reference to Ryan (1984: 97–8) who contends that, in the Republic of Ireland, Irish people perceive themselves as "basically a well-integrated, cohesive society with no great divisions of creed, class, colour or race", Ó Connell argues that, given that perception of themselves, it is not surprising that Irish people have little awareness of ethnicity as a possible phenomenon in Irish society. Ó Connell contends that lack of awareness allows us to continue to deny the separate cultural identity of our resident ethnic group – the Travelling community (Ó Connell 1994: 115).

Traveller Language(s)

McCann, Ó Síocháin, Ruane (1994: xv) claim that one important way in which Travellers preserve their ethnic "separateness" from mainstream Irish society is through language. That language is one of the most significant ways in which the Travellers maintain the boundary between themselves and the settled community is also asserted by Binchy (1995: 87), who states that, in addition to English, Irish Travellers speak Gammon or Cant, a language unique to their culture. McCann, Ó Síocháin, Ruane (1994: xix) consider that the study of Traveller language(s) is a sadly neglected topic. With regard to Travellers' use of English, they claim that the available literature to date has made only passing reference to the subject whereas others have made strong claims (unsupported by systematic research evidence) about the variety of English spoken by Irish Travellers. Ní Shuinéar (1994: 58) contends that Traveller English is a cohesive and distinctive entity. She claims that Traveller

English is so distinctive that settled people often have difficulty understanding Traveller speech even when Travellers are "trying their best to be understood". Binchy (1993: 146) suggests that Travellers' use of English is "pidgin-like". For her, they use a "restricted" form of English, learning only enough to make themselves understood to the settled host society. Ó Baoill (1994: 157) considers that, by a certain age, most Travellers have some basic knowledge of English. Interestingly, Travellers themselves perceive this difference in their speech, as can be seen from Nan Joyce in her biography, when she asserts:

> We're a different speaking people with our own traditions and our own way of life and this is how we should be treated. (Joyce 1985: 10)

The Distinctive Nature of Traveller Speech

Why is Traveller English so distinctive? Most authors on the subject of Travellers' use of English imply that Travellers' own language, Cant or Gammon, influences the variety of English that they speak. For ní Shuinéar (1994: 58) the distinctiveness and cohesiveness of Traveller English is due to its Cant underlay. She states that a familiar analogy to Travellers' English is Black English, just as Black English is a unique entity because of its West African substratal origins. Ní Shuinéar makes the explicit claim that, since the influence of Cant is so pervasive in the Travelling community, "it colours their use of a second language, English" (ibid.: 74). Ó Baoill (1994: 157) takes a more cautious approach on the influence of Cant on the variety of English that Travellers speak. While he claims that Travellers speak some form of Hiberno-English, he accepts that research is needed to discover "how the Cant relates to their use and knowledge of that variety of English".

The Influence of Cant on Traveller English

The influence of Cant on Traveller English raises a number of questions. The first relates to the linguistic status of Cant itself. From the research evidence to date, one can only conclude that its linguistic status is still in doubt. Two reasons for the failure conclusively to classify the linguistic status of Cant soon become apparent to the student who undertakes any in-depth study of Cant. First, there is an astonishing lack of Irish scholarly interest in Cant (Cleeve 1983: 252). Secondly, one has to take into account that, for a very long time, its existence has been so carefully concealed like a "religious arcanum" that "few, even among professional philologists, have ever heard of it" (Leland 1907–08: 73).

Cant has been variously described as "a language" (Binchy 1993: 148), a "restricted register" (Ó Baoill 1994: 160) and as "secret jargon" (Macalister 1937: 130) and Harper (1969: 79). The main contention against classifying Cant as a language hinges on the argument that present-day Cant does not have an independent grammar. An opposing view to that argument is that a language is not required to have an independent grammar to be recognised as a separate linguistic entity (Binchy

1993: 148). In support of her claim that Cant is a language, Binchy (ibid.: 148) points out that world languages such as Hindi and Urdu in India are recognised as distinct despite the fact that their grammars are almost identical. She argues that the criteria for defining what is and is not a language are motivated more by social and political considerations rather than purely linguistic factors. Hindi and Urdu are accepted as separate languages because their speakers are recognised as distinct ethnic groups. According to Binchy (ibid.: 148), an unwritten, non-standardised, relatively unknown language such as Cant spoken by a stigmatised minority group will have a difficult task in gaining recognition as a language because of the "generally held assumptions, both implicit and explicit, about what a language is".

While various authors (Leland 1881, Macalister 1937, Harper 1969, Binchy 1993, Ó Baoill 1994) debate the question of whether Cant is a language in its own right, they all agree on one critical point – that the linguistic structure of present-day Cant is entirely English or, more precisely, Hiberno-English. However, none has shown in any systematic way the correlation between present-day Cant syntactic features and those of Hiberno-English. By systematically comparing present-day Cant syntactic features with those of Hiberno-English, the main objective of this paper is to show that Cant shares an identical syntactic structure with Hiberno-English. Cant syntax should be investigated systematically before proceeding with any further study on the linguistic status of Cant. It is the evidence and results of systematic research rather than speculation that will provide the springboard for future study.

Hiberno-English

Hiberno-English speakers use a variety of the English language which sets them apart from all other speakers of English. Both the historical and linguistic evidence shows that it was the English of the Cromwellian planters in the seventeenth century along with the continuing influence of the Irish language which formed the basis of modern Hiberno-English. Bliss (1977: 19) contends that Hiberno-English is unique to the Irish people in that it accurately reflects the social, cultural and political history of their country. Henry (1977: 24), commenting on the uniqueness of Hiberno-English, states that, historically, the Irish people initially set out to learn English but that, by 1900, they had created their own variety – Hiberno-English.

Salient Features of Hiberno-English Syntax

Several salient features of Hiberno-English syntax serve to distinguish Hiberno-English from Standard English. Some of those features are:

1. The more extensive use of the definite article in Hiberno-English than in Standard English (Joyce 1910, Henry 1957, Sullivan 1976):

> (1)   **Hib.E.** He's the wise boy. (Henry 1957: 120–1)
>   **St. E.** He's a wise boy.

2. The use of reflexive pronouns to express emphasis in Hiberno-English where Standard English uses intonational means (Henry 1957, Sullivan 1976):

> (2) **Hib.E.** He'd like herself to see them. (Synge 1907: 141)
> **St. E.** He'd like her to see them.

3. Hiberno-English exhibits a number of special features in the use of prepositional structures which distinguishes it from Standard English (Sullivan 1976, Henry 1957, Bliss 1984):

> (a) The use of *on* as a dative of disadvantage:

> (3) **Hib.E.** When the rent was doubled on me. (Shee 1882: 373)
> **St. E.**   When my rent was doubled.

> (b) Use of *on* to describe transitory states such as hunger, tiredness, thirst, a cold, etc.:

> (4) **Hib.E.** What's on you? (Henry 1957: 148)
> **St. E.** What's the matter with you?

> (c) The process of naming something:

> (5) **Hib.E.** What name had they on him? (Henry 1957: 150)
> **St. E.** What did they call him?

4. The widespread use of *and* followed by a co-ordinate clause in Hiberno-English where Standard English normally uses a subordinate clause (Bliss 1984, Harris 1984, Kallen 1990):

> (6) **Hib.E.** It only struck me and you going out of the door. (Bliss 1984: 147)
> **St. E.** It only struck me when (as) you were going out the door.

5. In Hiberno-English, indirect questions frequently retain question inversion and lack the subordinator (*whether/if*) of Standard English (Bliss 1984, Filppula 1986, Kallen 1990):

> (7) **Hib.E.** She asked me were there many staying at the hotel."
> (Bliss 1984: 148)
> **St. E.** She asked me whether/if there were many staying at the hotel.

6. Clefting in Hiberno-English has a markedly higher frequency of use and a wider syntactic distribution than in Standard English (Harris 1991: 196). In Hiberno-English a cleft sentence can contain:

A VP:
(8)   It's doing his lessons that Tim is. (Stenson 1981)

A subject complement:
(9)   It's flat it is. (Henry 1957)

An adjunct of manner:
(10)   It's badly she'd do it now. (Henry 1957)

7. Topicalisation (the movement of a constituent to the beginning of a clause) is more frequently used in Hiberno-English than in Standard English (Filppula 1990: 44):

(11)   A watch Mary gave to John.

8. Standard English has only one present tense – *I am, you are, he is*, etc. Hiberno-English, on the other hand, distinguishes between non-habitual and habitual present. Habitual *be* in Hiberno-English is realised as finite *be/be's* or as *do/does* plus non-finite *be* (Harris 1984: 306):

(12)   Well, there be's games in it and there be's basketball, darts and
        all. (ibid.)
(13)   There does be fairies in it. (Henry 1957: 169)

9. The Standard English perfect rarely occurs in conservative Hiberno-English dialects. Instead, Hiberno-English speakers use a number of forms which do the work of the Standard English perfect (Harris 1984: 303–327). The four most important temporal and aspectual distinctions which are coded in Standard English are realised in Hiberno-English as follows:

(a) *Resultative*: past event with present relevance.

(14)   **Hib.E.** She's nearly her course finished.
        St. E. She's nearly finished her course.

(b) *Hot news*: event located at a point separated from but temporally close to the moment of speaking.

(15)   **Hib.E.** Al is after arriving.
        St. E. Al has just arrived.

(c) *Indefinite anterior*: events occurring at unspecified points in a period leading up to the moment of speaking.

(16)   **Hib.E.** I saw *ET* only once.
         St. E. I've only seen *ET* once.

(d) *Extended now*: situation started in the past and persists into the present.

(17)   **Hib.E.** I know Sam for some time.
         St. E. I've known Sam for some time.

A Comparison of the Salient Features of Hiberno-English Syntax with Cant Syntactic Features

For the purposes of comparing Cant syntactic features with those of Hiberno-English, I used examples from my own corpus (350 sentences and phrases), which was collected in 2000. The results of the comparison between the salient syntactic features of Hiberno-English outlined in 2.1 and Cant (Browne 2000) show that Cant shares with other Hiberno-English dialects a number of characteristic features:

1. Cant exhibits the same tendency as Hiberno-English to use the definite article more extensively than Standard English:

         Cant   I'll be able to wid her in *the* Gammon. (Maggie)
         Hib.E.   I'll be able to talk to her in *the* Gammon.
         St. E.   I'll be able to talk to her in Gammon.

2. The use of reflexive pronouns to express emphasis is also a feature of Cant syntax:

         Cant   Geig the beoir *your jeel* for another milk of the spunch. (Davey)
         Hib.E.   Ask the woman *yourself* for another piece of tobacco.
         St. E.   Ask the woman for another piece of tobacco.

3. Like Hiberno-English, Cant also makes use of special prepositional structures to denote transitory states and disadvantage.

         Transitory states:
         Cant   You'll die *with* the crolus agin you're home. (Kathleen)
         Hib.E.   You'll die *with* the hunger before you get home.
         St. E.   You'll die of hunger before you get home.

         Possession:
         Cant   He hasn't the geigin' *in him*. (Mary)
         Hib.E.   He hasn't the begging *in him*.
         St. E.   He doesn't know how to beg.

4. The Hiberno-English use of a subordinate structure with *and* is also evident in Cant:

> **Cant** He'd corrib you *and* the auld nides and the wobs glorchann out at us. (Jimmy)
>
> **Hib.E.** He'd hit you *and* the old people and the guards looking at us.
>
> **St. E.** He'd hit you (while) the people and the guards were looking at us.

5. The characteristic feature of the retention of subject-verb in indirect questions in many Hiberno-English dialects is also found in Cant:

> **Cant** Geig the beoir *will she shilt* you a pound of ide. (Davey)
>
> **Hib.E.** Ask the woman *will she sell* you a pound of butter.
>
> **St. E.** Ask the woman if she will sell you a pound of butter.

6. Clefting, a salient feature of Hiberno-English syntax, is also present in Cant:

> **Cant** *Twas a lorc that missled around in the muncaire.* (Davey)
>
> **Hib.E.** *Twas a car that travelled around the country.*
>
> **St. E.** A car travelled around the country.

7. Cant, like Hiberno-English also shows a tendency to topicalise phrases:

> **Cant** *A bottle of treap, I got.* (Mary)
>
> **Hib.E.** *A bottle of drink, I got.*
>
> **St. E.** I got a bottle of drink.

8. Like Hiberno-English, habitual *be* in Cant is realised as finite *be* or *do/does* plus non-finite *be*:

> **Cant** Mary, she does *be nakin'* the sweets. (Eileen)
>
> **Hib.E.** Mary, she does *be robbing* the sweets.
>
> **St.E.** Mary steals the sweets regularly.

9. The four important temporal and aspectual distinctions of the Standard English perfect are realised in Cant in the same way as Hiberno-English.

> (a) *Resultative perfect*:
>
> **Cant** I *have the inig parked.* (Jimmy)
>
> **Hib.E.** I *have the car parked.*
>
> **St. E** I have parked the car.

(b) *Hot news perfect*:
Cant   There's the feen *after falling* into the sgoch. (Bridget)
Hib.E.   The man is *after falling* into the water.
St. E.   The man has fallen into the water.

(c) *Indefinite-anterior perfect*:
Cant   I often *geiged* tugs at a cin. (Mary)
Hib.E.   I often *begged* clothes at a house.
St. E.   I have often begged for clothes at a house.

(d) *Extended now perfect*:
Cant   *My gatrum is treapin' all morning.* (Bridget)
Hib.E.   *My father is drinking all morning.*
St. E.   My father has been drinking all morning.

Convergence and the Question of Origin Revisited

The comparison that I have drawn between the salient features of Hiberno-English and present-day Cant syntax clearly shows that both languages share an identical syntactic structure. That conclusion raises other pertinent questions in the investigation of Cant. Did Cant ever have a fully developed grammar and syntax of its own? Is the present-day structure of Cant a case of convergence with Hiberno-English?

An attempt to answer these questions leads us directly to the subject of the origin of Cant (Ó Baoill 1994: 155). All theories on the origin of Cant are tentative, since records of it are scant and recent (Binchy 1993: 84). Some authors are convinced that it was a bona fide Celtic language (Leland 1881, Sampson 1890, Meyer 1891), while others argue that it has a relatively recent origin (Macalister 1937, Harper 1969, Ó Baoill 1994). To date, neither view has been proven conclusively (Hancock 1974: 131). Leland (1881) never presented any evidence for his claim, while Sampson (1890) and Meyer (1891) based their claims solely on the analysis of the vocabulary. It is unfortunate that they did not extend their study to an examination of the grammar and syntax of Cant.

Ó Baoill (1994) and Harper (1969) rely on evidence from the more recent recordings of the syntactic structure of Cant. They claim that, since Cant is essentially English in its grammatical structure with an extensively altered Irish lexicon, Cant must have been formed at a time when its speakers were bilingual in both Irish and English. This theory dates the origin of Cant to around the middle of the seventeenth century when English was introduced into Ireland. While these authors discuss the vocabulary of Cant, they do not include in their deliberations any consideration of the age and origin of vocabulary. It is surprising that they failed to take account of the earlier preliminary conclusions on vocabulary.

The comparison that I have drawn between the salient features of Hiberno-English syntax and present-day Cant shows that the structure is that of modern Hiberno-

English. However, there is a thread that leads us to a more distant past. There is some evidence to posit that Cant may have been spoken in an Irish grammatical framework at an earlier period in its history, and that its present-day structure is the result of convergence with Hiberno-English syntax.

Most authors on the subject of the influence of Irish syntax on Cant refer to the presence of Irish word order, with nouns frequently preceding adjectives in Cant. Some draw attention to the more frequent use of the Irish article *a* or *an* (sic) in the genitive case (Macalister 1937, Seaholm 1977).[1] Others note that the first- and second-person pronouns *muilsha*, *duilsha* are derived from Irish *mo thoil* and *do thoil* respectively (Sampson 1891: 210). The Cant words *stesh* and *nidesh* derived from Irish *tá sé* 'it is' and *ni ead* or *ní headh* 'is not' function as copulas, since there is no native copula (Grant 1994: 131).

The case for proposing a convergence theory for the syntactic structure of present-day Cant is further supported by the absence of any Irish structural influence on the more recent recordings. In my corpus, there was a marked absence of any of the Irish structural features listed above. This compares with Sampson's (1908) earlier recordings, which show the presence of all these features to varying degrees. In Sampson's corpus, which comprises 100 phrases and sayings in Cant, there were nine instances of *stesh* and *nidesh* in a copular sense. There were five examples of the Irish article used in the genitive case, four instances of the Irish word order for nouns and adjectives, and 31 cases of the use of the personal pronouns *muilsha* and *duilsha*. Those structures include:

(1)   *Stesh charp minkur bioer*
       Yes-is **true** tinker woman
       'That is a true tinker woman' (Sampson 1908: 274)
(2)   *Nus a Dhalyon*
       'Help of God' (Sampson 1908: 273)
(3)   *Ken-gop*
       House mad
       'mad house' (Sampson 1908: 273)
(4)   *Lesk muilsha, and muilsha lesk dhi-ilsha*
       'Tell me and I'll tell you' (Sampson 1908: 275)

Mac Gréine's (1931-34) corpus, comprising 127 phrases and sayings, is the next most significant collection of Cant and could be viewed as an intermediate stage between Sampson's collection and my own. Mac Gréine's corpus shows the near complete disappearance of Irish influence on the grammatical structure of Cant. In his corpus, there was only one example of the Irish order for nouns and adjectives and the use of the personal pronoun *muilsha*. In the case of the personal pronouns, convergence towards English can be seen in Mac Gréine's corpus in the most frequent use of the

---

[1] Editorial note: this could only really be *a*.

first and second person, singular pronouns, *my jeel*, *your jeel*, based on the English pronouns *my*, *your*:

> My jeel was gritch for sicir gratchuil
> 'I was ill for three weeks' (Mac Gréine 1932: 293)

In Mac Gréine's corpus, approaching convergence with English is evident in the use of the personal pronouns. In the case of the first person singular, *my jeel* is used only three times in the nominative case compared to thirteen instances of the English pronoun 'I' in the same case. All the other personal pronouns, singular and plural, are English, with only a few minor exceptions.

The evidence also shows that, as the structural influence of Irish on Cant declines, the influence of Hiberno-English increases. Sampson's (1908) recordings showed little influence from Hiberno-English syntax. Only single examples of three of the salient features of Hiberno-English syntax listed in 2.1 were evident, namely topicalisation, indefinite anterior and the hot-news perfect. Mac Gréine's corpus, on the other hand, showed the frequent presence of most of the salient features of Hiberno-English syntax. Only structures such as the use of *and* in co-ordinate clauses, retention of inversion in indirect questions, clefting and the resultative perfect were absent. My corpus of present-day Cant, in turn, shows the complete convergence of Cant syntax with that of Hiberno-English.

Conclusions

Although the evidence of Irish structural influence on Cant is scarce, it is possible to hypothesise that it was spoken at some stage in an Irish grammatical framework. The hypothesis that it had a grammatical system of its own at some point in its history is more problematic, since there is no solid evidence from the material reviewed to support this claim. Macalister (1937: 161) makes reference to the existence of what he calls "a few native inflexions" in Cant, but that claim can only be treated as speculation on his part, since it has not been supported by any systematic research to date. It is conceivable that we will never unearth the original state of Cant, particularly if we take into account that early written records of it are unlikely to emerge, as Travellers' tradition is oral.

Even though we have no direct evidence to date, it is still within the bounds of possibility that Cant may have had a grammatical structure of its own. It is quite possible that the origin and development of Cant mirrors that of Hiberno-English. Hume, in his work on Hiberno-English, warned in 1858 that "many of the characteristic terms of it are now disappearing". He called for further study of Hiberno-English because he feared that "if another generation were permitted to pass away, the character and interest of the Hibernic dialect would, it is to be feared, be practically lost forever". Could such a fate have befallen Cant?

However, there are some very definite conclusions which can be drawn regarding the nature of present-day Cant syntax. The comparison of Cant syntactic features with the salient features of Hiberno-English syntax outlined above indicates very clearly that present-day Cant is a combination of a non-English lexicon encoded in a Hiberno-English syntactic framework. The evidence from the material reviewed also points to the structural evolution of Cant along a continuum towards convergence with Hiberno-English syntax. The question that it is a language in its own right in its present-day form deserves the respect of more far-reaching research.

I hope this paper will show that the study of Irish Traveller Cant still remains an area ripe for linguistic research. Those interested in the study of the languages of Ireland should note Breathnach (1958: 67), who states that "in the mixed linguistic milieu which exists in Ireland, we have at hand a field of research which, properly exploited, could be the means of building up a thriving school of linguistic science" (quoted in Kallen 1985: 10). This paper presents the challenge to pursue the study of Irish Traveller Cant.

The Direction of Further Study

The evidence from this comparison between the syntax of Cant and Hiberno-English shows that the structure is essentially that of Hiberno-English. Is it not possible to imply that Travellers' English is also that of Hiberno-English? As noted in section 1.1 above, many authors on the subject of Travellers' use of English claim that Travellers speak a different variety of English than the 'mainstream' Irish population. Ó Baoill (1994: 157) called for research on the variety of English that Travellers speak. In response to Ó Baoill's recommendation for research into the matter, the present author undertook a preliminary study (Browne 1998) of the speech of school-going, urban Traveller children. The results of that study revealed that the Traveller children spoke Hiberno-English. However, the author concluded that, since the corpus was small (14 informants), there was a need for further research to support the findings of this preliminary study. In this study the author also took into account the fact that the children were participating in the mainstream education system. Therefore, the question of whether they were using a 'school register' must arise, since Mayor (1988: 113) points out that bilingual children learn to "recognise their different languages as separate and to keep them apart when necessary".

The focus of my current research is on the adult Traveller population which has predominantly remained outside mainstream education. Travellers are relative newcomers to the education system. The Commission on Itinerancy (1963) reported that a total of 1,642 Traveller children between the ages of six and 14 years were recorded in the 1960 census. The Department of Education's (1960) records indicate that, of those children of school-going age, only 114 were said to be regular attendees. Nunan (1993: 66) states that such negligible participation of Traveller children in education continued until the beginning of the 1980s. From that evidence we can assume that the majority of Traveller adults did not participate in the education system. In addition, Harper (1969) concluded that it was the adult Travellers in the 35+ age group who had an active knowledge of Cant. A study of adult Traveller English will not only establish conclusively the variety of English that Travellers speak, but also reveal if Cant is influencing that variety. Wolfram (1986: 88) points out that, when an ethnic group speaks another language, the influence of that language may be "incorporated into the differential basis of the English variety as well". It is on that issue that my current research is based.

References

Binchy, Alice. 1993. "The Status and Functions of Shelta". Unpublished Ph.D. thesis, Somerville College, University of Oxford
Bliss, A. J. 1977. "The Emergence of Modern English Dialects in Ireland". In ed. D. Ó Muirithe. *The English Language in Ireland.* Dublin: Mercier Press. 7–19
Bliss, A. J. 1984. "English in the South of Ireland". In ed. P. Trudgill. *Languages in the British Isles.* Cambridge: Cambridge University Press. 135–51
Breathnach, R.A. 1958 Review of Henry (1957). *University Review* 2.2: 67-69
Browne, M. 1998. "A Preliminary Study of the Speech of School-going, Urban Traveller Children". Unpublished M.A. thesis, University College Dublin
Browne, M. 2000 Corpus collected as part of current Ph.D. research
Cleeve, B. 1983. "The Secret Language". *Studies* 72: 252–63
Commission on Itinerancy. 1963. *Report of the Commission of Itinerancy.* Dublin: Stationery Office.
Filppula, M. 1986. *Some Aspects of Hiberno-English in a Functional Sentence Perspective.* Joensuu, Finland: University of Joensuu
Filppula, M. 1990. "Substratum, Superstratum, and Universals in the Genesis of Hiberno-English". *Irish University Review* 20: 41–54
Grant, A. 1994. "Shelta: The Secret Language of Irish Travellers viewed as a Mixed Language". In eds. Peter Bakker and Martin Mous. *Mixed Languages. 15 Case Studies in Language Intertwining.* Amsterdam:Utigave IFOTT. 123–49
Hancock, I. F. 1974. "Shelta: A Problem of Classification". In eds. D. De Camp and I. Hancock. *Pidgins and Creoles: Current Trends and Prospects.* Washington: Georgetown University Press. 130-37
Harper, J. 1969. "Irish Traveler Cant: A Historical, Structural and Sociolinguistic Study of an Argot". Unpublished M.A. thesis, University of Georgia.
Harper, J. 1971. "'Gypsy' Research in the South". In ed. K. Moreland. *The Not so Solid South: Anthropological Studies in Regional Subculture.* Southern Anthropological Society Proceedings No. 4. Athens, GA: University of Georgia Press Press. 16–24
Harris, J. 1984. "Syntactic Variation and Dialect Divergence'. *Journal of Linguistics* 20: 303–27
Harris, J. 1991. "Conservatism versus Substratal Transfer in Irish English'. In eds P. Trudgill and J.K. Chambers. *Dialects of English: Studies in Grammatical Variation.* London and New York: Longman. 191–210
Henry, P.L. 1957. *An Anglo-Irish Dialect of North Roscommon.* Dublin: Department of English, University College Dublin

Henry, P.L. 1977. "Anglo-Irish and its Irish Background". In ed. D. Ó Muirithe. *The English Language in Ireland*. Dublin: Mercier Press. 20–36

Joyce, N. 1985. *Traveller: An Autobiography*. Dublin: Gill and Macmillan

Joyce, P.W. 1998. *English as We Speak it in Ireland*, 3rd ed. Dublin: Wolfhound Press. First published 1910

Kallen, J.L. 1985. "A Global View of the English Language in Ireland". In ed. D.P. Ó Baoill. *Papers on Irish English, 63–77*. Dublin: Irish Association for Applied Linguistics

Kallen, J.L. 1990. "The Hiberno-English Perfect: Grammaticalisation Revisited". *Irish University Review* 20: 120–36.

Leland, C. G. 1891. "Shelta". *Journal of the Gypsy Lore Society* 2.4: 321–3

Leland C. G. 1907–8 "Shelta or the Lost Language of the Bards, and How it was Recovered" *Journal of the Gypsy Lore Society*, 11: 73-82

Macalister, R. A. S. 1937. *The Secret Languages of Ireland. With special reference to the origin and nature of THE SHELTA LANGUAGE, partly based upon the Collections and Manuscripts of the late JOHN SAMPSON*. Cambridge: Cambridge University Press. 130–224

McCann, M., Ó Síocháin, S., Ruane, J. (eds.). 1994. *Irish Travellers: Culture and Ethnicity*. Belfast: Institute of Irish Studies, Queen's University Belfast (for the Anthropological Association of Ireland)

McDonagh, Michael 1993. "Who are the Travelling People?" In *Do You Know Us at All?* Dublin: The Parish of the Travelling People. 9–19.

Mac Enrí, M. 1939. "Ceant agus Saoghal na dTincéirí". *Béaloideas* 1: 219–29

Mac Greil, M. 1996. *Prejudice in Ireland Revisited*. Maynooth: Survey and Research Unit, Department of Social Studies, St Patrick's College

Mac Gréine, P. 1931-4. "Irish Tinkers or 'Travellers'. Some Notes on their Manners and Customs, and their Secret Language or 'Cant'," *Béaloideas: The Journal of the Folklore of Ireland Society* 3:2 (1932): 170-186; "Further Notes on Tinkers' 'Cant'," *Béaloideas: The Journal of the Folklore of Ireland Society* 3:3 (1932): 290-303; "Some Notes on Tinkers and their 'Cant'," *Béaloideas: The Journal of the Folklore of Ireland Society* 4:3 (1934): 259-63.

Mayor, B. 1988. "What Does it Mean to be Bilingual?". In ed. N. Mercer. *Language and Literacy from an Educational Perspective*. Buckingham: Open University Press. 113–25

Meyer, K. 1891. "On the Irish Origin and Age of Shelta". *Journal of the Gypsy Lore Society* 2.5: 257–66

ní Shuinéar, S. 1984. "Macalister Debunked. The Case for Critical Assessment of Macalister's Assertions re. the Origins of the Shelta Language and of its Speakers, the Irish Travellers". Unpublished manuscript, privately circulated

ní Shuinéar, S. 1994. "Irish Travellers, Ethnicity and the Origins Question". In eds. McCann et al., 54–77.

Nunan, S. 1993. "Travellers and the Education System – An Overview". In *Do You Know Us at All?* Dublin: The Parish of the Travelling People. 65–77

Ó Baoill, Dónall P.. 1994. "Travellers' Cant: Language or Register?". In eds. McCann et al., 155–69

Ó Connell, J. 1997. *Travellers in Ireland: An Examination of Discrimination and Racism.* A report from the National Co-ordinating Committee for the European Year Against Racism

Ó Connell, J. 1994. "Ethnicity and Irish Travellers". In eds. McCann et al., 110–20

Ó Muirithe, D. (ed.). 1977. *The English Language in Ireland.* Dublin: Mercier Press

Ryan, L. (1984) *Irish Values and Attitudes: The Irish Report of the European Value Systems Study.* Dublin: Dominican Publication

Sampson, J. 1891. "Tinkers and their Talk". *Journal of the Gypsy Lore Society* 2: 204–21

Sampson, J. 1908. "A Hundred Shelta Sayings". *Journal of the Gypsy Lore Society* 1: 272–7

Seaholm, P. 1977. "Shelta and the Creole Classification Device". Unpublished term paper. University of Texas, Austin

Shee, G. 1882 "The Irish 'brogue' in Fiction: A Protest" *The Month* 45: 363–75

Stenson, N. 1981 *Studies in Irish Syntax.* Tübingen: Gunter Narr

Sullivan, J.P. 1976. *The Genesis of Hiberno-English: A Socio-Historical Account.* New York: Yashiva University

Synge J.M. 1907 *The Playboy of the Western World*

Wolfram, W. 1986. "Language Variation in the United States". In ed. O.L. Taylor. *Treatment of Communication Disorders in Culturally and Linguistically Diverse Populations.* San Diego, CA, College-Hill Press. 73–115

Hidden like a religious arcanum:
Irish Writing and Shelta's Secret History

Mary Burke

Shelta is the name by which the language of Irish Travellers is known in sedentary society. Shelta has been periodically subject to the colonial discourses of "discovery" and excavation, being constructed during the nineteenth century as a secret language with archaic roots. The discoverer or decipherer for an uninformed public or readership was always a sedentary writer, folklorist or academic. In an 1880 article entitled "Shelta, the Tinkers' Talk", the American scholar Charles Godfrey Leland claimed to have discovered the language whilst conversing with a beggar.[1] The language that academics and British Gypsylorists subsequently designated Shelta after Leland's lead was already (and still is) referred to by Travellers themselves as Cant or Gammon. Gypsylorists maintain that the origins of many "secret languages" (so-called thieves' cant, argots peculiar to certain occupations, etc.) are intertwined with those of the Traveller and Romany. In order to outline what has retrospectively been constructed as written references to Shelta before its "discovery", it is necessary to begin with the sixteenth-century classifications of England's petty criminals, inspired in part by the warning against vagabonds, *Liber Vagatorum*, since, in the wake of Shelta's supposed unearthing the 'Gypsylorist' John Sampson surmised an ancient origin for Shelta on the basis that the "cant/thieves' slang indices of such texts contained Shelta-derived vocabulary".[2] Those works, furnished with titles such as *The Fraternitye of Vacabondes*, which categorises the "tinkard" as one who "goeth abrode a begging"[3] and *A Caveat or Warning for Commen Cursetors Vulgarly Called Vagabones* (1567), which describes "dronken Tynckers" as "beastly people" who steal and cheat,[4] appear to be the first instance of the organised monitoring of the wanderers of the British Isles. Such writings routinely condemned "cant", a name given by the studies to the obscure languages of Gypsies, "tinkards" and thieves (although it has been surmised that in the Irish context the word may have

---

[1] Charles Godfrey Leland, "Shelta, the Tinkers' Talk", *New Quarterly Magazine* 3 (1880): 136–41.
[2] John Sampson, "Tinkers and their Talk", *Journal of the Gypsy Lore Society* 2 (1891): 204–21. In this article Sampson traces Shelta words back to slang/cant found in Thomas Harman's *A Caveat or Warning for Commen Cursetors Vulgarly Called Vagabones* (1567) and J.C. Hotten's *Slang Dictionary*, an 1864 publication that borrowed heavily from sixteenth-century studies of the underworld and its "cant".
[3] John Awdeley, *The Fraternitye of Vacabondes* (1560–01), *Awdeley's Fraternitye of Vacabondes, Harman's Caveat, Haben's Sermon &c*, ed. F.J. Furnivall (London: Early English Text Society, 1869) 5.
[4] Harman, *A Caveat or Warning for Commen Cursetors Vulgarly Called Vagabones*; Awdeley, *Awdeley's Fraternitye of Vacabondes*, 59.

independently arisen from the Gaelic *caint* "speech"[5]). A document of 1586 bemoans that Gypsies: "haue deuised a language among themselues which they name *Canting* [...] as none but themselues are able to vnderstand. The first deuiser thereof was hanged by the necke, – a just reward."[6] The definition of "Gypsy" in *Chambers's Cyclopaedia* of 1728 took exception to the "unknown, canting language" of Gypsies.[7] An early condemnation in Irish letters of utterances designated as "cant" occurs in Jonathan Swift's *A Proposal for Giving Badges to the Beggars in All the Parishes of Dublin* (1737) – the title being his suggestion for the scourge of vagrancy – where Swift dismisses as such the contrived tales of disaster proffered by beggars.[8] Certain classes of the indigents complained of in the text appear to be Travellers, though not clearly identified as such, since differentiation of Travellers from other peripatetic groups was not made in print until the early nineteenth century.[9] In this instance, Swift appears to conflate two separate, but ideologically entwined definitions of "cant": cant is simultaneously the language of the social outcast and an untruthful utterance.

---

[5] Ian Hancock, "Shelta and Polari", in *Language in the British Isles*, ed. Peter Trudgill (Cambridge: Cambridge University Press, 1984) 385.

[6] "Description of England", *Holinshed's Chronicles* (1586), quoted in *Awdeley's Fraternitye of Vacabondes*, xii.

[7] Angus Fraser, *Gypsies* (Oxford: Blackwell, 1992) 189.

[8] Jonathan Swift, *A Proposal for Giving Badges to the Beggars in all the Parishes of Dublin, The Prose Works of Jonathan Swift*, eds. Herbert Davies et al, vol. 13 (Oxford: Blackwell / Shakespeare Head, 1959) 135.

[9] The description of the "foreign" (non-Dublin) beggars Swift complains of appear to be Travellers, since Travellers rather than tramps travel *en famille*: "But when the spirit of wandering takes him, attended by his females and their equipage of children, he becomes a nuisance to the whole country" (ibid.: 134). That the "beggars" referred to are probably Travellers is also indicated by Swift's complaint that they marry young and penniless, a criticism levelled at Travellers by members of the settled community since at least the nineteenth century (Jane Helleiner, "'The Tinker's Wedding' Revisited: Irish Traveller Marriage", *100 Years of Gypsy Studies: Papers from the 10th Annual Meeting of the Gypsy Lore Society, North American Chapter, March 25–27, 1988, Wagner College, Staten Island, New York, Commemorating the Centennial of the Gypsy Lore Society*, ed. Matt T.Salo [Cheverly, Maryland: Gypsy Lore Society, 1990] 77–85). The beginning of the semantic shift of "tinker" from a term indicating occupation to one also suggesting insult, which had solidified in sedentary discourse by the twentieth century, is detectable in the title of a 1724 political poem by Swift referring to the Wood's half-pence scandal, which refers to itself as "A Serious Poem Upon William Wood, Brasier, Tinker, Hard-Ware-Man, Coiner, Counterfeiter, Founder and Esquire". Wood was an English entrepreneur who nearly succeeded in foisting a worthless coin upon Ireland with the support of the Crown, but for the opposition mounted by Swift's *Drapier's Letters* (1724–25).

Due to the rash of articles on the language which appeared in the *Journal of the Gypsy Lore Society* following Leland's "discovery" of Shelta and Sampson's subsequent linking of it to obscure and archaic vocabularies, it was fashionable enough to be included in the 1893 edition of *Chambers's Encyclopedia* as "a secret jargon of great antiquity spoken by Irish tinkers [...] descendants of the [...] bards" – an ironic contrast to the pre-"discovery" opprobrium heaped upon "canting language" in the 1728 edition. The colonial discourse of "discovery" or excavation of the hidden and ancient pervades nineteenth- and early twentieth-century considerations of Shelta; the title of a later Charles Leland article entitled "Shelta" is subtitled "or the Lost Language of the Bards and How it was Recovered". Within the article itself, Leland describes Shelta as being "hidden like a religious arcanum by the Tinkers".[10] During this period, Shelta becomes a cultural treasure to wrestle from its unappreciative possessors. The German scholar of Irish, Kuno Meyer, became interested in Shelta in the 1890s on the basis of its perceived antiquity and link to Old Irish,[11] a debased version of which belief is popular to this day.[12] Such colonial interest in the Traveller minority inspired Irish Literary Revival writers to turn their attention to such home-grown exotica, and a fashion was born for depicting "tinkers" (as Travellers are usually referred to in literature) as having little in common with the rising middle class and their growing obsession with land ownership:

> And so in Ireland our Abbey peasant-play now includes a foxy tinker as a stock type, together with the land-hungry mountainy farmer, the half-witted herd, the garrulous nosey-parker, and the psychic servant-girl.[13]

In his reckless unconventionality, the tinker, as portrayed, for instance, in W.B. Yeats's *Where there is Nothing* (1902), in which a "Country Gentleman" marries a tinker girl,[14] John Millington Synge's *The Tinker's Wedding* (1907), and James Stephens's *The Demi-Gods* (1914), where law-breaking yet charming tinkers are befriended by angels who have come to earth,[15] was a flattering mirror of the values of aristocratic disengagement, apparent freedom and marginal lifestyle which many of

---

[10] Charles Godfrey Leland, "Shelta", *Journal of the Gypsy Lore Society* 2 (1907–08): 73.
[11] Kuno Meyer, "On the Irish Origin and the Age of Shelta", *Journal of the Gypsy Lore Society* 2nd ser. 5 (1891): 260.
[12] The speech of interviewees in a magazine article on the wedding customs of Irish Travellers living in Britain was described as being "peppered with corrupt Gaelic" (Hannah Borno, "Caravan of Love", *Marie Claire* [August 2000]: 75).
[13] Leslie Daiken, "Parasites Without Power", in *Anvil: Life and the Arts*, ed. Jack Lindsay (London: Meridian, 1947) 30.
[14] W.B. Yeats, *Where there is Nothing. The Variorum Edition of the Plays of W.B. Yeats*, ed. Russell K. Alspach (London: Macmillan, 1966) 1064–165.
[15] James Stephens, *The Demi-Gods* (London: Macmillan, 1914).

the literati liked to perceive in themselves.[16] The growing engrossment with Traveller origins was also an Hibernicisation of the contemporary Continental fetishising of the Gypsy as symbolic cultural vagabond that Synge was undoubtedly exposed to in Paris.[17] Nearer to home, Synge may have been inspired by British polyglot George Borrow's semi-autobiographical picaresque narratives of his adventures with Gypsies, tramps and tinkers. Due to his alleged proficiency in the Romany dialects, Borrow claimed to have been able to "pass" for a Gypsy when "on the road". (The title of one of his most popular works, *The Romany Rye* (1857), refers to the Borrowesque main character, and translates from English Romanes as "the Gypsy gentleman". Amusingly, the phrase was glossed in nineteenth- and early twentieth-century dictionaries as "a gentleman who affects the society of gipsies".) Knowledge of and immersion in Gypsy and Traveller customs and language became a hallmark of a

---

[16] The decline of the Ascendancy was detrimental to the status of Travellers, since, in the popular imagination, they had long existed in an imaginative symbiosis. Consider the many ballads of the British Isles concerning Gypsy / tinker elopement with a member of the aristocracy. In Liam O'Flaherty's "The Tent" (*The Penguin Book of Irish Short Stories* [London: Penguin, 1981]), a tramping officer fantasises that the beautiful Traveller woman he stays with is "a gentleman's daughter. Lots o' these shots out of a gun in the county Wicklow". ("The Tent", 135). By locating the supposed mixing of Traveller and Ascendancy genes in the county of Synge's tramping, O'Flaherty points to the earlier writer as a progenitor of the literary discourse of the disdainful, aristocratic Traveller. Declan Kiberd defines the attraction of Anglo-Irish post-partition writers such as Beckett have for the wanderer as the recognition of one displaced group by another (*The Oxford Illustrated History of Ireland*, ed. R.F. Foster [Oxford and New York: Oxford University Press, 1991] 328). In the 1938 play *Purgatory*, W.B. Yeats uses the mixing of tinker and aristocratic blood as a fascist metaphor for the Anglo-Irish loss of vitality in the Free State. The thieving grandson of the fallen Anglo-Irish woman is "A bastard that a pedlar got / Upon a tinker's daughter in a ditch". Tinkers have lost the romantic aura they had for Yeats since the social distance between the minorities has lessened, and both are now threatened with cultural extermination in the homogeneous new state. Tom Murphy's *The Wake* tellingly refers to the post-Partition change in Protestant Irish status as "homelessness" (*The Wake* [London: Methuen, 1998] vi).

[17] Marilyn R. Brown's study contends that the ubiquitous artistic representation of Gypsies in nineteenth-century France was based upon a narcissistic conception of the Gypsy as being symbolic of all forms of "cultural vagabondage" (*Gypsies and Other Bohemians: The Myth of the Artist in Nineteenth-Century France* [Ann Arbor, Michigan: UMI Research, 1985], 2). As a self-conscious member of the artistic minority, Synge would have been exposed to such a pervasive cultural attitude, and was undoubtedly influenced in his choice of subject matter by the mania for Gypsies. However, Synge does subvert the stereotype to an extent, since his depiction of tinkers is far from idealisation.

certain bohemian constituent of the *cognoscenti* throughout the British Isles of the nineteenth century.

Although Revival-era representations of Travellers implied the existence of an innate aristocratic *insouciance*, in the colonial discourses of philology and Gypsylorism, it was only ever the language that was considered noble and not the Irish or Scottish Traveller speakers, who were constructed by Gypsylorists as being racially inferior to the more "pure-blooded" Gypsies of Wales and England. Sampson laments that such a rich language should be spoken by "shady characters".[18] Shelta lost its archaic mystique among Gypsylorists after the Revival era, when research concluded that it lacked the antique heritage suggested by Meyer and others. By 1914, the Cant of the "tinkers", as a minority culture commonly believed to be the descendants of Irish Traveller emigrants to Scotland are referred to, was constructed as being a pollution of the more pure and ancient language of the Romanies.[19] R.A. Stewart Macalister's 1937 study, *The Secret Languages of Ireland*, based on the late nineteenth-century notes of Sampson, suggests that the language was devised by druids dispossessed by Christianity and educated monks displaced by the Reformation, rather than Travellers.[20] In the decades after Partition, Shelta was rarely referred to in popular writings on Traveller culture and remained undiscovered outside academe until its unearthing by a nationally distributed February 1952 Irish Folklore Commission questionnaire entitled "Tinkers". (In the post-Partition era, Travellers were becoming increasingly subject to an *internal* colonial gaze in the form of sedentarist investigation by state-sponsored folklore projects and government commissions on the Traveller "problem".[21]) Olivia Robertson's 1953 novel, *Field of the Stranger*, satirises the Revival's othering of the tinker figure and its Gypsylorism-inspired fetishising of Shelta as a – to utilise Leland's description – hidden "religious

---

[18] Sampson, "Tinkers and Their Talk", 208.

[19] Alexander Russell, "Scoti-Romani and Tinkers' Cant", *Journal of the Gypsy Lore Society* 2nd ser. 8 (1914–15): 11–20. Russell surmises that Romani blood in Scotland has long been mixed with that of the tinker and that the "Romani tongue in like manner was debased by the cant or secret jargon of the Tinkers, losing not only all its inflexions but most of its roots as well" (12).

[20] R.A. Stewart Macalister, *The Secret Languages of Ireland with Special Reference to the Origin and Nature of THE SHELTA LANGUAGE, partly based upon the Collections and Manuscripts of the late JOHN SAMPSON* (Cambridge: Cambridge University Press 1937; facsimile ed., Armagh: Craobh Rua Books, 1996) 256-7.

[21] The 1963 *Report of the Commission on Itinerancy* recommended that the Traveller "problem", as the nomadic lifestyle of the Traveller was constantly referred to, be solved by settling or integrating the minority population. In the wake of the *Report*, a nationwide voluntary organisation, the Itinerant Settlement Movement, was established to help what were considered "drop-outs" to sedentarise. The ostensibly benevolent government policy towards Travelling people of the early 1960s was predicated upon the assumption that Travellers were at an economic disadvantage while their nomadism continued: the only good Traveller was a settled Traveller.

arcanum" whose revival would reveal a submerged and authentic pre-Gaelic Ireland. In Robertson's tale, an Irish National Theatre-style amateur dramatic society confounds the Mandoran villagers with the staging of the Yeatsian *Oedipus O'Hara*. The novel pokes fun at Titus, an amateur historian staying at Mandoran who holds predictably Revival-era views on the connections between tinkers and the aristocracy. Titus believes that "enchanting Irish tinkers have the romance inherent in all decaying aristocracies. [...] The tinkers are the rightful owners of Ireland."[22] Robertson's novel satirises the Revival rhetoric that would place the "Gaelic" or pre-Gaelic above the "progressive". The following proposal of Titus in *Field of the Stranger* is the logical conclusion of such Revival-era privileging of the ancient over the recent:

> I am ardently in favour of camogie and hurling: you are aware, of course, that hurling is pre-Celtic? An old pastime of the tinkers. Also, I am in favour of the Irish people once more speaking Gaelic. [...] Naturally, I should prefer the genuine Irish language, the tinkers' Shelta.[23]

In the wake of Macalister's debunking, Shelta lost the mystique bestowed upon it by colonial commentators and the very little academic attention that it received in the late twentieth century tended to contest its status as a language. Nonetheless, Shelta remains subject to periodic uncovering; Shelta's most recent excavation occurred in North America in the 1970s, when Jared Harper and Charles Hudson, "were surprised to *discover*" (my emphasis) that Irish-American Travellers (descendants of Travellers who had immigrated to the United States in the nineteenth century) spoke "an argot [...] which they call 'the Cant'" and which turned out to be similar to Shelta.[24] Traveller culture subsequently became an object of scientific interest to the North American academe: the anthropologists Sharon and George Gmelch produced an enormous body of work on Irish Travellers throughout the 1970s and into the 1980s.[25]

---

[22] Olivia Robertson, *Field of the Stranger* (Surrey: Peter Davies, 1948) 194. The novel's satire of sentimental views about tinkers reiterates Robertson's statement in a 1947 work that the "admiration which English anthropologists and Irish poets express for tinkers only annoys ordinary Irish people" (*It's an Old Irish Custom* [London: Denis Dobson, 1952] 47).

[23] Robertson, *Field of the Stranger*, 213.

[24] Jared Vincent Harper and Charles Hudson, "Irish Traveller Cant in its Social Setting", *Southern Folklore Quarterly* 37: 2 (1973): 101; Jared Vincent Harper, "Irish Traveller Cant", *Journal of English Linguistics* 15 (1971): 78–86.

[25] George Gmelch, "Economic Strategies and Migrant Adaption: The Case of Irish Tinkers", *Ethnos* 42 (1977): 22–37; George Gmelch, "The Effects of Economic Change on Irish Traveller Sex Roles and Marriage Patterns", *Gypsies, Tinkers and Other Travellers*, ed. Farnham Rehfish (London: Academic Press, 1975) 257–69; George Gmelch, *The Irish Tinkers: The Urbanization of an Itinerant People* (Menlo Park, CA: Cummings Publishing Company, 1977); George Gmelch, "Settling the Irish Tinkers", *Ekistics* 43 (1977): 231–9; George Gmelch and Sharon Bohn Gmelch,

Shelta's existence was uncovered by Irish literary practitioners only after the 1960s and the growth in Traveller activism of that era.[26] One of the results of the growing politicisation of Traveller issues was that depictions of Traveller culture could no longer be apolitically presented as representations of a charming and contented community. The contested concept of Traveller ethnicity that was to emerge in the 1980s was embryonic in the new awareness of the radical implications of the distinct nature of the minority's culture. Literary works concerned with Traveller culture from the Partition era to the 1960s generally ignored the existence of Shelta and tended to romanticise the Traveller lifestyle as an easily unveiled subculture into which disaffected members of the settled community could merge – a virtual continuation of the Revival-era bohemian appropriation of the tinker lifestyle as a representation of *bourgeois* rebellion. A good case in point is that of Maurice Walsh, whose idealised depiction of Travellers and rural life in general contrasts sharply with that of fellow Kerry writer Bryan MacMahon's lyrical realism when dealing with the same subject matter. That two authors from the same place could take such differing stances in their representation of an equivalent theme is comprehensible in light of Terence Brown's analysis of the creative climate of post-Partition Ireland:

The Irish artist, writer or poet who in the early decades of independence chose to remain in Ireland had two roles available to him. He could furnish

"Begging in Dublin: The Strategies of a Marginal Urban Occupation", *Urban Life* 6 (1978): 439–54; "The Emergence of an Ethnic Group: The Irish Tinkers", *Anthropological Quarterly* 49 (1976): 225–38; George Gmelch and Sharon Bohn Gmelch, "Ireland's Travelling People: A Comprehensive Bibliography", *Journal of the Gypsy Lore Society* 1:3 (1977): 159–69; George Gmelch and Sharon Bohn Gmelch, "The Irish Tinkers: When Wanderers Settle Down", *Human Nature* 3 (1978): 66–75; George Gmelch and Sharon Bohn Gmelch, "The Irish Travellers: Identity and Inequality", *World Minorities*, ed. Georgina Ashworth, vol. 2 (Middlesex: Quartermine House, 1978); George Gmelch and Sharon Bohn Gmelch, "The Itinerant Settlement Movement: Its Policies and Effects on Irish Travellers", *Studies: An Irish Quarterly Review* 63 (1974): 1–16; George Gmelch and Ken Kroup, *To Shorten the Road: Traveller Folk-tales from Ireland* (Dublin: O'Brien, 1978); George Gmelch and Ann Saddlemeyer, *In Wicklow, West Kerry and Connemara* (Dublin: O'Brien, 1980); Sharon Bohn Gmelch, "An Exodus of Travelling People", *This Week* (December 1971): 9–13; Sharon Bohn Gmelch, *Nan: The Life of an Irish Travelling Woman* (London: Souvenir Press, 1986); Sharon Bohn Gmelch and Pat Langan, *Tinkers and Travellers* (Dublin: O'Brien, 1975).
[26] In 1963 a makeshift primary school for Travellers was established by Travellers themselves, who felt that the state system offered little to Traveller children. The first large Traveller demonstration occurred in Dublin in Febraury 1964 in response to the school's destruction during an eviction (Katrina Reemtsma, "Travellers in Ireland", *Pogrom: Magazine for Threatened People* 121 [1986]: 13).

the new order with an art, which whether in its self-conscious nativism or idyllic celebration of the rural folk tradition would nourish the dominant essentialist ideology of the state; or disgusted with the unreality of such programmatic artistic endeavours, he might seek to define his artistic identity in terms of opposition and dissent.[27]

Maurice Walsh was born into a Kerry farming family in 1879, the year the Land League was founded by Michael Davitt to procure a reduction in rents, and to promote the substitution of peasant proprietors for landlords. Small farmers were invested with symbolic "Irishness" during the Land League struggle when a nascent Irish state coalesced around the ambition of land ownership.[28] Problematically, this consensus excluded those Irish people who had no wish to own or cultivate land. The common Land League phrase, "the land for the people", implied a homogeneous land owning and sedentary majority and ignored those unconnected to the soil. By the early twentieth century, the Land League had succeeded in its aims, and Ireland was a society dominated by the interests and values of peasant proprietors. Property was perceived to facilitate access to political and moral structures and was the foundation of citizenship itself; the 1937 Bunreacht na hÉireann / Constitution of Ireland, which replaced the 1922 Constitution of the Irish Free State, enshrined land ownership as a virtual right.[29] Land possession gained an emotional resonance and an entanglement with national identity only comparable to the American attachment to the right to bear arms, a constitutional right which could be said to be similarly grounded in the traumas of a colonial, inter-ethnic, conflict-ridden past. According to Philip Bull, Post-Partition Ireland consisted of two agriculturally based sectarian monocultures, which, despite apparent difference, had more in common with each other than with those cultures, such as that of the Traveller, which were excluded by the shared agricultural and sedentary values of both.[30] Walsh must be considered as a writer from a small-farming background who came to public prominence in an era when sedentarist values antithetical to the Traveller lifestyle began to hold sway, and as an author whose work does not challenge the new orthodoxy.

Walsh began writing while working as an excise officer in Scotland, and his first major success came in 1926 with *The Key Above the Door*, a romantic novel set in the

---

[27] Terence Brown, *Ireland: A Social and Cultural History 1922–1985* (London: Fontana, 1985) 312–13.

[28] "[T]he status given to land as the symbol of liberation from oppression was such that those who had little or no land were unable to see either their individual identity or their national and social identity in terms other than as landholders and farmers" (Philip Bull, *Land, Politics and Nationalism* [Gill and Macmillan, 1996] 179).

[29] "The State shall, in particular, direct its policy towards securing that [...] there may be established on the land in economic security as many families as in the circumstances shall be practicable" (Article 45.2.v, Bunreacht na hÉireann / Constitution of Ireland [Dublin: Stationery Office, 1964] 150).

[30] Bull, *Land, Politics and Nationalism*, 191.

Scottish Highlands. Most of Walsh's novels rehash the twin themes of romantic love and manful fights in outdoor Scottish and Irish settings replete with tinkers, tramps and other "colourful" outdoors types.[31] In Walsh's novels the subversion of state discourse inherent in tinkers' lifestyle is contained by their construction as a jolly, uncomplicated subset of Gaelic, nationalist Ireland, always willing to aid members of settled society who wish to appropriate their lifestyle. The exceptional nature of their manner of living – such that it functions as a suitably picturesque subject for action narratives read by the literate, sedentary majority to begin with – is contained by the sentimentalising of that lifestyle, which serves, in the end, merely to reinforce dominant values. Such unthreatening idealisation was embraced by the reading public: Walsh was the best-selling author in Ireland during the 1930s, and the new government acknowledged his celebration of post-Partition nationalist discourse by sanctioning the use of his *Blackcock's Feather* (1932, the story of a Scottish mercenary soldier in Elizabethan Ireland), as a text in Irish schools from 1933 onward.[32] Walsh had jumped at the chance to transfer from the British to the Irish Civil Service with the founding of the Free State[33] and defended Irish neutrality during the Second World War in the *Saturday Evening Post*, so his enthusiasm for the new order was never in doubt.[34] Walsh also enjoyed huge success in America from the 1930s to the 1960s, and experienced a surge in popularity worldwide after John Huston filmed his short story "The Quiet Man" (1933) in 1952 and transformed it into the Hollywood "Oirish" film *par excellence*.

Walsh's 1934 novel *The Road to Nowhere* was antecedent to the explosion of the Travellers' rights movement of the 1960s and 1970s; this composition in an era prior to the politicisation of Travellers is most notable in the absence of ideas of Traveller ethnicity embryonic in MacMahon's (admittedly later) *oeuvre* and the celebration of what Pat Sheeran terms the *itinérant* cultural and linguistic values that suffuse the texts of writers intimate with Traveller life (as MacMahon famously was). Walsh's novel glorifies the "tinker" lifestyle and is presented as a "guide" to such,[35] though the

---

[31] Titles include *While Rivers Run* (1928), *The Small Dark Man* (1929), *Green Rushes* (1935), *And No Quarter* (1937), *Sons of the Swordmaker* (1938), *The Hill is Mine* (1940), *The Spanish Lady* (1943), *Castle Gillian* (1948) and *Trouble in the Glen* (1950).

[32] Steven Matheson, *Maurice Walsh, Storyteller* (Kerry: Brandon, 1985) 71.

[33] Walsh first entered the British Customs and Excise Service as an Excise Officer or Gauger in 1901 and worked in the Scottish Highlands, transferring to the Irish Free State customs service after the Treaty.

[34] Maurice Walsh, "Ireland in a Warring Europe", *Saturday Evening Post*, 3 June 1940: 27. Walsh's work was approved of by that other bastion of post-Partition ideology, the Catholic Church. "The Quiet Man" was reprinted in *Stories of Our Century by Catholic Authors*, eds. J.G. Brunini and F.X. Connelly (Philadelphia: Lippincott, 1949).

[35] Maurice Walsh, *The Road to Nowhere* (London and Edinburgh: Chambers, 1949), unsigned preface.

novel's idealisation of Travellers provoked controversy even at the time.[36] Given that autumn is referred to as "fall" and that even the simplest Gaelic phrases are rendered phonetically and repeated in English, it can be surmised that it was aimed at the lucrative American market. Walsh's representation of life on the road seems to be informed by second-hand sources: he presents "jumping the budget" as the marriage ceremony of Travellers (as does Yeats's *Where there is Nothing*), though this custom has been described by a Traveller informant as a fabrication which has been used to placate persistent settled investigators who wished to construct the minority as an exotic or pagan subculture.[37] *The Road to Nowhere*, which sold well in Ireland and the United States, and which was discussed as a potential film script at the time, revolves around Scottish Rogan Stuart and Irish-American Elspeth Tandy who improbably join a "tinker camp" in order to escape, respectively, the police and the intrigues of life in a Big House. Walsh strips away the linguistic and cultural markers of Traveller ethnicity, bar that of wandering: after four months Stuart, who has merely begun to sprinkle his speech with Gaelic, considers that "he could talk like a tinker, drink like a tinker, think inside a tinker's skin".[38] The flimsy boundary between Traveller and dominant culture effortlessly and willingly yields to the penetration of the sedentary adventurer. In *The Road to Nowhere*, Shelta is not a lost or hidden tongue; rather, it does not appear to exist (though the year in which the novel emerged saw the publication of the third of folklorist Pádraig Mac Gréine's articles on the language).[39] In Walsh's text, Gaelic – not Shelta – functions as the private language of Travellers, though few Travellers speak Gaelic since it is a language that is, for the vast majority of the sedentary population, acquired in school. The marriage ceremony is performed in Irish by the Traveller patriarch, an awkward construction of Travellers as authentic Gaels in a novel set in the early years of the Free State when the discourse of ethnic and religious homogeneity was in the ascendant. Shelta, an obscure tongue of dubious, possibly foreign, origin, academically instated by British Gypsylorists, cannot function as an authentic Irish language in Walsh's decolonised fictional world. "Running away with the tinkers" is a potent fantasy of evasion of sedentarist values and the institutions of sedentarist control. In Walsh's novel, the potential subversion of such a reverie is defused when the seemingly impenetrable minority turn out to be

---

[36] The *Times Literary Supplement* was bemused by "the unreality" of Walsh's "rough but noble-minded tinkers, the broken-hearted hero and the dark, muttering villain" (Review of *The Road to Nowhere*, *Times Literary Supplement*, 21 June 1934: 444).

[37] Artelia Court, Alen MacWeeney and Thomas Munnelly, "Patrick Stokes", *Puck of the Droms: The Lives and Literature of the Irish Tinkers* (Berkeley, CA: California University Press, 1985) 118.

[38] Walsh, *The Road to Nowhere*, 125.

[39] Pádraig Mac Gréine, "Irish Tinkers or 'Travellers'", *Béaloideas: The Journal of the Folklore of Ireland Society* 3:2 (1932): 170–186; Pádraig Mac Gréine, "Further Notes on Tinkers' 'Cant'", *Béaloideas: The Journal of the Folklore of Ireland Society* 3:3 (1932): 290–303; Pádraig Mac Gréine, "Some Notes on Tinkers and their 'Cant'", *Béaloideas: The Journal of the Folklore of Ireland Society* 4:3 (1934): 259–63.

little more than a wandering subset of an imagined nationalist, Catholic, Gaelic-speaking dominant population; by joining the tinker camp Elspeth Tandy, Anglicised mistress of the local Big House, is reconstituted as Ailish Conroy, her authentic Gaelic self.

Bryan MacMahon's 1967 *The Honey Spike*, based on his critically acclaimed 1961 Abbey play of the same title,[40] concerns the journey to Antrim of Traveller couple Breda and Martin Claffey and their race home from Antrim to get the pregnant Breda to what she believes to be a fortuitous hospital, the "honey spike" of the title. *The Honey Spike* is one of the few novels in which Traveller characters are depicted as speaking Shelta amongst their own and in which speech in Shelta is reported, and is the only major Irish novel with a title in Shelta. MacMahon strips Shelta of its colonial-era mystique as an archaic tongue steeped in secrecy and presents it for what it is to its speakers – a utilitarian, quotidian language.

Bryan MacMahon was born in Kerry in 1909, and continued to work as a schoolmaster and sporadic teacher of Traveller children in the Kerry town of Listowel throughout his successful writing career. He was on intimate terms with Kerry Travellers and may be the only recent Irish writer from a settled background who could actually speak Shelta.[41] An anecdote he relates in his autobiography intimates that he considers Shelta to be a language of equal status with the traditional languages of literature,[42] rather than being a creole or pidgin, as has been suggested by academe.[43] MacMahon prided himself on his opposition to the dominant discourse of Irish life. He contributed to the Irish journal of letters, *The Bell*, described by Roy

---

[40] "*The Honey Spike* is impelled by much real observation and intimate knowledge; its realism is lifted by waves of lyricism and emotion and enchantment and song. It is one of the most masterly pieces of theatre that the Abbey has ever produced" (Robert Hogan, *After the Irish Renaissance: A Critical History of the Irish Drama Since* The Plough and the Stars [Minneapolis: Minnesota University Press, 1967] 73).

[41] Reviews acknowledged this fact: "Perhaps because he speaks the private language of the tinkers he appears warmly sympathetic to their bloody brawls and trickery; there is no detached anthropological observation here" ("Tinker Stinker", review of *The Honey Spike*, *Times Literary Supplement* 14 September 1967: 813).

[42] MacMahon's autobiography details an incident which occurred in a local harnessmaker's shop, where on one occasion he spoke in Latin to a priest who entered, conversed in Irish to a schoolteacher who arrived soon after and later conversed in Shelta to "an old traveller friend". When he was finally alone with MacMahon, the harnessmaker, who had remained silent throughout the conversations, "looked out the window and said dryly, 'The priests have Latin, the schoolmasters have Irish, the tinkers have gammon – 'tis' only ignoramuses like meself speak English now'" (*The Master* [Dublin: Poolbeg, 1992] 106–07).

[43] The Romani specialist Ian Hancock's consideration of Shelta situates it within the field of pidgin and creole studies: Ian Hancock, "Shelta: A Problem of Classification," in *Pidgins and Creoles: Current Trends and Prospects*, eds. I. Hancock and D. De Camp (Washington: Georgetown University Press, 1974).

Foster as "the record of an alternative culture",[44] and clashed within the educational and clerical Establishment throughout his teaching and writing career. In his autobiography, he gleefully relates how a mildly anti-clerical article he contributed to an American study of contemporary Ireland caused him to be denounced from "at least three pulpits".[45] Like fellow Listowel writer, John B. Keane, MacMahon's narratives engaged with, though never sought to dismantle, the essentialist oppositions of Irish life; tellingly, MacMahon endorses Sean O'Faolain's explanation of the creative process as the product of the coupling of "a male idea and a female idea".[46]

Travellers, of necessity, employ the alternative spatial languages or "tracings" of kinlines, tradelines and memory lines, rather than conventional maps. Travellers camp on sites "dictated by the calendar of annual fairs, births, deaths and marriages".[47] According to Gilles Deleuze and Félix Guattari, nomadic peoples utilise limitless, boundless "tracings" rather than maps, which are a manifestation of the limited "gridded" sedentary understanding of space.[48] Travellers thus negotiate a separate identity and sense of place from beneath monocultural, sedentarist Ireland by their employment of such non-textual and non-scriptural modes of representation. According to a glossary of Traveller usage, the community's definition of the word "country" is radically different from that which is understood by sedentary society: "a region characterised by family or cultural unities, not necessarily coinciding with county lines and not necessarily rural".[49] A Traveller writer describes this alternative mapping, performed after meeting a generous individual: "To meet such a kind person was to make their particular house a very good mark. [...] by a [*sic*] easy landmark of the house being taken and noted."[50] This practice, which also entails communicating information by leaving sticks or rags in a "highly peculiarised manner", is called *patrin*.[51] Such non-textual modes of representation challenge reductive sedentarist assumptions of what constitutes script. It is a measure of MacMahon's familiarity with Traveller custom that *patrin* is accurately depicted in *The Honey Spike*: "Watch out for the grass I'll throw at the crossroads [...]. If you see a red rag tied to a bush, skedaddle like the wheels of hell."[52] The illiterate Martin is perfectly capable of comprehending the signs and signifiers of hostility: he interprets the fact that "well done" printing on a public poster indicated that "it was a

[44] Roy Foster, *Modern Ireland: 1600–1972* (London: Penguin, 1988) 548.
[45] MacMahon, *The Master*, 25.
[46] Ibid.: 157.
[47] Bettina Barnes, "Irish Travelling People", in *Gypsies, Tinkers and Other Travellers*, 236.
[48] Gilles Deleuze and Félix Guattari, *A Thousand Plateaus: Capitalism and Schizophrenia*, trans. Brian Massumi (London: Athlone, 1988) xiii, 24.
[49] Court, MacWeeney and Munnelly, *Puck of the Droms*, 255.
[50] Seán Maher, *The Road to God Knows Where* (Dublin: Talbot Press, 1972) 58.
[51] Barnes, "Irish Travelling People", 236.
[52] MacMahon, *The Honey Spike* (Dublin: Talbot, 1972) 45.

Government notice. Together notice and barrier said: Get the hell out of here!".[53] Hoping to convince Martin of the value of learning to read, Breda intriguingly suggests that with literacy, the "whole country would be a book".[54] While traversing the border the Claffeys very reluctantly aid an I.R.A. man from Kerry who reminds them of the debt of previous kindness they owe his father in order to enlist their aid. In exploring the detachment of Travellers from the political concerns of sedentary society, North and South, and in depicting Shelta being spoken and spatial language being employed by Traveller characters, MacMahon tentatively acknowledges that Travellers constitute a cultural and ethnic minority on the island.

MacMahon's apparently benevolent attitude to Travellers and their language is far from unproblematic, however. In his description of his annexation of the tongue in *The Master* (the apparently benign paternalism of the autobiography's title now begins to take on more sinister associations), MacMahon unashamedly boasts of the "subterfuge" of passing himself off as a Traveller that he employed in order to learn the language:

> I went to the trouble of learning the secret language of the travelling people. It is known by various names: Shelta, Sheldru, Gammon, Cant or even Ould Nock – "the old thing." I learnt it because I wished to understand the traveller's mind and how it operated under shifting circumstances. Having mastered the basics I travelled to the west and introduced myself to the travellers there as a Kerry O'Brien (a member of a Kerry Traveller family) […]. By this subterfuge I increased my vocabulary and recorded the leading linguists. I studied Macalister's *Secret Language of Ireland* (sic) and found that the gammon had changed […] indeed, it is always being changed in certain ways with the aim of preserving secrecy.[55]

This secrecy was necessary since, according to Alice Binchy, Travellers are understandably reluctant to allow outsiders to breach what they consider to be a linguistic frontier between the Traveller lifestyle and the pollution of dominant culture:

> Older Travellers are jealous of the secrecy of Shelta – they do not want it known, and with few exceptions, they do not want it recorded. […] Many Travellers feel that, if settled people got hold of the language, they would use it to humiliate Travellers.[56]

---

[53] Ibid.: *The Honey Spike*, 51.
[54] Ibid.: 53.
[55] MacMahon, *The Master* (Dublin: Poolbeg, 1992) 132.
[56] Alice Binchy, "Travellers' Language: A Sociological Perspective", *Irish Travellers: Culture and Ethnicity*, eds. May McCann, Séamus Ó Síocháin and Joseph Ruane (Belfast: Institute of Irish Studies, Queen's University Belfast, 1994) 137-38.

MacMahon becomes an agent of dominant culture, infiltrating the minority community and appropriating its language. MacMahon's stance toward the Travellers is, ultimately, ambivalent. By virtue of its references to the practice of *patrin* and inclusion of Shelta phrases (and exclusion of a Shelta glossary), *The Honey Spike* investigates the inferior and latent status of the languages of a peripatetic and oral culture in a literate and sedentary society. MacMahon's account of the circumstances of his acquisition of Shelta nonetheless reinscribes the language's otherness by intimating that it is a cultural resource to be plundered by the dominant, sedentarist culture. The stated aim of the uncovering of the "traveller's mind" partakes of the Gypsylorist discourse of tinker culture as religious arcanum to be revealed and appropriated by the adroit sedentarist explorer / writer / academic. Gypsylorism has been subject to the discourse of the wily colonial capable of passing for a native since its inception. Charles Godfrey Leland admired Professor Palmer, the academic in whose company he "investigated" Shelta, for his ability to "pass for an Indian among Indians, a Persian among Persians, and a gipsy among gipsies".[57] George Borrow likewise boasted that the Gypsies among whom he wandered in Britain "always believed me to be a Romany"[58] and one of the heroes of his adventure novels purchases a destitute tinker's cart and tools and subsequently "passes" for a member of that community.[59]

Paradoxically, MacMahon bestows equivalence upon the oral culture of the minority and simultaneously depicts Travellers striving for literacy. Clever, resourceful Breda endeavours to teach her husband to read in *The Honey Spike*, and MacMahon unproblematically iterates the theme of the benefit to be derived by the Traveller from literacy throughout his autobiography:

> On the occasion of the First Communion day I selected a traveller lad for the honour of reading from the brass lectern on the altar steps. It was a time when there was some local friction about the housing of the travellers […]. I shall not easily forget his declaiming in clarion tones a line taken from one of the earliest disciples: 'It is not because of my people that I wear the badge of shame.'[60]

The teacher author of *The Master* here privileges the text above non-scriptural modes of representation noted and given equivalence in *The Honey Spike*. MacMahon's sedentarist assumption that literacy is a necessary and good thing for Traveller children is challenged by Traveller writer Juanita Casey, the theme and style of whose writing elucidates the ambivalent relationship of the nomadic subject to textuality. The written word is overwhelming and even murderous in Casey's 1971 novel *The Horse of Selene*:

---

[57] Leland, "Shelta, the Tinkers' Talk", 137.
[58] George Borrow, *Lavengro* (London: Ward and Lock, n.d.) xxii.
[59] Ibid.: 308.
[60] MacMahon, *The Master*, 136.

Newspapers were liable to fight; pages shifted from back to front, and when replaced, some demon managed to whisk them round upside-down. They suddenly grew paper arms and tried to strangle her with the power of the printed word.[61]

Juanita Casey was born in England in 1925 of an Irish Traveller mother and Romany father and spent many years travelling as a circus animal trainer. The novel was written in a tent on Achill Island, Co. Mayo, and John Huston was, at one point, interested in directing a film version.[62] In his consideration of Casey's novel, "The Road, the House, and the Grave: A Poetics of Galway Space, 1900–1970", Pat Sheeran considers Casey's ethnic background as pivotal to an understanding of her place within the female literary counter-tradition of celebration of placelessness and motion, as does a recent study of Irish women poets.[63] Casey's mytho-poetic novel (Selene is Greek and is referred to as a "goddess" throughout) is set on an Irish island populated by untamed horses and repressed humans, which is invaded by a group of hippie wanderers. (Casey's choice of title and subject matter are self-conscious: horses are a topos pivotal to Traveller culture and self-perception.) Selene, who masters the island's untameable "tinker" stallion and the islander Miceal equally, has a Gypsy past and tinker associations. Miceal, acceding to the demands of hearth and nation, finally rejects Selene – and becomes the sacrifice necessary to Selene's development when killed by the stallion whilst attempting, according to the author's recent consideration of her own novel, "to dominate it [and] take on Selene's magic".[64] Casey's work, which, according to Sheeran, "offers a striking contrast between, on the one hand, the fluidity of young women, wild horses, tinkers and the sea, and on the other the rigidity, not to say petrification of men,"[65] is predicated upon the binary oppositions of nomadism / land cultivation, Traveller / settled, freedom / domestication, non-human noise / human speech and, ultimately, animal / human.

---

[61] Juanita Casey, *The Horse of Selene* (Dublin: Dolmen; London: Calder and Boyars, 1971) 16.

[62] "An Interview with Juanita Casey", *Journal of Irish Literature* 1.3 (1972): 47.

[63] Casey's poetry, published as the collection (*Eternity Smith and Other Poems* [Mountrath: Dolmen, 1985]), is similarly conceived as deconstructing male literary myths in the consideration of her in Patricia Boyle Haberstroh's *Women Creating Women: Contemporary Irish Women Poets* (Dublin: Attic, 1996) 202–03. Casey is ambivalent about her identification as a "Traveller writer": "The only reason why I'll stress it is because, in a small way, if I get success, then in some way I can pass it on to them – because people say, 'Oh fancy that, a Traveler! Well, I never knew they had it in them'" ("An Interview with Juanita Casey", 51).

[64] Juanita Casey, personal correspondence, 9 March 2001.

[65] Pat Sheeran, "The Road, the House, and the Grave: A Poetics of Galway Space, 1900–1970", *Galway: History and Society* (Dublin: Geography Publications, 1996) 771.

Sheeran reads Casey's novels as an attempt to transform Aran space from the realist / hard pastoral vision and masculine *espace rayonnant* (radial / domicentric space) of the writings of Liam O'Flaherty and island poets such as Máirtín Ó Direáin into feminised landscape of desire and *espace itinérant* (itinerant / travelling space).[66] Sheeran's reading of Casey's re-mapping of Aran / Achill and the western seaboard (it becomes "Aranchilla" in her novel) perceives it as an attempt to "amend the near exclusive popular reception of it as literature of place and rootedness rather than, as it often appears, a literature of motion and travel".[67] Thus, Shelta is symbolically rather than actually present in her novel, with its subversion of dominant discourse, its linguistic *patrin*, although Casey elsewhere makes an explicit connection between the Traveller language and Traveller ethnicity.[68] By her refusal to yield to the artifice of representing Shelta scripturally, Casey evades the categorical binary separating oral from written that inscribes Shelta as the other of English and Gaelic; Shelta is invariably examined by linguists in terms of its relationship to either or both languages. Music represents the utterance that challenges: Miceal's fixed sedentary identity threatens to disintegrate under the influence of the evocative Gypsy music played by Selene's friend:

> Miceal was bewildered and shaken by the lure and fierceness of the music. It seemed to writhe in the fire, and to lead you into ice and burning so that the hairs crawled on you like a dog's. He felt a new country of the spirit lying before him as a traveller, yet was afraid to leave the island of himself. The occasional dance, the traditional bands, the ballads and the radio, these were straight roads enough, this other a path which if you stepped on it would turn and fang you.[69]

---

[66] Ibid.: 752.

[67] Ibid.: 749. Casey's method of composition evokes the French feminist concept of the fluidity of *écriture feminin*. The following is a description of the writing of the novel given to Gordon Henderson: "And I find that, when I do start writing, I release fountains of words, which is awful. I can't think of anything else, I get obsessed with my writing, and I do it at all the wrong times, you know, when I'm preparing soup, for instance. Suddenly a sentence or a line of poetry will come up. I can't sort of sit down from like nine to five, steady writing. It has to come in a bang, come in a rush" ("An Interview with Juanita Casey", 45).

[68] "Or are they the remnants of the ancient itinerant smiths [...] or are they the last of the fighting tribes of Ireland [...]. Some may be a distinct race, from the same Asiatic stock as the Lapps, as many have similar physical characteristics, and there are [...] certain words of their Shelta tongue which are the same in the Lapp's language." ("You who Walk Upon Earth...Walk Not Upon One Road", *Ireland of the Welcomes* 20.6 [March/April 1972]: 7).

[69] Casey, *The Horse of Selene*, 63.

The Doran tinker clan, who at one point are observed "spreading out over the furze like rabbiting dogs"[70] are associated with the animals that figure so prominently in the novel[71] and are outside the articulations of elite discourse. In Casey's detailed description of the family's preparations for a ferry journey, their utterances mingle with those of their animals to create a cacophony that is beyond the symbolic and speaks also of their status as those who operate on the borders of sedentary, literate culture:

> And the tinkers, on the edges of the island, always on the edges of the lands and the settled society, prepared to move on. The young boys were ordered out of the lake where they had been bathing, their skinny white bodies silvery as sand eels. [...] Hysterical dogs ran under all feet, there were shouts, whinnies, brayings, barks and children's laughter.[72]

Like the Dorans who have no dialogue in the text, even the domesticated animals of the islanders are beyond the subjugation of naming: "The dog has no name. We don't go in much for naming beasts here."[73] Casey considers the mores of the restless emigrant a subversion of the tenets of fixity and literary origin emanating from settled society. The effect of the voice of Paudi, Miceal's wayward immigrant brother and shadow self, is associated with the destabilisation engendered by Gypsy music: "Paudi was a magpie with language; he picked out bright phrases and glitter-laughter, he stole from literary nests. Such a voice naturally charms the ears off women and horses, and can lead a man away [...]. Paudi was an Irish Orpheus, his voice his lute."[74] In *Horse of Selene* the oral is privileged above the printed, the wanderer (be it human or animal) above the settled, and, by implication, the language of the wanderer above that of the sedentary person.

Maurice Walsh's novel was written in an era when there was little awareness of Traveller ethnicity and language and Travellers were depicted in literature as residing

---

[70] Ibid.: 15.

[71] The novel opens with a long description of the movements and unnerving habits of the island's wild horses, and animal "characters" are delineated with perhaps more detail than those of the human beings, who are occasionally mere Syngian stereotypes. Casey lovingly details the horses' comic affronts to sedentary pieties, as in this description of the behaviour of the horses when grazing in the graveyard: "the big black, with the lightning blaze, rocked gently back and forth with his behind digging into the pleasantly sharp edge of a Celtic cross, and the white, raising his tail, sighed, and Mary, beloved wife of Fintan Duffy, received an unexpected tribute which would guarantee a powerful growth of grass around her for a good year" (Ibid.: 11). The world of animals, like that of the mute tinkers, coexists with but is often oblivious to the pieties of sedentary society.

[72] Ibid.: 41.

[73] Ibid.: 43.

[74] Ibid.: 20.

or operating in rural settings. Since the 1960s, Travellers have increasingly moved to urban areas,[75] and certain towns in the Republic of Ireland are famous (or infamous, depending on one's political stance) for their high Traveller populations. Would the literature emanating from such places reveal the complexities of cultural hybridity, the ethnic, social and linguistic intertwining that occurs in such a setting? Tuam, a medium-sized town of 6,000 people in Co. Galway, is one such locale. In comparison to an average of a 0.5% Traveller presence within the population as a whole,[76] 6.5% of the population of Tuam is Traveller.[77] According to a well-known Tuam Traveller activist, there has always been an above-average degree of contact between the Traveller and settled communities, an interaction evident in the number of Shelta words found in what is presumed to be "Tuam slang".[78] Fintan O'Toole's *The Politics of Magic*, a study of Tuam playwright Tom Murphy, posits that the town was also historically associated with the wanderer / Traveller:

> Tuam is in the West of Ireland, but to some observers it seemed more like the Wild West than the Irish West. [...] But the flatness [of the surrounding land] gives to Tuam the feeling of being open to the world around it, unlike the enclosed air of hill-ringed towns, and this has been reflected in its culture. An American journalist visiting the town in 1897 found it "a sort of headquarters of every tramp going the road who, no doubt, looks upon it as a haven of rest and a valley of tears". Unlike most Irish towns with their suspicion of "blow-ins", Tuam has a history of welcoming the outsider, even placing the outsider on a pedestal of awe.[79]

The town of Tuam also has the distinction of producing the only popular Irish music group to take their name from a Traveller-associated term. The SawDoctors, according to their official website, is the title given to "travellers who earned money by sharpening saws in old Ireland".[80] The SawDoctors refer to their home town in

---

[75] Gmelch, *The Irish Tinkers*.

[76] Patrick Williams, "The Travelling People", *The Furrow*, January 1986: 21.

[77] *Tuam's Community of Travellers in the International Year of Shelter 1987* (n.p. [1987?]).

[78] Mary Moriarty, personal interview, 31 January 2001.

[79] Fintan O'Toole, *The Politics of Magic* (Dublin: New Island; London: Nick Hearn, 1994) 21–22.

[80] "The SawDoctors", 18 December 2000 <www.Sawdoctors.com/index.html>. Travellers have long been associated with the sharpening of cutting implements: "Thus they mend with solder etc. kettles, and pans, or any other small wares of metal, sharpen knives and scissors" (Charles Godfrey Leland, "The Tinkers", *Journal of the Gypsy Lore Society* 2nd ser. 1 [1907–08]: 76). Itinerant knife-grinders and Travellers are believed to have spoken a related language (A.T. Sinclair, "The Secret Language of Masons and Tinkers", *Journal of American Folklore* 32.26 (1909): 359–60).

many of their songs,[81] and the name of their own label is Shamtown Records.[82] In Murphy's drama, *On the Outside*, Joe refers to Frank as "sham" in his first line of dialogue as both are waiting outside a dancehall pathetically hoping to get in for free, a word which, according to O'Toole, "in the Tuam idiom is used to indicate another Tuam person. It is used so much that even outside of the town, Tuam people are called 'shams.'"[83] In fact, "sham" is a Shelta word meaning "man" or "settled man", [84] and the assumption that the word is Tuam slang indicates the generally unacknowledged influence that Shelta has had upon the dialect spoken in the town.

Tom Murphy wrote his first drama, *On the Outside*, in 1959. He retired from his teaching job in 1962, relocated to England, and returned to Ireland in 1970 a successful playwright. He was born in Church View, Tuam in 1935, the son of a carpenter, and Tuam or its rural hinterland is the setting for some of the plays.[85]

---

[81] The SawDoctors's debut single in the early 1990s, "N17", was a paean to the Tuam-Dublin road and a bittersweet consideration of the lot of the contemporary emigrant, and their second album entitled *All the Way from Tuam*, appeared in October 1992.

[82] The SawDoctors, a "rock 'n' country band" who, according to Kieran Keohane, "play at being a pack of lads from small-town Ireland" and whose lyrics celebrate the minutiae of Irish rural life, reveal "the elements of an Irish proto-fascist traditionalism" which would "seek to protect the sanctity of the Irish family from 'foreign' influences like divorce and feminism, which would be intolerant of 'strangers coming over here and disrupting our way of life', and 'dirty' travellers 'overcrowding' our parishes and townlands" (Kieran Keohane, "Traditionalism and Homelessness in Contemporary Irish Music", *Location and Dislocation in Contemporary Irish Society: Emigration and Irish Identities*, ed. Jim Mac Laughlin [Cork: Cork University Press, 1997] 278–79. It has been said of the SawDoctors that "future historians and archaeologists will get a better picture of life in late twentieth-century Ireland from the SawDoctors' albums than they will from anything by U2 or the Pogues" (Simon McKenzie, "The SawDoctors at Edinburgh Liquid Rooms", *Edinburgh Evening News* 15 November 1999; http://www.sawdoctors.com). Yet Keohane detects in that very celebration of the inanities and excesses of contemporary rural Ireland a mockery of and ambivalence towards institutions of the establishment; The SawDoctors biggest hit, "I Useta Love Her", details a young man's erotic fantasies about a girl he watches each Sunday during Mass. This inherent contradiction allows the SawDoctors to appropriate Shelta terms while apolitically ignoring the speakers of that language in their detailing of rural society, a very real indication of the exclusion of Travellers from the hearty masculinist bonhomie celebrated. Music may be not quite the force for revolution and liberation that Casey's novel assumes it to be.

[83] O'Toole, *The Politics of Magic*, 42–43.

[84] Maher, *The Road to God Knows Where*, 155.

[85] *A Crucial Week in the Life of a Grocer's Assistant* (1969) and *A Thief of a Christmas* (1985).

Murphy's childhood home was solid and detached, but surrounded by the cramped, thatched cottages of the shanty poor and backing onto the working-class estate of Tierboy. According to O'Toole, the "sense of a social underbelly to the town runs through Murphy's work, with its concern for the outsiders, the dispossessed, the unrespectable".[86] Murphy's stage is littered with outsiders railing against bourgeois values: tinkers, circus performers, prostitutes, magicians, bitter and excluded emigrants. (Murphy's deployment of the tinker figure is not exceptional; the late twentieth-century plot that substantially features a tinker is usually concerned with the acquisition of property or property rights, and the tinker's presence is a tool with which to interrogate sedentary values.[87]) In Murphy's *The Wake*, premièred at the Abbey Theatre in 1998, a triumvirate representing the minorities inimical to the interests of the post-Partition propertied Catholic middle class – Traveller Finbar, directionless Anglo-Irishman Norman, and returned emigrant Vera – attempts to destroy the hotel that Vera has inherited. Vera is, her sister is disgusted to note, "Living with the tinkers. [...] With that old thing, that old sponger, that old layabout, Reilly, Finbar Reilly"[88] Henry snubs the family he has married into by carousing with Finbar and Vera and by "sleeping in that dirty fella's dirty house".[89] Murphy's most recent play, *The House* (2000), revels in the destructive consequences to one's property of allowing a Traveller into one's affections.

Murphy has never found an easy acceptance of his *oeuvre* in Ireland, despite, or perhaps because of the fact that it forms "a kind of inner history of Ireland since the momentous changes which were set in motion in 1959".[90] O'Toole considers that this political antipathy to the playwright originates in the perception that "there were no such people in Ireland and that if there were, to show them was to demean the theatre".[91] Murphy represents on stage those who have no desire to enter a theatre, and represents their inability to fit the mould with speech syntax that is fractured, hesitant and incomplete.[92] In his plays, violent navvies and restless emigrants share the predilection of his more overtly "tinker" characters for references to or phrases in Shelta, deployed to indicate their linguistic and social exclusion. In *The Wake* the

---

[86] O'Toole, *The Politics of Magic*, 24.
[87] Marina Carr's *By the Bog of Cats*, premièred at the Abbey Theatre during the 1998 Dublin Theatre Festival, similarly celebrates the destruction of the holdings of the settled by the outcast "tinker" figure. In John Banville's novel *Birchwood* (1973), the chaotic existence of the Gypsy characters contrasts with the continuity of the Big House. In Molly Keane's novel *Time After Time* (1983), Travellers threaten the (literally and socially) collapsing borders between the Big House and the native rabble.
[88] *The Wake* (London: Methuen, 1998) iv.
[89] Ibid.: ix.
[90] O'Toole, *The Politics of Magic*, 19.
[91] Ibid.: 12.
[92] Anthony Roche, *Gill's Studies in Irish Literature: Contemporary Irish Drama: From Beckett to McGuinness* (Dublin: Gill and Macmillan, 1994).

Traveller Finbar refers to a priest as a "coonic", a word used in many Murph
Coonic is another Shelta word that has percolated from Traveller to general us
Tuam.[93] Murphy avows the joint and unacknowledged – Shelta and Hiberno-Eᵣ ᵤₛn
– linguistic heritage of the socially, politically and ethnically exiled. However, the
language of Murphy's plays threatens to encode Shelta as the language of the
dispossessed. Such a reductive and pessimistic configuration allows no space in
which to construct Shelta as a language with other potentials.

A very recent novel which portrays the current situation of Travellers and Gypsies
in the British Isles, John F. McDonald's *Tribe* (1999), embraces Shelta's liberating
potential. McDonald, born in Carlow and later resident in London, is a hybrid and
relatively youthful figure who moves between the world of the Traveller and the
settled: as well as having been an analyst in the City of London, he has worked side
by side with Travellers in the traditional occupations of horse-breeding,
tarmacadaming and scrap-dealing.[94] If Walsh's novel may be read as an attempt to
construct Travellers as a colourful community not ethnically distinct from what
conservative post-Partition writers wished to construct as the homogeneous
population of the Free State, McDonald's, on the other hand, partakes of the ideology
of ethnicity that has, according to Judith Okely, suffused Gypsy and Traveller activist
discourse since the late 1980s.[95] *Tribe* attempts to situate Travellers as part of a
transnational ethnic group having more in common with Romanies and nomadic
peoples of the former Soviet Union than with the sedentary populations of the nations
they happen to have been born into. *Tribe* details the struggle of Traveller Owen to
make his living from the traditional nomad's occupation of horse-breeding. Owen
speaks Gaelic, Shelta and Romanes and works with Romanies and a nomadic
Mongolian, thereby gleefully dismantling the boundaries and categorical separations
painstakingly erected between the "secret languages" by the nineteenth-century
Gypsylorists. McDonald's linking of Travellers to other peripatetic communities is
germane, given that the Romany has become the newest Irish pariah since the refugee

---

[93] To take just one instance, in *The Wake* Finbar refers to a 'priest' as a *coonic* (vi).
This Shelta word is also used in many of Murphy's other plays, such as *On the
Outside* (1962), *The Morning After Optimism* (1971), *The Sanctuary Lamp* (1976) and
The J. Arthur Maginnis Story (1976). Pádraig Mac Gréine's index of Shelta words
lists 'priest' as *cúinne* ("Irish Tinkers or 'Travellers'", 181). Seán Maher glosses
'priest' as *cúnia* and 'monk' as *cunic* in the index of his memoir *The Road to God
Knows Where*, 156.
[94] Biographical sketch of author taken from the hardback edition of *Tribe* (Dublin:
Wolfhound Press, 1999).
[95] Judith Okely, "Some Political Consequences of Theories of Gypsy Ethnicity: The
Place of the Intellectual", in *After Writing Culture: Epistemology and Praxis in
Contemporary Anthropology*, eds. Allison James, Jenny Hockey and Andrew Dawson
(London; New York: Routledge, 1997) 224–43.

influx into the Republic of Ireland commenced.[96] Post-industrial Traveller culture is shown to be vibrantly merging with other nomadic and minority lifestyles in the urban melting pot of *Tribe*. The opening of the novel challengingly fires word after word of unexplicated, unitalicised Shelta, Romanes, Irish and street slang at the reader: "Almost unnoticed, the unconscious pav is carried away [...]. And to most Gorgios this little scene of bare-knuckle buileam would be cause enough to call the fucking wobs."[97] Significantly, unlike many works citing Shelta phrases, *Tribe* does not include a Shelta glossary – McDonald registers Shelta's non-scriptural nature by refusing to uncover it to the penetration of the sedentarist academic gaze, thereby subverting the paradigm of Shelta as a language that periodically lies in secret and passive darkness awaiting the illumination and explication of the pioneering scholar. The substantial representation of oral languages in the text disrupts the hegemonic nature of textuality, and its role in reinforcing the sedentary, literate Western paradigm, and dismantles the categorical binary that separates oral from written and the supposedly adumbrate from that which claims to be transparent. On the levels of both linguistic content and subject matter, *Tribe* posits the potentiality of Traveller–sedentary and oral–textual cultural hybridity; by the final page Owen is about to move happily into a house with his settled girlfriend, while her bigoted father has finally accepted that his daughter will marry a Traveller. As a text produced by another literate, sometime member of the Traveller community and a novel that celebrates Romany and Traveller culture, *Tribe* does not flee from Shelta's ambivalent relationship with textuality (and the problematic status of a *writer* from an oral culture) – as Casey's work perhaps does – but engages with it and points to the potential of the future; that Shelta might be recognised as a language of equal status to, rather than the obscure other of Ireland's official languages, and be heard on radio and television, taught in schools and substantially or wholly utilised in contemporary novels.

[96] Mícheál Ó hAodha, "Roma Immigration to Ireland", *Patrin*, 3 December 1999; <http://www. geocities.com/Paris/5121/ireland2.htm>.
[97] McDonald, *Tribe*, 7.

Exoticising the Gypsies:
The Case of Scott Macfie and the Gypsylorists

Mícheál Ó hAodha

In this essay, I would like to examine how some of the idealisation of the "true-blooded Gypsy" as portrayed by the Gypsy Lore Society and its leading intellectuals such as Scott Macfie manifested itself in the literature and led to a strange form of prejudice whereby those many thousands of Gypsies and Travellers who did not fulfil the criteria of the full-blooded Romanichal were deemed unworthy of study by the British Gypsy Lore Society. I would also like to examine how that same categorisation and stereotyping continues to have repercussions for the image of Gypsies and Travellers even today, over a century after the Gypsy Lore Society was founded. To examine how this prejudice operated, it is possible to trawl through the pre-Second World War correspondence of the Gypsy Lore Society searching for references to "noble" or "true Romanichals" and occasionally demeaning comments regarding other Travellers and Gypsies (often referred to as "half-breeds" or "wild" or "dirty types" – the latter two adjectives used in particular in relation to Irish tinkers). I decided instead, however, to read through Scott Macfie's account of his trip through Bulgaria with a group of Gypsy horse-dealers in 1913. Macfie kept a diary while on his travels and wrote a lively account of his adventure for the Gypsy Lore Society entitled "With Gypsies in Bulgaria". In that account, he expressed many of the stereotypes and romantic idealisations of Gypsies which were common amongst his peers in the Gypsy Lore Society at the turn of the last century.

Macfie's Background

As with his peers in the Gypsy Lore Society, it is likely that the origins of many of Macfie's opinions and stereotypes regarding race, class and the existence of a graded "hierarchy" of differing Travelling and Gypsy groups were typical of his time and a reflection of his class – i.e. Britain's upper-class at the turn of the twentieth century. Indeed the concept of "race" as a distinguishing factor between different peoples (including "true Gypsies" and other wanderers) can be linked to the colonial discourses of British imperialism and Orientalism and to the way in which the colonial project was ideologically justified in countries like Ireland and India. Macfie himself was very much a part of this upper-class or "colonial" elite having been educated at Cambridge, Edinburgh and Göttingen Universities before taking over the running of his family's Liverpool-based sugar refining business. He fought with the Liverpool Scottish regiment during the First World War and retired from the family business on his return to go and live at Hawes on the Yorkshire Moors. He became one of the first members of the distinguished University Club in Liverpool. His association with the University Club brought him into contact with the group of well-known scholars who were, at that time, building up the University College, a number of whom were also keen gypsylorists. Amongst his friends in this group were the noted Celtic scholar from Germany, Kuno Meyer, Consul Harald Ehrenborg, the Swedish gypsylorist and John Sampson, the Librarian at the University of Liverpool, as well as the artists Augustus John and Anning Bell. Through Sampson, Macfie became interested in gypsy Studies and the Romani way of life and, in 1907, Sampson and fellow gypsylorist David MacRitchie persuaded Macfie to revive the Gypsy Lore Society which had been defunct for the previous 14 years.[1] For the next thirty years or so, Macfie became the inspiration and driving force behind the publication – the *Journal of the Gypsy Lore Society*. He was secretary and editor of the Journal from the year of its resurgence in 1907 to 1914 and, for many years afterwards, continued much of the editing work, though not allowing his name to appear officially as editor. It is no exaggeration to say that he devoted his every waking moment to the development of the Gypsy Lore Society. As a wealthy and successful businessman, he was lucky to be in the privileged position to do this. That said, the man was an incredibly hard worker – often writing up to 30 handwritten letters a day to various different members of the society – while maintaining the bulk of the editing work on the *Journal of the Gypsy Lore Society* for the best part of 40 years. He was a driven man who was fascinated – "obsessed" some might say – by Gypsies and the Gypsy way of life. Along with other scholars and amateur collectors who were members of the Gypsy Lore Society, he made the recording of what they saw as a fast-disappearing culture his life's mission.[2]

In his day, Macfie was regarded as one of England's leading authorities on Roma Gypsies and their language, recording large quantities of dialect, folktales and songs from various bands of Roma Gypsies in Britain. Amongst the different groups of Gypsies from whom he collected material were the Lovara or "German" Gypsies, who visited England in 1906, and the "Coppersmith Gypsies", who came into the country in 1912. There is no doubt that he and his colleagues in the Society saw

---

[1] The Society had originally been founded in 1888 and its first members included the explorer Sir Richard F. Burton, Whistler's biographer Elizabeth Robins Pennell, and Archduke Joseph of Austria-Hungary.

[2] On his death, Macfie bequeathed his large collection of works about Romany and Gypsy lore to the Gypsy Lore Society. The Society was based at the University of Liverpool Library until 1974, when it was dissolved following the death of Dora Yates. The Gypsy Lore Society, North American Chapter was founded in the United States in 1977 and, since 1989, has continued as the Gypsy Lore Society. The archives of the Gypsy Lore Society can be accessed online at the University of Liverpool's "Gypsy Collections" website: http://sca.lib.liv.ac.uk/collections/gypsy/intro.htm

themselves as engaged in a great cultural project where they were recording the folklore, customs and language of a "non-literate" group so that future generations of both Gypsies and settled people could appreciate that rich heritage.[3]

While the bulk of the Gypsy Lore Society's members were British, its membership was worldwide and attracted other Europeans and Americans who sought confirmation or elaboration of their independent researches into "Gypsy matters" in their own local areas. In Britain itself, having an interest in a minority or different cultural group was not such an unusual hobby or activity for many of the upper-class at this juncture. The then social and intellectual climate and the colonial project itself fostered a whole spectrum of similar activities whereby groups of British scholars and amateur enthusiasts attempted to unveil the unofficial or "unlettered" history of British and other peoples. The folklorist Richard Dorson has written of "the golden century from 1813 to 1914" inventing the concept of folklore, "when diverse intellectual pursuits flourished during the the the Pax Britannia and the physical scope of Empire afforded special bonuses to the folklorists of Britain [...] until the dislocation of the Great War, coincident with the passing of a brilliant generation" (Dorson 1968, i-x). For wistful "settled" admirers and the gypsylorists, in particular, Gypsy culture represented the survival of long lost, premodern values of human "high spirits", "racial purity" and "individual liberty". The peculiar nature of this fascination with the Gypsies, however, necessitated a cautionary attitude to any person or group who did not fulfil the criteria for racial Gypsy "purity" – i.e. anyone who did not look the part of the pure-blooded, fluent-speaking, Anglo-Romani ideal. According to these criteria, a host of people were not really worth enquiring into including those labelled "mumpers", "hedgecrawlers", "posh-rats", "didakais", or Romany people who had married Irish tinkers or non-Gypsies ("gaujos"). A cautionary attitude was necessary in relation to the seemingly impure Irish tinker, for instance. John Sampson – one of the few members of the Gypsy Lore Society to evince an interest in Irish tinkers and their language Shelta – wrote in the *Journal of the Gypsy Lore Society*:

> The Tinker has already been introduced to us by Mr. MacRitchie [the society's president] and as he is undoubtedly a good fellow, and worth

---

[3] The upsurge of interest in Gypsy life at the end of the nineteenth century was not confined to Britain, of course. Gypsy fads and fashions flourished in many parts of Europe from the eighteenth until the twentieth centuries. Pushkin and Tolstoy were but two of the prominent nineteenth-century Russians infatuated with Gypsy life. As young men, they spent much of their time patronizing Gypsy gambling games, singers and dancers. The habit was not confined to writers. An 1889 *Harpers' Magazine* article reported that in Moscow "no fete is considered complete without the Bohemiennes; no prodigality in money or jewelry can satisfy their rapacity; reserved, disdainful, inaccessible to the enterprises of gallantry, these Gypsy women drive the gilded youth of Russia wild with enthusiasm, and stir their torpid souls." (*Journal of the Gypsy Lore Society* 2: 204-21)

knowing, there can be no impropriety in further cultivating his acquaintance. Although his less reputable [...] connections [...] may perhaps cause him to be somewhat coldly received by the more exclusive of our members [...] yet he still comes of a good old stock, rich, if in nought else, in hereditary and developed characteristics [...] an inviting field for the labours of the missionary and social reformer.[4]

Gypsylorists like Sampson reinforced their "prejudiced" attitude by alleging that the principal objects of their study - the coveted British Gypsies themselves - evinced an antipathy towards the Tinkers, particularly Irish Tinkers, as opposed to tinsmithing Gypsies or "tinkers" who had become "Scottish" and were slightly more acceptable. The gypsylorist Brian Vesey-Fitzgerald, who was probably the most influential writer of "literary" works on Gypsies in the 1940s, surmised that:

> [...] the Gypsy dislike of the tinker springs very largely from the similarity between the two in the way they live and the way they earn a living, and because wherever the two meet the Gypsy is blamed for sins that more often than not are the tinker's. (Vesey-Fitzgerald, 1944: 42)

Vesey-Fitzgerald may have been correct in attributing some of this alleged "antipathy" to the fact that both groups were often competing in the same commercial arena. How much of the Gypsies' alleged "antipathy" was, in reality, the projections of the views of this second-generation group of Gypsy Lore Society gypsylorists such as Vesey-Fitzgerald himself, Edward Harvey and Rupert Croft-Cooke, amongst others, is an even more interesting question. As Thomas Acton has showed in his book *Gypsy Politics and Social Change* (1974), many county councils and local government officials in Britain accepted the thesis of racial "purity" in relation to Gypsies as fact from as early as before the Second World War.

The categorisation of Gypsies into sub-groups undertaken by the gypsylorists of the "Romany Rai"[5] tradition and other so-called experts and advisers on Gypsy matters (many of whom were members of the Gypsy Lore Society) in the early part of the century "justified" local authorities in building up their own "inventories" of how many "true" Gypsies as opposed to "mumpers", "half-breeds", "didakais" and "tinkers" there were in a particular area of the U.K. These bizarre classifications would have been amusing except for the devastating results they had for Gypsies and Travellers still living on the road, particularly in the period after the Second World War. The belief that the "true-blooded Gypsy" was a dying breed lived on in the literature of gypsiology and officialdom alike and the romantic idealized Gypsy of literary and gypsylore fame became a millstone around the necks of those Gypsies

---

[4] *Journal of the Gypsy Lore Society* 2: 204–21.
[5] "Romany Rai" means Romany "king" or "expert" or "gentleman". "Romany Rai" seems to have been a term which some Gypsylorists took as a "title" to refer to themselves.

and Travellers agitating for their rights. Gypsy "experts", many of whom were members of the Gypsy Lore Society, warned in their writings of the demise of the "real" Gypsy and the upsurge of those whose claims to a Gypsy lifestyle were perceived to be spurious. The romantic literary myth of the "true" Gypsy continued to be propagated as various "experts" on Gypsies warned of the imminent demise of this "true" Gypsy type in areas which have been synonymous with Gypsies for centuries, including Hampshire's New Forest area. As Acton (1974: 191) points out, the literary myth is likely to have influenced those various bodies responsible for local affairs because, even in the 1960s, a report of the Hampshire Association of Parish Councils states:

> The old Romany stock is diluted and there has been an infiltration of "poor white". The majority of these people have wandered all their lives. Though, in the past, they had the their proud traditions, they, and we too, as thinking people, are faced with the problem that besets a decadent stock. They belong to neither past nor present.[6]

The continuing strength of the "racial" stereotype allowed some local authorities the possibility to absolve their responsibilities towards Gypsies completely on the pretext that they would help "real" Romanies but not the crowd of "pretenders" who were then on the road. In many instances, the reports of the "true" Gypsy's demise may have aided local government in it's efforts either to totally "assimilate" Gypsies and Travellers or to practice so-called "rehabilitation" on them, at the same time absolving themselves from any charges of ethnic oppression. Acton (1974) points out that some local councils in Britain actually made surveys during the 1950s and, in the process, attempted to distinguish between the number of so-called "true" Romanies and those others "on the road" – a process with uncomfortable echoes of the categorisation of Gypsies into sub-groups and their subsequent ethnic cleansing by the Nazis in the concentration camps only a few years before. When one considers the practical consequences of the literary tradition, it is no surprise to find that present-day Gypsy activists are increasingly critical of the whole gypsylore genre and the persistence of its stereotypes in the public consciousness.

To marvel at the longevity of this stereotype tradition, and the frighteningly precise nature in which the cult of the "true Gypsy" or "true Romany" persists from one generation of public policy-makers to another all we have to do is read the comments made by the then British Home Secretary, Jack Straw, in 1999.

> Now the first thing we have to say is that people have got to stop being sentimental about so-called "Travellers". There are relatively few Romany Gypsies left who seem to be able to mind their own business and don't cause trouble to other people, and then there are a lot more people who

---

[6] From a report of the Hampshire Association of Parish Councils (1960), quoted in Acton 1974: 191.

masquerade as Travellers or Gypsies, who trade on the sentiment of people, but who seem to think because they label themselves as Travellers that therefore they've got a licence to commit crimes and act in an unlawful way that other people don't have [...] In the past there has been rather too much toleration of Travellers. [...] (Jack Straw, British Home Secretary, in a radio interview, 22 July 1999.)

The gypsylorist tradition is likely to have infiltrated the culture of the Gypsies themselves. While it was the Romany Rai tradition which first propagated the myth of the "true" Gypsy, it is also likely that some Gypsies and Travellers were themselves not averse to manipulating the "gaujo"[7]-created distinctions between the mythologised "real" Gypsy of literary creation and the alleged "mix-bloods" as a defence mechanism or when the occasion was opportune to do so. That some Gypsies or Travellers may still use the use the ethnic perceptions of gaujos (non-Gypsies) as a defence function from time to time has been hinted at in some reports of recent gatherings of Travellers or Gypsies in Britain. In January 2000, a very large group of Travellers – one of the biggest ever seen according to various British newspapers – gathered at the town of Great Yarmouth on the east coast of England to celebrate the Millennium. Over the best part of a week, a number of British and Irish newspapers gave reports of this unusually large gathering. When questioned by some journalists on arrival, one spokesman for the Travellers said that they were all Romanies while, later in the week, it emerged that the Travellers were all descendants of three different Traveller families originally from County Limerick in Ireland. In the same vein, some regional newspapers in England occasionally describe the professional boxer Francis Barrett, who has been consipicuous in the assertion of his Irish Traveller identity, as a Romany boxer. The "stereotype" tradition which Macfie and his fellow gypsylorists propagated appears to be alive and well even today. This is hardly surprising given the longevity of the same tradition. The myth of the "true" Gypsy has had a long tradition in Britain and in other countries from the seventeenth century onwards. Popular fiction by writers on Gypsies such as Bampflyde Moore Carew in the 1700s and British philantrophists such as Harriott, Hoyland and Crabb, all of whom were influenced by the widely-circulated work of Grellmann; all to one extent or another perpetuated certain stereotypes and theories about Gypsies, theories that were often based on little knowledge or acquaintance with the people themselves. Many of these same stereotypes and categorisations of Gypsies later found themselves into the writings of later gypsylorists such as Borrow, Smart and Crofton, Leland and Macfie.

Gypsy Stereotypes and their Manifestation in Macfie's Text

Macfie's journey in Bulgaria took place in June 1913 and was in the company of a small handful of Zagundzi Gypsies whom Macfie described as horse-stealers. He and

---

[7] "gaujo" is Romany for a 'non-Gypsy' or 'settled person'.

his companions travelled in horse-drawn wagons on the journey from Varna to Rustchuk, which took less than a week. Macfie's travel account provides interesting descriptions of the people and places through which they passed and gives a brief but vivid snapshot of rural life, including the markets common in country towns.

His travel diary slots neatly into a tradition of travel writing which was very much in vogue throughout Europe for at least two centuries before he made his trip. Travel accounts were seen as an important source of reflection on human diversity. In sixteenth- and seventeenth-century Europe, members of the elite, educated, versed in Latin and other foreign languages, and fond of travelling, met individuals like themselves on their tours and felt a degree of transnational community. Foreign travellers often gave the most interesting proto-ethnographic accounts. For example, Goethe, in his travel journal of 1788–89, gave a celebrated account of the Roman carnival and of Venetian and Roman melodies, one of which he transcribed in musical notation. French travellers in the eighteenth and early nineteenth centuries, visiting the distant provinces of their country, wrote accounts in which much exotic information of ethnographic interest was given, usually explained in terms of its antiquity. In Germany, late-eighteenth-century travel literature brought together the dominant objectives and topographies which would prevail in the future field of folklore research.

Travel writers raised the question of the specific character of the population of a place, the understanding of which had rested on stereotypes deriving from classical times and from dissertations written for that purpose which influenced the travellers' own accounts. Many such accounts portrayed the character of the different classes in the region visited. The laziness or otherwise of the local inhabitants was a favourite topic of interest, particularly for visitors to countries such as Ireland and Spain, as were descriptions of superstitions and the use of magic. Macfie, who had a fine ethnographic library at his disposal and who was himself a noted book collector, would have been very familiar with travel literature of this type, and his travel diary is filled with notes on the margins, where he quotes the descriptions of other travel writers who visited the Balkans. These he uses to buttress some of his opinions or generalisations as well as reinforce stereotypes about the different nationalities and ethnic groups he encounters on his journey. His perspectives are well in accordance with the mainstream of Victorian racial thought, much of which formed the background to the formation of the Gypsy Lore Society in 1888.

In his travel journal, Macfie divides his notes and quotations from previous visitors to the Balkans into sections which read like a manual for good conduct for a Victorian gentleman. These include headings such as "Truthfulness and Honesty", "Justice", "Toleration", "Sobriety", "Chivalry", etc. Quotes such as the following regarding the character of the Turks from a travel book entitled *Turkey in Europe* by a Lieutenant-Colonel James Baker (8th Hussars), published in 1877, abound in the commentaries and glosses which Macfie includes all over the pages of his travel diary. Under a section of notes entitled "Character of the Turks", the author remarks:

A nation may change its character, but not its nature; and there is one point in common with both the past and the present, and that is the Turkish rank and file were then (fourteenth century), as now, distinguished for their patience, discipline, sobriety, bravery, honesty, and modesty, and to these qualities I may also add that of humanity, although I know it will excite an indignant exclamation from many at the present moment. (Baker 1877: 155)

Or a note on the Bulgar character from another travel writer, an Englishman named John Foster Fraser, author of *Pictures from the Balkans*:

You must look beneath the surface for the qualities of the Bulgar. He is dour, even sullen. There is little refinement about him. He carries himself slovenly. His brusqueness of manner, and the polite "thank you" rarely enters his speech. He hates the idea of subservience [...] But he is a good worker, zealous, plodding, and is one of the best agriculturalists in the world. (Fraser 1912: 69)

Or another negative picture of the alleged dishonesty of Greek traders from Keppel, author of a work entitled *Narrative of a Journey across the Balcan*:

All commercial transactions between Turks and English are carried on without any written documents; a proof of the mutual confidence they repose in each other's honour, more especially when it is to be considered, that experience has taught both these nations to have no dealings with Greeks without receiving all the security that writing can give. (Keppel 1831: 289)

Macfie himself gave detailed and interesting descriptions of towns, markets, monuments and the dress and food of the people he encountered on his travels, and those are the principal reasons why his journal is worth reading. He also bemoaned what appeared to him to be any decline in the vestiges of ancient civilisation as he came across them. This world view was very common among the intellectuals of his generation. It is interesting that, roughly at the same time that Macfie was idealising the Gypsies and the rural way of life he saw in the Balkans, a similar cultural project involving the idealisation of rural life was taking place amongst folklorists in Ireland. Here the "authentic" west of Ireland and the illiterate but folklore-rich, Irish-speaking country people of that region were the people that folklorists and ethnographers gravitated towards in a cultural project that bore remarkable similarities to that of the Gypsy Lore Society – i.e. gathering stories, folklore and the various dialects of the Irish language.

Like Macfie and his contemporaries, those scholars who idealised rural landscapes were members of the upper middle class or upper class. Some of the leading intellectuals who shaped Irish folkloristic discourse in the late nineteenth and early twentieth century, people such as Lady Augusta Gregory and William Butler Yeats (who, interestingly, was a member of the Gypsy Lore Society for a number of years), all took a strong position against the materialism of a modern, urban industrial world and a fatalistic view, coloured by a nostalgic Romanticism, of the inevitable decline of folklore communities. Like many members of the Gypsy Lore Society, the attraction of such communities for the writers of the Irish Literary Renaissance, who felt themselves marginalised by the materialism and urbanisation of Europe, was the strength of the oral tradition and the magical powers of poets and poetry. In the rural society of the west of Ireland, they saw their ideal live realised, the image of the Ireland which they wished to fashion: a rural society led by a new aristocracy, that of the mind. Education and rural development were the enemies of folklore, and various writers understood that "to save folklore was to preserve underdevelopment". The idealisation of the west of Ireland country person originated in the same Romanticism as that of the Gypsy Lore Society. Macfie describes his fascination with the Gypsy group with which he is travelling – the Zagundzis – as follows:

> If I have dwelt unnecessarily on the affection I cherished for the filthy Zagundzis, eaters of carrion, importunate beggars, it is not because I am blind either to their faults or to the virtues of other Gypsies; but rather because I have been blamed for this affection and wish to record my gratitude to these friendly people for being so happy and so beautiful. (Macfie 1916: 7)

For some Irish intellectuals, the peasant became a type of "aristocrat in disguise". That form of idealisation also has remarkably similar parallels in Macfie's romantic descriptions of the Gypsies whom he came across on his Bulgarian journey. He describes the king ("thagar") of the (Bulgarian) Rustchuk Gypsies, Milano Nikoloff, as:

> a remarkable man who was not tall, but was sturdily built. He wore ordinary western clothes and his face was so pitted with smallpox that he would have been repulsive in appearance, had it not been that the Gypsy glitter of his eye and his extreme vivacity distracted one's attention and suspended one's judgement. (Macfie 1916: 47)

His idealistic description of a Gypsy named Turi, his main guide on the journey who accompanies him on a visit to an ancient baths, approaches the heights of romantic eloquence:

> And Turi, as he sat there [...] head bowed, clasping his knees, might well have been the god of the place, mourning that the present generation of Bulgar Christians have done nothing to maintain its beauty and protect it from decay except to add a miserable deal paygate at the main entrance. [...] Even when, seventeen days afterwards, I recall the picture with delight, and

not without pride because I am brother, more than brother (po-phral), to a god, I see no reason why he should not deal steal horses if he so desired. (Macfie 1916: 32)

It is noticeable that he ties in the idealisation of the Gypsy in the above description with a bemoaning of any signs of modernisation or development. For Macfie and other members of the Gypsy Lore Society, as for the folklorists of the Anglo-Irish revival, all of whom belonged to the upper landowning class, their social position meant that they felt a repugnance at accepting any evolution of the rural world.

The romanticisation of the "aristocrat in disguise" led to a wish for identification with the group under study – an identification which at times led the folklorist or gypsylorist to wish that he was in fact one of the group that was the source of his fascination. Describing a visit to a market in the town of Razgrad, Macfie writes:

> Threading our way through the dense throng we entered a small khan to drink tea and rakia – coffee they did not sell. It was full of Gypsies, and my companions were immediately involved in an animated exchange of family news and gossip, while I was introduced as a sort of a curiosity, but a curiosity who might be trusted. Here, as elsewhere, among both Gypsies and gadze, people marvelled most that I neither spoke nor wished to speak either Bulgarian or Turkish, and the wonder of the Gypsies was mixed with approval. That I should choose to travel in such company was not to them remarkable, for all assumed that I was myself some kind of Gypsy, a member of the kingdom, an inhabitant of Romanipe, which is to them just as real as Xoridanipe (Turkey) or any other territorial nation. But that I should come to Bulgaria to see the Roma, depending only on an imperfect knowledge of Romani, won their admiration. (Macfie 1916: 28)

The wish to be admitted to some kind of inner circle of "true Gypsies" of course has a long tradition in gypsylorism and is something that certain Gypsies used to their advantage on occasion. The Romany Rais felt flattered to be admitted to some closed "inner circle", and only too often, as a result, they accepted at face value unfavourable stereotypes of other Gypsies who were presented as "didakais" or not true Romanies.

The alleged distinctions between "true" Gypsies and those deemed less worthy of consideration appear again when Macfie and his Gypsy friends meet a Gypsy who apparently cannot speak Romany. Macfie comments:

> They made us coffee and we sent a boy to fetch rakia, which we all drank with great ceremony. One man, apparently a true Gypsy, spoke no Romany; and, to the amusement of the tribe, I did my best to abuse him in the language he could not understand. (Macfie 1916: 36)

This attempt at belonging often took on the form of an attempt at ownership of a particular group by the Romany Rai. On arriving at one village called Pisantza, the local schoolmistress asks Macfie why he is dressed like the Gypsies, suggesting (suspiciously) that it is "to escape observation". The mayor of the town then arrives to meet them and:

> [...] somewhat indelicately, since Turi was the interpreter, inquired how I ventured to travel in such company as that of Gypsies, a race notorious even in Pisantza for their thieving propensities. I protested strongly against this accusation and maintained that even if other Gypsies stole, mine did not; and in order that he might himself be witness to their scrupulous honesty I invited him to accompany us to the tent and drink coffee. If he did not accept the invitation with alacrity, he did at all events accept it, and returned with us in the dark. (Macfie 1916: 44)

The mayor becomes the guest of honour, and they all drink rakia, the sole subject of conversation being "the uncorruptible integrity of Gypsy morals". Macfie mentions that during the conversation he hears every now and then the "smothered fluttering" of a hen which the Gypsies recently acquired as an "involuntary gift from some gadzo neighbour". On the departure of the Mayor, Macfie indicates that they visited the houses of the local Gypsy smiths to "discuss the incurable folly of the gadzos".

All is not fun and games for Macfie, however. Occasionally in his diary the difficult side of his ethnographic project comes through. About halfway through the trip, which lasted only six days, he comments:

> The last two days had been too strenuous for me, and in the morning I awoke feeling very depressed. My journey seemed a failure: I was learning nothing, I was not even a spectator of the normal life of these Gypsies. We travelled at such a rate that conversation was impossible; and, when we halted, fatigue prohibited any serious attempt at enquiry or investigation. The excursion was costly; and I was not even enjoying myself. (Macfie 1916: 25)

Echoes of Macfie's slightly egoistic and paternalistic attitude appear not only in the comments just quoted but also in other passages throughout the travel diary. It is as if "his" Gypsies are only interesting as long as they remain exotic, and that they are only there to entertain him and stimulate him intellectually. Macfie, for example, has little empathy with the Gypsies with whom he is travelling on those occasions when they are forced to continue travelling even though they are weak with hunger, despite the fact that he seems to have eaten and drunk well (plenty of good wine) in the towns when they reached them. Similarly, in Ireland, it could be said that, unlike the Gaelic Revivalists who tried to arrest the decline of the Irish language and the rich culture that went with it, Yeats, Lady Gregory and other Anglo-Irish writers, whose world view was similar to the intellectuals of the Gypsy Lore Society, didn't really have a dialogue with the world they were attempting to engage. In many ways, what was happening was actually an egoistic use by the intellectuals and writers of the poetic spectacle which the peasant or Gypsy offered. As one writer commented about the condition of the poorest of the Irish country people towards whom the intellectuals gravitated for artistic sustenance: "Misery for them was never poverty, and transformed itself into rich tapestries." The Anglo-Irish literary intelligentsia rarely involved themselves in any initiatives for the development of rural Ireland or to stop the constant emigration which was haemorrhaging it.

Likewise, apart from one letter-writing campaign to government ministers in relation to the implementation of a Moveable Dwellings Bill in Britain, the Gypsy Lore Society never involved itself in any political campaigns on behalf of the people who were the object of their studies.

Is it time for a reassessment of the role of the Gypsy Lore Society in the history of Gypsy Studies? I have spoken to a few Romany activists who – resentful of the gypsylorists' central role in perpetuating certain erroneous stereotypes and myths, many of which are still common currency, and many of which have justified economic and cultural discrimination against Gypsies – admit that they would rather the Gypsy Lore Society had never recorded the material it did or collected its huge archive of photographs. Is it true that Gypsies and Travellers would be better off if the British branch of the Gypsy Lore Society had never existed?

References

Acton, Thomas 1974. *Gypsy Politics and Social Change*. London: Routledge and Kegan Paul

Baker, James 1877. *Turkey in Europe*, London: Cassell, Petter & Galpin

Dorson, Richard M. 1968. *Peasant Customs and Savage Myths*. Chicago: University of Chicago Press

Fraser, John F. 1912. *Pictures from the Balkans*, London: Cassell and Co. Ltd.

Grellmann, Heinrich M.G. 1783. *Die Zigeuner*, Dessau and Leipzig (English translation by M. Raper, 1787, and E. Wilson, 1807)

Keppel G. 1831. *Narrative of a journey across the Balcan, by the two passes of Selimno and Pravadi, also at a visit to Azani, and other newly discovered ruins in Asia Minor, in the years 1829-30*. London

Macfie, Robert A.S. 1916. *With Gypsies in Bulgaria*, University of Liverpool

Vesey-Fitzgerald, Brian. 1944 *Gypsies of Britain*. London

Collecting the Cant

Ricca Edmondson and Níall Ó Murchadha

This article outlines empirical work among groups of Travellers in three national settings – Ireland, Scotland and America – which was undertaken in the course of a project to reconstruct their language, Cant. We describe the inception and aims of the project, emphasising the methods used for contacting the Travellers who contributed to it. Outlining some of the difficulties which confronted the study, we comment on the influence of modes of access on relations with members of the communities being researched. In this project, Travellers who spoke Cant were often identified using "alternative geographies" – world networks as perceived by social workers, police or clergy. Introductions via such networks often involved the researcher in forms of interaction he would have preferred to avoid – but this did not inevitably have the deleterious results which might have been predicted. Thus, in addition to explaining some of the problems the project confronted, we are able to point to some of its successes.

Cant was long treated as a secret language (Leland 1880, Thurneysen 1886, Macalister 1937, Clement 1981), and its original extent is not now known – though all that was said by Travellers participating in this project emphasises that it has contracted considerably over time. The language, which was derived in various ways from a combination of English and Irish origins, has now become so fragmented that no one now alive is able to speak it in its entirety. Though Cant was formerly jealously guarded from non-Travellers or "countrymen", Travellers contacted in the course of this research preferred to have the language restored rather than see it decline further. Even though this work was undertaken by an outsider, the fact that they saw the language as part of their cultural heritage and identity led them to support the project. Participants in the study were aware that there is a noticeable age-related decline in knowledge of Cant. As a rule, the older the Traveller, the better his or her knowledge of Cant. Some older Travellers might have a relatively thin grasp of the language, and occasionally one might encounter a child who has been taught it thoroughly (Binchy 1985, 1994). But many younger people know only a few words (Wiedel and Ó O'Fearadhaigh1976, Ó Briain 1986).

Developing a picture of Cant's grammar and vocabulary is, however, a demanding undertaking. It requires, besides the techniques of linguistic and historical reconstruction, extensive practical enquiries with considerable geographical spread. Fragments of Cant need to be sought in far-flung settings so that they can be reassembled to show the extent and structure of the language. To date, over 100 groups of Travellers in Ireland, England, Scotland and America have been visited in the course of the research. It is in the context of Níall Ó Murchadha's efforts in that regard that a range of further information about Travellers' culture was acquired.[1]

The project was started at the beginning of the 1990s, investigating the status of Cant, asking what was distinctive about it, and who was speaking it. Was it associated with the languages of other travelling peoples? As the project developed, it began to appear more likely that Cant might fall completely into disuse. Níall Ó Murchadha's interest in Irish had led him to be sensitive to such dangers, and he wished to save for future generations whatever was extant of Cant. The fact that he was working in the field of education and had a number of Travellers in his school lent an additional interest to this work. It was a point of *rapprochement* with their parents for the headmaster to be able to speak some Cant, and was intended to show respect for their culture.[2]

At the start of the project, recourse was taken to former collectors of Cant, who included other primary school teachers such as Pádraig Mac Gréine (1931), Brian MacMahon (who was also a playwright), Nioclás Breathnach, and Micheál Mac Enrí (1931). Mac Mahon and Breathnach had worked in Munster, Mac Enrí and Mac Gréine nearer to the west of Ireland. They collected from Travellers who camped near where they lived or taught and did not travel about to discover further speakers of the language. Moreover, those early investigators in the field did not use phonetic transcription but employed versions of English or Irish in their notation, so that it is not always possible to say what pronunciation they intended. Nonetheless, they were relatively accurate in their suggestions of the sounds they heard, as far as those can be distinguished. Other recorders were less skilled in listening and were unable to differentiate between related sounds. Even the work of Macalister (1937), which is often referred to as definitive, often evinces confusion between Irish Traveller Cant and Romany.

In the face of the incomplete nature of earlier work, Ó Murchadha's background in linguistics meant that he saw it as an intriguing challenge to try to discover the origin of the language of Cant. The more he read, the clearer it became that those origins had not been dealt with adequately in existing literature.[3] Like his predecessors in the field, he began to work in his home area of Galway, but the

---

[1] The linguistic research constituting the bulk of this project was carried out by Níall O Murchadha. Ricca Edmondson's role was limited to providing ethnographic support in relation to questions of the use of language as such and its relation to community.

[2] A tape-recording on Cant made by Níall Ó Murchadha at an earlier stage in the research was issued by the Department of Education to all schools in the Republic with Traveller pupils.

[3] A recent article by Dónall Ó Baoill (1994) comes closest to an appreciation of the background of the Travellers. His article, though it uses them with skill and insight, unavoidably employs a small number of examples. But although it is so important to extend the range of instances used for linguistic analysis, we prefer not to offer a final analysis of the structure of the language until the present project is nearer completion.

project came to develop a life of its own as questions posed themselves which could not be answered on the basis of local knowledge alone. Thus the work was extended to cover the whole of the country and, eventually, to include areas inhabited by Irish Travellers[4] abroad.

In former times particularly, it was strictly enjoined on Travellers not to share their knowledge of the language. At the beginning of this project, a breakthrough was achieved when one Traveller became sufficiently convinced of the worth of the study that he shared with the researcher everything he knew. This occurred in the course of some ten visits in all, which had been embarked upon in the investigation of Travellers' culture in general. It enabled the researcher to go on elsewhere to display some knowledge of Cant, which helped allay any mistrust which might be felt in some cases. Later, when he was sent from person to person in search of the language, his knowledge of it conferred upon him a certain cachet and became less of an issue. When participants teased him by coining a pretend word on the spot, they were amused by his ability to differentiate between the invention and the real thing.

The methodology adopted for the project was influenced by the fact that Níall Ó Murchadha had previously worked with Prof. P.L. Henry in the National University of Ireland, Galway, on the linguistic survey of Ireland, investigating the various dialects and subdialects of English used in various parts of the country. But here the difficulties in studying Cant began. In keeping with the criteria of linguistic studies in general, it seemed necessary to collect samples of Cant which were spread as evenly as possible over the country so that they could be used to represent each adjoining area. However, difficulties in identifying people fulfilling the necessary criteria meant that rules had to be adapted for the purposes of the project. It was originally intended to collect samples at approximately thirty-mile intervals, but, in the event, people speaking Cant might be encountered at spaces of ten miles or fifty miles apart. In the North of Ireland in particular, Travellers proved comparatively scarce. Moreover, in keeping with accepted linguistic techniques, the original goal was to locate people who had occupied their areas since 1900 and could thus be classified as representing their regions. In Northern Ireland it was particularly difficult to locate people with this consistency of habitation: in any given place the original inhabitants might well have moved on and others moved in. However, this difficulty in collecting evenly spread samples is in part compensated for by the fact that Cant speakers use the language relatively infrequently with people outside their own immediate milieu. The samples of language collected to date indicate that speech in Cant remains relatively stable in intonation, accent and vocabulary, even if it declines in extent. That affords some compensation for the fact that a perfect geographical spread of speakers proved impossible to collect. Someone who was born, say, sixty years ago in Kilkenny appears likely to retain local linguistic markers for his or her entire lifetime. That has made it possible to reconstruct a "virtual" spread of samples in the absence of a strictly actual one.

---

[4] The older people used the term 'tinker' and did not regard it as a term of abuse, whereas younger people dislike it and consider it insulting.

The outcome of the project will be to display the range and variety of Cant as it exists at the beginning of the twenty-first century. It is hoped also to show how the language originated and what influences developed it. In this way it will become possible to substantiate hypotheses about the origins of the Irish Travelling people and Travellers in the Irish tradition in Scotland and America (Baird 1822, Simson 1865, Henry 1995). All the available Cant it has been possible for the project to trace has now been collected, except in one part of Scotland which was initially visited in the course of 2001.

Tracing Participants for the Study

Seeking participants in this project – Travellers who might be able to contribute to the reconstruction of Cant – imposed its own considerable constraints on the methods chosen for the work (cf. Bulfin 1915, Evans 1957, Bachmann O'Toole 1973, Barnes 1975, Court 1985).[4] There is no administrative or automatic way of finding out where groups of Travellers happen to be living on any particular occasion or whether they speak Cant; nor should there be. Access must first be acquired, then, starting out from serendipity – stopping at the side of the road when groups of Travellers are noticed, and conversing with them. As the project progressed, lacunae in the linguistic information gathered at a particular date would dictate the need to seek informants in some particular geographical region. That area would simply be toured in a search for Travellers, or journeys undertaken for other reasons would be adapted into search expeditions. That was cumbersome for the purpose of gaining acceptance, for reasons which are obvious. The next most common approach was to go from one Traveller with an introduction to another in a different part of the country, who would usually be a relative. On such occasions the person sending the researcher on never informed the relative of the impending visit; but when the researcher arrived and announced the source of his recommendation that would generally be accepted without question. The procedure had the virtue of being socially acceptable but brought with it the disadvantage of producing similar types of linguistic information to those already acquired.

Here it should be pointed out with gratitude that by far the most active and positive agents in the whole process of discovering respondents were Travellers themselves. Thanks must be recorded for their generous and forthcoming welcomes. Often, participants in the study offered the researcher a bed to sleep in, assuming that travelling at night was an unpleasant option; they were anxious for him to stay until

---

[4] For further information on the background of the Irish Travellers, see Carleton 1844, Neligan 1968, Gow 1971, Gmelch 1977, Gmelch and Gmelch 1978, Joyce 1985, McLoughlin 1995, MacGréil 1998, plus the unfortunately named 1963 *Report of the Itinerant Settlement Commission.* Crawford (1975) went so far as to use blood typing in an effort to discover the origin of various European Traveller groups including a number of Irish Travellers, who appeared to possess similar blood types to settled people elsewhere in the Irish population.

morning rather than travel home. On occasion the offer was gratefully accepted, for example, from a group of by no means wealthy Irish Travellers in Scotland, who saved the researcher from having to spend the night in his car waiting for a delayed ferry sailing.

A third source of introductions amounted to using what we term "alternative geographies": local, national or international networks linking groups of Travellers – either in their own perception or in informal maps of the social world constructed by different types of outsider. That was, inevitably, the mode of access used for contacting Travellers in America (Harper 1969, O'Malley 1991), who were too distant for more *ad hoc* methods to be used. "Alternative geographies" are devised informally for their own use by the groups who make them, and take on different compositions accordingly. Police, social workers and clerics all have their own criteria for acquiring and evaluating what they see as relevant information about the worlds in which they move. Their lines of connection and points of significance differ from conventional ones – although, it was illuminating to discover, not always in expected ways.

Social workers, in particular, were important sources of introductions in both Ireland and Scotland, but the impact of that source of contact on the research was highly dependent on the relationship between a group of Travellers and the specific social worker in question. In some areas of the Republic, moreover, social workers were in general unresponsive to attempts to locate Travellers, for reasons which were never established; it was, though, noticeable that there were differences according to district. In contrast to police introductions, social workers would arrange meetings in advance and, when the relationship with Travellers was good, this was by far the most relaxed and productive of starting points. Housing authority workers in Scotland were particularly helpful, even though the researcher arrived unannounced and unknown to them, and often directed him to extraordinarily positive and informative respondents. Many social workers in Ireland, however, were surprised to hear of the purpose of the research, having had no idea that Travellers spoke Cant.

The need to use "alternative geographies" often involved applying for information on Travellers' locations to the police, since their work specifically entails moving around a region and taking note of who lives in it. In addition to embarrassment at the tactlessness of beginning any new acquaintance under such auspices, one might expect introductions derived by such means to exercise a distorting influence derived from justifiable annoyance on respondents' parts. Moreover, given the conventional frameworks within which Travellers are frequently perceived, as well as the history of prejudice against Travellers in urban and rural Ireland (Ó Riain 2000), one might assume that the agents of mainstream society would tend to reflect such prejudice. It was, however, often the case that the researcher's expectations both about Travellers' reactions and the activities of the police proved to be unjustified.

It became clear that "alternative geographies" could function in more ways than expected. Police in particular were often spoken of as serving to bring messages, especially important ones concerning matters of life and death, from one Traveller or group of Travellers to another. In Scotland, searching in vain for a particular Traveller who he had heard was an authority on Cant, the researcher gave up in frustration and applied at the local police station to find where he might be located. The police were able to tell him where this man took a walk with his terrier at just that time of day, in a pleasant Victorian park in the town. In the course of the subsequent encounter, the respondent appeared reassured because the researcher had provided credentials for himself by arriving by those means. The ensuing conversation was of special interest, since the researcher had read about Travellers living in caves in Scotland but never met anyone who had done so. The participant described living in a cave near the seaside as a child, information well worth having.

On another occasion, the researcher was interviewing a Traveller in his caravan by the side of the road in Scotland when a police car arrived at speed, and the researcher himself anticipated some unfriendly purpose from the visit. In fact the policeman had driven out to bring the Traveller news of the death of his sister. This is not, however, to imply that relations were universally so benign. In the North of Ireland, the police again gave the researcher information on where to find a particular Traveller, evincing intimate knowledge of all his movements. The Traveller said drily, "They should know where I am, they've been here often enough." We should note that we are unable to speculate here on how often members of police forces behave benevolently or otherwise. We are, rather, drawing attention to the ways in which they are thought of as behaving by the people interviewed for the project.

In the North of Ireland, there was usually no need to visit the police because Travellers there are relatively few and they live in a small number of urban settings, so that introductions could usually be obtained from relatives. In the Republic, it was more often necessary to apply to the police, who on occasion drove out to an encampment so that the researcher could follow them. The Travellers in question did not seem to object and, on the contrary, showed satisfaction that they were known about and recognised. Traveller informants often referred to the police as having been significant points of reference in former times – showing that this "alternative geography" with the police was to some extent a mutual one. If a Traveller died on one side of the country, the police would contact relatives on the other; even today this still occurs if people do not possess telephones, and nearly always in the case of deaths or serious accidents. Nonetheless, many informants also viewed the police with suspicion because of the law compelling them to move Travellers on, which they were often seen as enforcing rigorously at the behest of the settled population. Some informants spoke bitterly about being moved on in extremely adverse circumstances, when the weather was bad or there was sickness in the family.

Travellers in America

Although in such a system of alternative geographies the clergy were used least overall as sources of contact, they were crucial in obtaining links to America. The academic authors of a number of articles on American Travellers did not reply when applied to for information where they might be found, except for one who wrote suggesting they were dangerous people and best avoided! Many subsequent letters to a variety of possible informants went unanswered, and the researcher would have taken recourse to the police again but for a telephone call at short notice from an American priest resident in a Traveller community. The priest, known to his flock as "the pastor", had been alerted by his bishop that the project was under way, and proved extremely supportive, if sometimes in unexpected ways.

The priest met the researcher at the airport and supplied him with accommodation in his own trailer. This was a double trailer like many in the community, by the researcher's standards luxuriously furnished and complete with ensuite bathrooms. Immediately on reaching home he took up the telephone and required members of his flock to attend for interview. That appeared to the researcher abrupt, but his clerical informant indicated that he knew that a number of people were due to leave on long journeys and did not wish the researcher to miss them. Fortunately, informants did not appear to take this method of access ill, and the community known as Murphy Village supplied the researcher with all the help that could be desired.

As elsewhere, the researcher used a tape-recorder so that the flow of conversation might be as unrestrained as possible. It was very rare that an informant would express any objection to the method, and after the opening period of conversation people often appeared to forget the existence of the machine. On occasion, Travellers videoed the researcher taping them. Most of the Travellers interviewed in America did not, however, speak very much Cant (see also Harper 1969, Harper and Hudson 1971, Hancock 1974), especially if they were aged under 50 – though one particular child of seven had been taught as much of the language as was locally available. The younger participants in the project regard Cant as a badge of their identity, but older people report that the generations preceding them knew much more of the language than they do. Looking back on Cant, an American participant expresses particular pride.[6]

> It is a distinct language. You know, there was a word for everything. A lot of it I've forgotten. I don't care what it was: they had a word for it. I'll tell you a true story. There was a fellow, Brian Carroll, and a fellow named Dewey Costelloe. This was back during World War II. They wanted to get information to a kind of people over there without letting know what they were trying to do. If they sent it in code, they knew they could break the code. Brian heard them talking about it. And he said "See if you can get Dewey Costelloe over there." They got Dewey over there. Brian told Dewey. He said "The gammy nioks ['gamr nʲɔks] is firing with the tome nioges [toːm nʲɔgəz]. Misley ['mɪslr]." ('The evil men are firing with the big guns. Get out.') He said we got to get out of here and get out right now. The Japanese could intercept it, but there was no way they could break that code. That's the only incident that I ever knowed of it being used like that. They were on some island, but they were coming, some

---

[6] Editorial note: the putative Irish transcriptions in this paper were created by Níall Ó Murchadha in consultation with the Editors.

ships and a bunch of men. They knew that if they stayed right there, they'd be slaughtered.

In addition to such tales, the fact that the Travellers in America have had no contact at all with Ireland for 150 years underlines the tenacity with which they have held onto the Cant in a sometimes hostile environment (see also Leland 1880, Arnold 1898). Moreover, even the depleted state of the language in America still shows a vocabulary strikingly similar to that of Irish Travellers who have never left the island.

Both Georgia and Mississippi Travellers interviewed in the study emphasised that they see themselves as specifically Irish, and distinguish between themselves and English and Scottish Travellers, recognising no kinship as such between them. Differences in the Cant spoken by those groups can be recognised (see below), as well as discrepancies in religious practice and common memories. The burial arrangements in the oldest cemetery in Memphis exemplify this. On one side are buried English Travellers, some as far back as the 1860s, and on the other side the more recently arrived Irish.

Participants in the study in Murphy Village arranged for the researcher to visit a second community of Irish travellers in Memphis. The members of this community live in a trailer park, close beside each other, but the majority of the inhabitants are not Travellers, and there are many hundreds of others. Again, the caravans appeared to the researcher to be very luxurious and beautifully kept. Many residences had statues of the Virgin Mary outside – the bigger the residence, the bigger the statue! The Travellers here were highly successful in material terms and showed a very strong consciousness of being Irish Travellers. They were glad to get news of Traveller life in Ireland, though many of their views of the country showed signs of having been derived from sources such as the film *The Quiet Man*.

The Mississippi Irish Travellers have been in the region since approximately the 1930s, whereas they have been in Georgia since the 1850s. In both regions they began as mule traders rather than tinkers. But in America the mule trade ceased to exist after the Second World War (Riordan 1950), and this had been the mainstay of Traveller communities. The mould of Traveller culture seems to have been broken somewhat at that stage; the decline of the mule trade parallels the decline in Cant.

The Cant

The Second World War appears to have been a watershed both in the use of Cant and in specifically Traveller occupations, in Scotland and Ireland as well as in America – though for somewhat different reasons. One American Traveller recalled the contrast between past and present use:

> Years ago we used the Cant a lot; now the Cant is hardly ever used; we're just talking in English. It's just not the need for it now as we had years ago. We were out more. Here we're all together, and whenever we're around here together we hardly ever use it. The Cant is just dying out. We

were up in Michigan. There was a little old café there. We used to eat there. Most of the people up there were Polish. So they were all talking in this Polish Language. So me and this cousin of mine were talking in the Cant and all of a sudden I could hear, the only thing I could hear was me and him. Everybody else had done talking. They could hear us, and they quit talking.

The change in occupations which accompanied the decline in Cant in America is paralleled in Scotland (Gentleman and Swift 1971), where Travellers joined the British Army in not inconsiderable numbers (some as a result of conscription). They became employed in tasks to which they had not previously been used, such as truck driving or gardening. Those avocations could then be pursued in peacetime. Thousands of Irish Travellers had joined the British Army in World War I, but they consider, in contrast, that it changed them relatively little, for they resumed the lifestyle of tents and donkeys as before. (Informants report that the first caravan for Travellers appeared in Ireland in about the year 1900.)

Scottish Travellers participating in this project do not regard themselves as identical with Irish Travellers, though American Travellers do. This discrepancy is reflected in their language, for Cant in Scotland differs considerably from that in the other two countries (for an excellent early work on Scottish Cant, see MacRitchie 1889). The Cant to be found in America can be heard in Ireland too. Examples include the word for a woman – transcribed in Irish as *beor* [bʲoːr] – which is the same in America and all over Ireland. In the areas so far visited in Scotland it does not exist, though it probably did years ago. When the researcher mentioned it to participants in the research, it sounded familiar to some. The word for 'a hand' – *máille* [mɑːʎə] – is one used in common among Americans and Irish, but is not employed in Scotland. The word for a young girl, one of the commonest words with which almost everyone who knows some Cant would be familiar, is *laicín* ['lakʸɪːn]. It is also shared by Irish and American Travellers, but not by the Scots. The same applies to the word for 'house', *cín* [kɪːn] or *cínne* [kɪːnʲə].

Similarly, the Irish and the Americans have a word for 'a guard, policeman or sheriff' – *séideog* ['ʃeːdʲoːg] – often abbreviated to *shade*. The Scots use a Romany word, *musker*, and their language is strongly influenced by Romany, although in social terms they look on themselves as perfectly distinct. (In the Memphis cemetery, Irish Travellers are buried in a quite different area from English and Scottish Romanies.) The Americans and the Irish have almost no words for plants or trees, though they do have a word for 'hay' *réb* [reːb], but neither do the Scottish. In all three, adjectives are relatively scarce. Examples which are used include *tóm* [toːm] 'big', or *biní* ['bʲɪnʲɪr] 'small', or *láiseal* ['lɑːʃəl] 'pretty'. These three have so far been discovered among Irish and American Travellers, but not Scottish ones. The remnants of the language still extant therefore include mainly nouns and verbs, and the verbs are usually explicitly verbs of action.

From a linguistic point of view, the fact that Cant in many respects exhibits a uniformity throughout Ireland and those parts of the USA where it is spoken is an almost unique phenomenon. These are areas so geographically distinct that it is to be wondered at that many a Cant word is pronounced virtually identically. Thus: *camra* ['kamrə] 'a dog'; *lárc* [lɑːrk] 'a cart, car'; *ríospún* ['rɪːspuːn] 'a prison'; *niúp* [nʲuːp] 'urine'; *mislí* ['mɪslɪ] 'to go'; *stéis* [steːʃ] 'to stay'; *lois* [loʃ] 'to eat, drink'; *carb* ['kɑrəb] 'to beat, kill'. However, considerable phonetic variation can occur in the pronunciation of certain words. Thus: *cúinne* ['kuːnʲə] and *cúinic* ['kuːnɪk] 'a priest'; *rúmóg* ['ruːmoːg] and *rúmac* ['ruːmək] 'an egg'. The Cant word for 'shoe' has a wide phonetic range, with *golamóg* ['gɪləmək], *golamac* ['goləmək], *golamar* ['goləmər], and *gileamac* ['gɪləmək] displaying some of this variety. Of course, forms can be quite different depending on place, as, for example, *drípear* ['drɪːpər] and *sruidéal* ['srɪdʲeːl] 'a bottle', and the terms for an English Traveller, which in the USA is *cipín* ['kʲɪpɪːn] in Ireland *Gypsy*.

In contrast to Romany (see Okely 1983), Cant seems always to have been used as a secret language, and that has led to a number of misapprehensions about it (but see Seaholm 1977). It is often forgotten that, until the twentieth century, secret languages were relatively common in Europe, often associated with particular trades or societies (cf. O'Shaughnessy 1978). Because Travellers lived on the outskirts of society, a secret language seems to have been additionally important to them for at least two reasons. It did, of course, provide a means of discreet discussion in the presence of outsiders, in particular that of enforcers of the law. Cant has indeed been used, as all languages on occasion are, to bamboozle outsiders. Nonetheless, the way it is spoken of by participants in this study suggests that its role in establishing and reinforcing intimacy has been most important to them. Cant created a bond between Travellers, and between them and their ancestors. Current participants in the project are proud of their forebears' accomplishments: "They could say anything, they had a word for everything." They were proud that the language existed and pleased that efforts were being made to reconstruct it – those on which we have begun to report here.

Acknowledgement

For support during recent stages of this project, we are grateful to the Millennium Fund, the National University of Ireland, Galway.

References

Arnold, Frederick S. 1898. "Our Old Poets and the Tinkers". *Journal of American Folklore* 2: 210–20

Bachmann O'Toole, Electa. 1973. "An Analysis of the Lifestyle of the Travelling People of Ireland". *Journal of the Gypsy Lore Society* 3rd ser. 52.1–2: 54–80

Baird, John. 1822. *The Scottish Gipsy's Advocate*. Edinburgh: John Lindsey & Co.

Barnes, Bettina. 1975. "Irish Travelling People. In ed. F. Rehfisch. *Gypsies, Tinkers and Other Travelling People*. London: Academic Press. 231–56

Binchy, Alice. 1985. "A Linguistic Description of the Speech of Urban Travelling Children". Unpublished BA thesis, National Institute of Higher Education, Dublin

Binchy, Alice. 1994. "Travellers' Language: A Sociolinguistic Perspective". In eds. McCann et al., 134–55

Bulfin, William. 1915. *Rambles in Eirinn*. Dublin: Gill & Son

Carleton, William. 1844. *Traits and Stories of the Irish Peasantry*. Gerrards Cross: Colin Smythe. Reprinted in 1990

Clement, David. 1981. "The Secret Languages of the Scottish Travelling People". *Frazer Linguistische Studien: Sprachliche Sonderformen* 15: 17–25

Court, Artelia. 1985. *Puck of the Droms: The Lives and Literature of the Irish Tinkers*. Berkeley, CA: University of California Press

Crawford, Michael H. 1975. "Genetic Affinities and Origin of the Irish Tinkers". In *Biosocial Interactions in Population Adaptation*. The Hague: Mouton. 93–103

Evans, E. Estyn.1957. *Irish Folkways*. London: Routledge and Kegan Paul

Gentleman, Hugh, and Swift, Susan. 1971. *Scotland's Travelling People: Problems and Solutions*. Edinburgh: HMSO

Gmelch, George. 1977. *The Irish Tinkers: The Urbanization of an Itinerant People*. Menlo Park, CA: Cummings Publishing Company

Gmelch, George, and Gmelch, Sharon. 1977. "Ireland's Travelling People: A Comprehensive Bibliography". *Journal of the Gypsy Lore Society*, 4th ser. 1.3: 159–69

Gmelch, George, and Gmelch, Sharon. 1978. "The Emergence of an Ethnic Group: The Irish Tinkers". *Anthropological Quarterly* 49: 225–38

Gow, James. 1971. "The Irish Tinkers". *Ulster Folklife* 17: 90–3

Hancock, Ian F. 1974. "Shelta: A Problem of Classification". In eds. David de Camp and Ian Hancock. *Pidgins and Creoles: Current Trends and Perspectives*. Washington: Georgetown University Press. 130–7

Harper, Jared V. 1969. "Irish Traveler Cant: An Historical, Structural and Sociolinguistic Study of an Argot". Unpublished M.A. thesis, University of Georgia

Harper, Jared, and Hudson, Charles. 1971. "Irish Traveller Cant". *Journal of English Linguistics* 15: 78–87

Henry, Patrick Leo. 1995. "Tain Roscada". *Zeitschrift fuer Celtische Philologie*. 32–75

Joyce, Nan. 1985. *Traveller*. Dublin: Gill and Macmillan

Leyland, Charles G. 1880. "Shelta, the Tinkers' Talk". *New Quarterly Magazine* new ser. 3: 136–41

Macalister, R.A. Stewart. 1937. *The Secret Languages of Ireland. With special reference to the origin and nature of THE SHELTA LANGUAGE, partly based upon the Collections and Manuscripts of the late JOHN SAMPSON.* Cambridge: Cambridge University Press

McCann, May, Ó Síocháin, Séamus, and Ruane, Joseph (eds.). 1994. *Irish Travellers: Culture and Ethnicity.* Belfast: Institute of Irish Studies, Queen's University Belfast (for the Anthropological Association of Ireland)

Mac Enrí, Micheál. 1939. "Ceant agus Saoghal na dTincéirí". *Béaloideas* 1: 219–29

MacGréil, Micheál. 1998. *Quo Vadimus? Report on the Pastoral Needs and Resources of the Archdiocese of Tuam.* The Archdiocese of Tuam

Mac Gréine, P. 1931. "Irish Tinkers or 'Travellers'; Some Notes on their Manners and Customs, and their Secret Language or 'Cant'". *Béaloideas* 3: 170–86

Mac Laughlin, Jim. 1995. *Travellers and Ireland: Whose Country, Whose History?* Cork: Cork University Press

MacRitchie, David. 1889. "Irish Tinkers and their Language". *Journal of the Gypsy Lore Society*, 1st ser. 1: 350–7

Neligan, David. 1968. *The Spy in the Castle.* London: MacGibbon and Kee

Ó Baoill, Dónall P. 1994. "Travellers' Cant: Language or Register?". In eds. McCann et al., 155–69

Ó Briain, Tomás. 1986. "The Education of Travellers Reviewed". Unpublished M.Ed. thesis, St Patrick's College, Maynooth

Okely, Judith. 1983. *The Traveller Gypsies.* Cambridge: Cambridge University Press

O'Malley, Mary. 1991. "Emigration of Irish Travellers". In eds. Mary Clancy, John Cunningham and Alf MacLochlainn. *The Emigrant Experience.* Galway: Galway History Group. 102–10.

Ó Riain, Seán. 2000. *Solidarity with Travellers.* Dublin: Roadside Books

O'Shaughnessy, Patrick. 1978. "A Glossary of Market-Traders' Argot". *Lore and Language* 2.8: 20–4

*Report of the Itinerant Settlement Commission.*1963. Dublin: Government Publications

Riordan, Marguerite. 1950. "The Irish Mule Traders". *American Cattle Producer* (October): 9–10, 25–8

Seaholm, Per. 1977. "Shelta and the Creole Classification Device". Unpublished term paper, University of Texas, Austin

Simson, Walter. 1865. *A History of Gypsies.* Edinburgh: Sampson, Low & Son & Marston

Thurneysen, Rudolf. 1886. "Du Langage Secret Dit Ogham". *Revue Celtique* 7: 369–74

Wiedel, Janine and O'Fearadhaigh, Martina. 1976. *Irish Tinkers.* London: Latimer New Dimensions

Travellers' Cant in Scotland

Sheila Douglas

Scottish Travellers, especially in the north, are an aboriginal people, who have been in the country since time immemorial, unlike the Gypsies who came into England and the borderlands in the sixteenth century.[1] They were the armourers and metalworkers to the clans, making the weapons and ornaments that went with Highland garb, competent silversmiths and later tinsmiths, and bearing clan names. Down the centuries they have been joined by those dispossessed and marginalised by historical change,[2] have mixed with Romanies from the South and have chosen in some areas to settle and be integrated into the community. Some, however, continue to travel to find seasonal work or other opportunities to earn a living. The two areas I am most familiar with, and where I have friends among the travelling people, are Perthshire and Aberdeenshire.

Many Travellers are now settled in houses, although there are those who still travel and some who stay on Travellers' sites, which the government is bound by law to provide in accordance with the official policy of non-harassment. That sounds better than it really is, since many local authorities neglect their duty, some misunderstand the difference between genuine Travellers and the so-called "new age Travellers", who are mostly society dropouts and others provide sites that are not very satisfactory. In Perth, a site on the outskirts of the Inveralmond industrial estate has been one of the most successful. It was built, however, only after protracted wrangling with the local council.

Members of the Traveller family I know best, the Stewarts of Blairgowrie,[3] a country town in the middle of the fruit-growing area of Strathmore, who have been settled for most of the twentieth century, have served on the Secretary of State for Scotland's advisory committee on travelling people. It is a well-meaning body, which

---

[1] Duncan Campbell of Glenlyon once wrote "I think the Travellers were in Scotland before any Lord of Little Egypt imposed upon the court of James V." Duncan Campbell, *Reflections of an Octogenarian Highlander* (Inverness, 1910) 5.

[2] Especially because of the breakdown of the clan system.

[3] The late Alec and Belle Stewart, their cousin, Willie MacPhee, their daughters, Cathy and Sheila, and their grandsons, Ian and Roy, are the ones who have performed their music in public, but the family is extensive both locally and in other parts of Scotland. The two people from whom I have learnt about Cant are Belle Stewart, who died in 1997 aged 92, and her husband's cousin, Willie MacPhee who was born in 1910, who has never lived in a house and who has a trailer on the Doubledykes site on the outskirts of Perth. Willie has more relations than anyone I know and is seemingly always attending funerals. I also had a "wee crack" with Sheila Stewart, who is a close friend of mine, before writing this paper.

often says the right things but, because it is by definition only there to advise, has no real power to do anything. For that reason, a branch of the Gypsy Council, set up in England, has also been established in Scotland, although Scotland's Travellers, while they have mixed with and even intermarried with Gypsies, and have the same problems, are not Gypsies, but a native people.

When I collected and recorded the stories told by the Perthshire Stewarts, I found that Travellers had been accepted by country people for centuries but were misunderstood and discriminated against by people in urban areas. In the past 50 years, members of the travelling community in Scotland have become recognised as tradition-bearers and custodians of oral culture, for which two of them, the late Jeannie Robertson of Aberdeenshire and the late Belle Stewart of Perthshire, have been honoured by the Queen. This meant that those members of the settled population who were involved in the folk revival of the 1960s and 1970s came to have a high regard for the Travellers, who sang ballads and traditional songs, played the pipes or fiddle and told stories. They also learned songs and stories from them and looked on the Travellers as having given them back their heritage. It is against this background that the Cant language in the second half of the twentieth century should be considered. Here are two well-known Scottish songs in Cant:

"Dance to your Daddy"[4]

Grib tae yer naiscoull, my beneship kinchin
Grib tae yer naiscoull till the beerie bings anee
An ye'll feek a flattrin, aney a teepnie mazie
If ye grib tae yer naiscoull till the beerie bings anee.

"Big Jimmy Drummond"[5]

O ma name it is big Jimmy Drummond
Ma name I will never deny
I'll moolie the gannies in dizzens
For there'll be naebody there for tae tell

---

[4] I got this song from the lips of the late Belle Stewart. The only bibliographical reference for "Grib to your naiskel (naiscoull)" is Ewan MacColl and Peggy Seeger, *Till Doomsday in the Afternoon* (Manchester: Manchester University Press, 1986) 146.
[5] I got this song from the lips of the late Big Willie MacPhee. The only bibliographical reference for "Big Jimmy Drummond" is Ewan MacColl and Peggy Seeger's Travellers Songs from England and Scotland (London: Routledge and Kegan Paul, 1977) 295.

Last nicht I lay in the cauld granzie
The nicht I lie in the stardie
My mort and my kinchins are scaittert
An I dinna jan whaur they may be.

An if ever I dae bing a-chorin
I'll be shair for tae bing be masel
I'll moolie the gannies in dizzens
For there'll be naebody there for tae tell.

Belle's family were "discovered" in the 1950s and were recorded for the School of Scottish Studies in Edinburgh by local folklorist and writer, Maurice Fleming,[6] and Dr Hamish Henderson.[7] They were later recorded and made known in England by singer and folklorist Ewan MacColl,[8] who encouraged them to exploit the more exotic features of their Traveller identity to create a public image that would get them invited all over Europe and the States. One of those features was the Cant language.

Anyone who has met and become friends with travelling people knows that they have a gift for words. They have had to be articulate and persuasive in order to survive for centuries, pleasing the public and using their wits to deal and swap, buy and sell, entertain and manipulate. That last word may sound derogatory, but it is not meant to be. Travellers use the term "work" for this skilful dealing with people to make them do what you want them to do. They can tell stories and take their listeners on all kinds of imaginary journeys. I can think of no better company for an evening than a roomful of Travellers conversing, joking, riddling, bantering, arguing and reminiscing. They enjoy using language in all kinds of ways, better than many who are educated and practised in using words.[9]

---

[6] Maurice Fleming, writer, playwright, folklorist and collector, edited the *Scots Magazine*.

[7] Hamish Henderson, scholar, poet, singer, songwriter, collector, one of the founders of the School of Scottish Studies, and a leading lights of the Scottish folk revival, particularly active in revealing the importance of the oral tradition of the Travellers for Scottish culture.

[8] Ewan MacColl, born Jimmy Miller, involved in agitprop theatre, became one of leaders of the folk revival in both Scotland and England and was interested in the oral culture of the Scottish Travellers and English Gypsies.

[9] I once took Belle Stewart with me when I gave a talk to an international group at a Conference of University Women at Stirling University. My talk was carefully prepared and read and went down quite well. Then Belle stood up, tall and queenly, and talked fluently and without a note for nearly an hour – and also sang – and had the group completely under her spell. She ended by saying, "It's a great privilege for an old Traveller woman like myself to address ladies of your standing. You see, I can't put words together the way you can!" An American lady sitting at the front

The Cant used by Belle's people comprises a list of perhaps a few hundred words, all connected with the practicalities of everyday life and without any abstract nouns, apart from *shannas* meaning 'badness' and adjectives like *bene, barrie* and *shah* meaning 'good' and 'bad'. Such words, mainly nouns and verbs, are slotted in as required to act as a code to render their speech incomprehensible to outsiders. That was the function of Cant, as confirmed to me by Willie MacPhee and Belle Stewart.

Willie commented further that Travellers nowadays find the use of Cant counterproductive when they deal with officialdom or the law, and that, while, in the past, it was used in the presence of non-Travellers for strictly practical purposes, it was never used as a medium of conversation when no outsiders were around. I have also the feeling that, for people like Sheila Stewart, it has a nostalgic association with her parents and her younger days, when the family did a certain amount of travelling in summer. At the same time, I have noticed that there is a generation gap between Sheila and her mother, Belle, in that the former knows fewer Cant words, as demonstrated by the Cant list in Ewan MacColl's book elicited from Belle's generation.

Although Belle Stewart was born Belle MacGregor in a bow tent on the banks of the River Tay, her father, a pearl-fisher and tinsmith, died when she was only a few months old, and her mother took what is called a "single end" (a one-roomed house) in Blairgowrie. Belle grew up in a house, and Alec Stewart's family were croft-based Perthshire Travellers; that is, they lived in cottages on small bits of land and travelled around in summer to pursue their trades. Alec's father was a great piper who won medals at the Highland Games, played for the Atholl Highlanders and was engaged as personal piper by Lord Ward of Dudley when he stayed in Dunkeld House on the Atholl Estate. In the First World War, like many Scottish Travellers, the Stewarts came over to Ireland to avoid conscription. They did not feel like fighting for a country in which they were not respected. That had changed by the time the Second World War came along, when their menfolk all served in the armed forces. In Ireland, the Stewarts travelled in bow-topped horse-drawn wagons and later in cars. They travelled back and forward between Scotland and Ireland a good deal, and took squads of seasonal workers back to Scotland with them to pick berries or lift potatoes.[10]

It was Hamish Henderson who pointed out, at an oral history conference in the School of Scottish Studies some 20 years ago, that quite a number of Cant words correspond to the slang used by Elizabethan Travellers or "common cursitors", as they were called by Thomas Harmon, in whose book, first published in the sixteenth century, *A Caveat for Common Cursitors*, they can be found. These include: *bing*

---

turned to the rest and said, "Whom is she kidding?" Of course, kidding is one of the things Travellers are very skilled at doing.

[10] Cf. Sheila Douglas, 'Next of kin: A Study of the History, Background and Recorded Material of a Perthshire Traveller Family's Links with Ireland', in eds. John M. Kirk and Colin Neilands *Images, Identities, Ideologies* (Enfield Lock: Hisarlik Press, 1994) 69-79.

('come', 'go'), *vile* ('town'), *ken* ('a house'), *lour* ('money'). It is fascinating to speculate how this came about, but I suspect there is only one answer to the question: human contact and word of mouth – in other words, oral tradition. William Motherwell[11] was right when he defended the power of oral transmission in the foreword to his *Minstrelsy*. This certainly applies to Travellers' Cant.

The Perthshire Cant used by the Stewarts and their family and Willie MacPhee which I have taken down includes the following words (the lexical origins of these words are accounted for in an appendix by John Kirk and Gavin Falconer): *anee* 'in', 'back', *avree* 'away', *bammins* 'clutter', 'mess', *barracade* 'large tent, with stove and chimney', *barrie* 'good', *beerie* 'boat', *bene* 'good', *bene patren* 'minister', *bene patren's ken* 'church', *bene yerram* 'blood', *beneship davies* 'good day', *bing* 'come', 'go', *bing avree* 'go away', *blaswag* 'bag', *blinkum* 'match', *bow-tent* 'tent made from cloth-covered bent hazel boughs', *brickets* 'trousers', *broskin* 'car', *buffert* 'dog', *carnis* 'meat', *chate* 'thing', *chatterie* 'goods', 'stuff', *chore* 'steal', *chourie* (Romany) 'knife', *cluishes* 'ears', *coull* 'man', *country hantle* 'settled people', *deek* 'look', 'see', *dilly* 'girl', 'young woman', *dodder* 'doctor', *doomie* 'back', *drom* (Romany) 'road', *drookerin* 'reading palms', 'telling fortunes', *faizen* 'hair', *feek* 'give', *femmels* 'fingers', 'hand', *fichles* 'rags', *flattrin* 'fish', *gadgie* 'man' (derogatory), *gannie* 'hen', *geddie* 'boy', 'young man', *gellie* 'a bow tent' (a Scots word for a 'bothy'), *glimmer* 'fire', *granyie* 'ring', *granzie* 'barn', *grenum* 'corn', 'grain', *grib* 'take', 'hold', *gruffie* 'pig', *gry* (Romany) 'horse', *haain chates* 'cigarettes', *haben* 'food', *hornie, feekie* 'policeman', *jan* 'know', 'understand', *jeer* 'excrement', *jurival* 'genitals', *keer* 'house', *ken* 'house', *kinchin* 'child', *kip* 'bed', *lour* 'money', *lour chates* 'jewellery' ('money things'), *magelum* 'potato', *mang* 'speak', *mangin chate* 'phone' ('speaking thing'), *manishee* (Romany) 'woman', *mazie* 'cup', *mazies* 'dishes', *megget* 'sheep', *miaowin chate* 'cat' ('mewing thing'), *moich* 'fool', *monticleer* (Perthshire) 'water', *mookie* 'kiss', *moolie* 'kill', *morricans* 'belly', 'body', *mort* (Perthshire) 'woman', *mush-feeker* 'umbrella-mender', *mutyie* 'rabbit', *naiscoull* 'father', *naiscoull coull* 'priest', *naismort* 'mother', *naken* 'traveller', *pannie* (Romany) 'water', *peeve* 'drink', *peevin kain* 'pub', *pennam* 'bread', *persteejie* 'cart', *pluffer* 'pipe', *pooskie coull* 'gamekeeper', *poris* 'pocket', *rowtler* 'cow', *ruffie* 'Devil', *shan* 'bad', *shannas* 'badness', *snottam* 'hook for hanging pot over fire', *sprach* 'beg', *stall* 'stop', *stardie* 'prison', *strammel* 'straw', *stumerer coull* 'piper', *stumers* 'bagpipes', *sweetnie* 'sugar', *test* 'head', *tramplers* 'feet', *trash* 'afraid', *tuggerie* 'clothes', *tullum* 'spoon', *vile* 'town', *wanner* 'buy', 'sell', *weed* 'tea', *whammlin cacavie* 'a boiling kettle', *winklers* 'eyes', *yarra* 'eggs', and *yerram* 'milk'.

---

[11] William Motherwell wrote, "The tear and wear of three centuries will do less mischief to the text of an old ballad among the vulgar, than one short hour will effect, if in the possession of some sprightly and accomplished editor of the present day, who may choose to impose on himself the thankless and uncalled-for labour of piecing and patching up its imperfections... " William Motherwell, *Minstrelsy Ancient and Modern* (Paisley: Gardner, 1827) iv.

Several comments can be made about the Cant contained in this list. First, it is clear that it was not a fully developed language with syntax and grammar but a limited code language with a very practical purpose. At the same time, in view of the long history of the travelling people as a marginalised social group, it is understandable why they cherish Cant as a distinctive feature and a means of maintaining solidarity in their families and communities. It is the same instinct that has made both Gaels and Lowland Scots cling onto their mother tongues.

Two other things have to be pointed out. The incidence of Romany words is an indicator of how the Scottish Travellers have mixed with Gypsies, both in the Borders and further south. Their similar lifestyles have meant that they have found themselves pursuing the same seasonal or casual work in hop fields and other harvest fields and building sites. One branch of the Stewart family, for example, has inter-married with English Gypsies, called Hilton, encountered on trips to the south of England to pick hops or work on building sites.

Secondly, the Cant used by the Perthshire Travellers varies from that used by the Aberdeen ones. For example, 'tea' is *weed* in Perthshire but *slab* in Aberdeenshire, 'money' is *lour* in Perthshire, but *lowie* or *lowdie* in Aberdeenshire. A 'pig' is a *gruffie* in Perthshire and a *guffie* in Aberdeenshire. 'Eyes' are *winklers* in Perthshire but *yaks* in Aberdeenshire. A 'fool' is a *moich* in Perthshire, but a *corach* in Aberdeenshire. The term *naken* for a 'Traveller' in Perthshire is rendered as *nyakim* in Aberdeenshire, as in the title of Stanley Robertson's book, *Nyakim's Windows*. Actually *naken* means 'self'.[12]

During the preparation for this paper, Sheila Stewart remarked that her grandmother had told her that words like *gadgie* and *barra* are what she called "slang Cant" and were used to help keep the true Cant a secret. The "real Cant", to her, was *coull* and *bene*. Hamish Henderson recalled that he had been told that *gadgie* was used of a 'man', meaning 'one other than a Traveller'. Cant has the ability to form new name words as required by using the all-purpose word *chate* – 'thing', as in *miaowin chate* ('cat'), *whuddin chate* ('radio'), *lowpin chate* ('frog'), *nab chate* ('hankie'), *stallin chate* ('chair'), *glimmer chate* ('match'), *bavver chate* ('needle'), *lour chate* ('valuable or piece of jewellery'). Other words can be made by using *gadgie* or *coull*, in the same way, as in *sprachin gadgie* ('beggar'), *carnis gadgie* ('butcher'), *stumerer coull* ('piper') and *strod cowl* ('shoemaker').

There is also a Gaelic backslang used in the far North of Scotland by travelling people. This Cant is called *Beurla Reagaird* or 'the language of the metalworker', as Calum McLean translated it, which hints at an ancient origin, and is akin to the *Beurla na Saor* in Ireland. There are also Gaelic words or words with possible Gaelic connections in Perthshire Cant, including *cluishes* ('ears'), *shan* ('bad'), *fichles* ('rags') (from *fughell*) and *snottam* ('pot-hook'). Willie McPhee also uses *gourach* for

---

[12] Editorial note: Gavin Falconer reminds us that the name hunter-gatherers use for themselves is also their name for "human beings".

'the fork of a tree', which corresponds to the Gaelic word for a 'fork' or 'crotch'.[13] In Ewan MacColl's book on the Stewarts, *Till Doomsday in the Afternoon*,[14] he includes in his list of Cant words *cailleach*, which is Gaelic for 'an old woman', *ruadh* which is Gaelic for 'red', and *clach* which is Gaelic for a 'stone'. There are three words in *Beurla Regaird* which correspond to words in Perthshire Cant: *fidileas* ('rags', also *fichles*), *caineag* – 'hen' (also *gannie*), and *cian* ('a house', also *kain*). Since the latter also relates to the Elizabethan slang word *ken* which Hamish Henderson found in the *Caveat for Common Cursitors*, it can only be speculated how it came about or in which direction it spread.

There are Scots words still used by Travellers who think they are Cant because they are no longer used by the settled people. These include *lerrick* ('larch tree'), *mowdit* ('buried'), *hantle* ('part or piece'), *siskin* ('a type of bird'), *mools* ('earth'), *mazer* ('a [wooden] cup'), *gellie* ('a bothy'), *rowt* ('bellow'), (cf. *rowtler* 'cow'), *screeve* ('write'), *speugie* ('sparrow'), *coories* for 'blankets' (to *coorie* is 'to crouch down, curl up, as people do in bed').

Although its usage may be less nowadays, Cant still lives on the memories of older Travellers and used only for nostalgic or light-hearted reasons. I have a recollection of an Inverness relative of the Stewarts whom Belle had told, *She can mang the cant, ye ken*, flattering me shamelessly, when I told him I was *a barra manishee* 'a great woman', by saying I was a *barra deekin manishee* 'a great-looking woman'.

---

[13] For this information, I am indebted to Morag McLeod of the School of Scottish Studies.

[14] "Till doomsday in the afternoon" was a phrase used by Belle Stewart in speaking of how she thinks there will always be Travellers. Ewan MacColl and Peggy Seeger's book *Till Doomsday in the Afternoon* (Manchester: Manchester University Press, 1986), while it contains a good deal of excellent recorded material and commentary on it, is also riddled with errors and unfortunately – and unintentionally – caused deep offence to some Travellers, which led to all kinds of threats being made against the Stewarts, whom they held responsible. One of its main faults is that it illustrates foregone conclusions that were reached before the work of interpreting the recorded material was even begun.

Appendix: Scottish Cant Words

John M. Kirk and Gavin Falconer

In this glossary of 106 words, we attempt to provide brief explanations for the source or origin of the Scottish Cant words listed by Sheila Douglas. The following sources of help are acknowledged: *The Concise Scots Dictionary* (CSD). *The Scottish National Dictionary* (SND) and the *Oxford English Dictionary* (OED).[1] During this exercise, we observed that, for some reason, some words (e.g. *barrie, geddie, haben, manishee, pannie* and *shan*) are listed in CSD as still being current in Roxburghshire, which is not at all near Perthshire – perhaps an example of uneven decline in the use of certain words, although it could theoretically show that Perthshire Travellers have connections with south-east Scotland too. The words have a lot to say about Traveller society. For example, if *bene patren* is of Latin origin, it suggests that the word was coined at a time when the Travellers, or those from whom they acquired it, were Catholic. Overall, it is a mixed vocabulary, as mixed in origins as other Scots dialects along the Highland line. Examples which for Gaelic may have been the source or the use of which Gaelic may have reinforced are *cluishes, coull, dodder, drookerin, granyie, jeer, shan, shannas, yaara* and possibly *vile*. Macafee[2] calculates the Gaelic element accounts for only 0.8% of Scots vocabulary; Dareau[3] shows that the debt "Scots owes to Gaelic has been underestimated" but does not provide any overall figures. On the basis of the sample of Perthshire Travellers Cant presented to us by Sheila Douglas, we speculate that the Gaelic element at about 20 per cent – stronger as that of Romany (see below) – thus reinforcing Gaelic as a substratal ancestral tongue of Scottish Cant, as claimed by Kirk and Ó Baoill in the introduction to the present volume. Germanic words appear to be *gruffie, kinchin, mazie, pluffer, pooskie (coull)* and *sprach*, whereas Romance or Latinate words are *bene, bene patren, beneship davies, carnis, granum, pennam, strammel, test*. The Perthshire Travellers word list has numerous cognates with English words or colloquial or slang forms in English: *anee, barracade, beerie, blaswag, bow-tent, dilly, dodder, flattrin, glimmer, grib, lour, miaowin (chate)*, and *weed*. Several words were identified as entering Scots from Cant – *barrie, deek, drom, gadgie, manishee, monticleer, pannie* – or as

---

[1] We also thank Tom Clarke of the Northern Ireland Assembly for his assistance with some of the Gaelic etymologies and Pauline Cairns-Speitel, who compiled the glossaries in Betsy Whyte's autobiographies *Yellow on the Broom* and *Red Rowans and Wild Honey*, for comments on our preliminary analysis.

[2] Macafee, C.I. 'Older Scots Lexis'. In *The Edinburgh History of the Scots Language*. ed. C. Jones. Edinburgh: Edinburgh University Press 1997. 182-212 [p. 190].

[3] Dareau, M.G. 'The Scots/Gaelic Interface: A New Perspective'. In *Language Links: The Languages of Scotland and Ireland*. eds. J.M. Kirk and D.P. Ó Baoill. *Language* Belfast: Cló Ollscoil na Banríona 2001. 237-256. Belfast Studies in Language, Culture and Politics 2. [p. 251].

being used only by Travellers: *granzie, haben, mort, ruffie*. We are grateful to Sheila Douglas for compiling this list, for it lets us see the diversity of sources which make up the vocabulary of Scottish Cant. It makes us reconsider in particular the extent to which Scottish Cant has Gaelic origins which may in turn be shared with the Cant of Ireland, and also the extent to which Travellers continue to share an Indo-European vocabulary, traceable back to Romany and ultimately Sanskrit and shared by Travellers throughout Europe. Hamish Henderson's claims that Scottish Cant – at least in Perthshire – is made up of no more than 15% of Romany words, and that some words of Scottish Cant are evidenced by Gaelic and shared with Irish Travellers, are in general – even if only impressionistically – confirmed by the present short analysis.[1]

Anee 'in', 'back', is probably a Scots cognate of English *anigh*.
Avree 'away' is possibly a north-east Scots cognate of English *awry*.
Bammins 'clutter', 'mess' may be related to the onomatopoeic use of Scots *bum* 'to throw away carelessly or noisily' (cf. CSD).
Barracade 'large tent, with stove and chimney' may be from English 'barricade'.
Barrie 'good' is acknowledged as a Scots word of gypsy origin by CSD.
Beerie 'boat' is possibly derived from English *bear* / Scots *beir* with the meaning 'that which bears'.
Bene 'good' is the Scots word *bien*, probably from French *bien* (cf. CSD).
Bene patren 'minister'. *Patren* is possibly the metathesised variant of Scots *paittern* in the sense of 'a model of virtue'; alternatively, it may be from Latin *bonus pater* with the literal meaning of 'good father'.
Bene patren's ken 'church' is a compound of *bene patren* 'minister' + *ken* 'house'.
Bene yerram 'blood' is a compound of *bene* 'good' + *yerram* 'milk'.
Beneship davies 'good day' is derived from *bene* 'good' + suffix *-ship*, possibly jocularly based on the formula 'good ship x'. *Davies* is possibly a jocular form based on *day* by analogy with the name *Davies*, although the final *-s* could betray a Romance origin, cf. Latin *dies*, Spanish *días*.
Bing 'to come', 'to go' is recorded in this sense in the OED as obsolete.
Bing avree 'go away' combines *bing* and *avree*, each glossed separately.

---

[1] The full quotation is: "Unlike the true gypsies, whose language is (or used to be) Romany, the tinkers use a cover-language known as 'cant'. The cant of the tinkler-gypsies of Galloway and southeast Scotland has quite a strong admixture of Romany in it, but north of the Forth-Clyde line the amount of recognizable Romany in the cover-tongue is hardly ever more than 15 per cent. The tinkers of the north and west, whose native language is Gaelic (or was, until very recently), have a cover-tongue of their own which resembles one of the secret languages of Ireland. Their name for it is 'Beurlacheard' or 'lingo of the cairds' (the tinkers). That this is a very ancient cover-tongue is shown by the fact that some of the vocabulary which it reflects and deforms is archaic Gaelic." From Hamish Henderson, "The Tinkers", in *A Companion to Scottish Culture*, ed. D. Daiches. London: Edward Arnold 1981: 377-8.

Blaswag 'bag' is a conflation of English *bag* and *swag*, possibly reinforced by English *blag*.

Blinkum 'match' is probably the Scots word *blink* 'to give a spark to or of' + suffix -*um* (cf. CSD).

Bow-tent 'tent made from cloth-covered bent hazel boughs' is probably a compound of English *bow* + English *tent*.

Brickets 'trousers' is Scots *breek* 'breech, trousers' + diminutive suffix (cf. CSD).

Broskin 'car'.

Buffert 'dog' is probably Scots *bouff* or *bouffer* (cf. CSD).

Carnis 'meat' is Latin *carnis*.

Chate 'thing' is probably Scots *chat* 'a snack' or 'a morsel' (cf. CSD).

Chatterie 'goods', 'stuff' is *chate* + group suffix -*erie*, but cf. obsolete Scots *chatterie* 'crockery' (cf. SND).

Chore 'steal' is acknowledged as a Scots word of gypsy origin by CSD.

Chourie 'knife'.

Cluishes 'ears' is Scottish Gaelic *cluas*, probably in dative form *cluais*.

Coull 'man' is a shortened form of Scots *cowlie* or *coulie* described by CSD as 'a contemptuous term for a man'. It may be reinforced by Scottish Gaelic *cèile* (cf. Old Irish *céle*), which is the first element in Scots *culdee*, and/or Scottish Gaelic *gille* 'a lad', 'a servant' (whence Scots *gillie*). It is also related to English slang *cully*.

Country hantle 'settled people'. Scots *hantle* 'a considerable quantity (of things)', 'a large number (of people)', 'a great deal' is probably a reduced form of Older Scots / Middle English *handfull* (cf. SND).

Deek 'look', 'see' is Scots *deek* 'to catch sight of', and is acknowledged as a Scots word of gypsy origin by CSD.

Dilly 'girl', 'young woman' may be a hypocoristic abbreviated form of *daffodilly*; alternatively, it may be a reversed form of Scots *leddie* 'lady'.

Dodder 'doctor' is based on English *doctor*, perhaps influenced by the Scottish Gaelic form *dotair*.

Doomie 'back'.

Drom 'road' is described as an obsolete slang word for 'a street' by OED which cites an 1889 slang dictionary: "*Drum* means also a street, a road ... It may have come directly from the English gypsy *drum* (old form *drom*), which is, truly, from the Greek *dromos*".

Drookerin 'reading palms', 'telling fortunes' may be related to Scottish Gaelic *draoidheachd* / Irish *draíocht* 'magic'.

Faizen 'hair' may be based on the obsolete Scots form *fas* 'a border', 'a fringe' (cf. OED).

Feek 'give' may be a reversed form of Middle Scots *gif*.

Feekie 'policeman' is Scots *feekie* 'a policeman' and may be related to Scots *fykie* 'restless', 'fidgety'.

Femmels 'fingers', 'hand'.

Fichles 'rags' may be from the Scots exclamation of disgust *feech* or *fich*.

Flattrin 'fish' may be from English *flutter*, cf. *flounder*.

Gadgie 'man' is Scots *gadgie* 'a man', 'a fellow', acknowledged by CSD as a Scots word of Romany origin – from Romany *gadgi* 'a man', chiefly 'a non-gipsy', cf. English *gadjo*.

Gannie 'hen'.

Geddie 'boy', 'young man' is from a hypocoristic form of *Gideon*, a not uncommon name in the Borders, + diminutive suffix (cf. SND).

Gellie 'a bow-tent' is a Scots word for a 'bothy'.

Glimmer 'fire' may be from English *glimmer*.

Granyie 'ring' may be from Scottish Gaelic *fàinne* with prefix *gr-*, similar to prefixation processes in Irish Traveller Cant.

Granzie 'barn' may be an altered of English *grange* and is acknowledged as a Scots word of gypsy use by CSD.

Grenum 'corn', 'grain' is Latin *granum*.

Grib 'take', 'hold' is related to English *grab* and *grip*.

Gruffie 'pig' is Scots *guffie* 'a pig', hence 'fat' and may be onomatopoeic, possibly of Scandinavian origin – cf. Norwegian dialect *goffa* 'grunt' and *guffa* 'yelp' (cf. CSD).

Gry 'horse' is Scots *gry* 'a horse' and is acknowledged as a Scots word of gypsy use by CSD.

Haain chates 'cigarettes'. *Haain* may be derived from Scots *haw* 'of a bluish, leaden, livid or dull colour' (because of the colour of the smoke produced) + verb participle ending *-in* and compounded with *chates* 'things', although, in *Exodus to Alford*, Stanley Robertson glosses *haain* as 'having' (cf. CSD).

Haben 'food' is Scots *haben* 'bread' and is acknowledged as a Scots word of gypsy use by CSD.

Hornie 'policeman' is Scots *hornie* 'a constable', 'a policeman' (cf. CSD).

Jan 'know', 'understand' may be an altered form of Scots *ken, kan*.

Jeer 'excrement' may be related to Scottish Gaelic *todhar*, Irish *tuar* 'dung'.

Jurival 'genitals'.

Keer 'house'.

Ken 'house' is related to Irish Traveller Language *cēn* 'house' and is described by OED as possibly the same as cane, an obsolete form of *khan* 'an eastern inn or caravanserai'. Stanley Robertson's preferred form is *kane*.

Kinchin 'child' is described by OED as a Cant word "used by [sixteenth-century] tramps to denote respectively a boy and girl belonging to their community". The form of the word and the history of some other early words of the same class suggest that it is a form of German *kindchen*.

Kip 'bed' has come into modern slang (cf. OED).

Lour 'money' is English *lucre*, each form having come into modern slang, and is from Latin *lucrum* related to O.Ir. *log, luag*.

Lour chates 'jewellery' is a compound of *lour* + *chates*, literally 'money things'.

Magelum 'potato'.

Mang 'speak' is obsolete English slang *mang* 'to speak or talk' (cf. OED).

Mangin chate 'phone' is a compound of *mangin* + *chate*, literally 'speaking thing'.

Manishee 'a woman' is acknowledged to be of gypsy origin by CSD. Cf. Sanskrit *mánusí*.

Mazie 'cup' is Scots *maise* or *maze* 'a unit of measurement' (cf. CSD).

Mazies 'dishes' is the plural of *mazie* 'cup'.

Megget 'sheep'.

Miaowin chate 'cat' is a compound of English 'miaowing' + *chate*, literally 'miaowing thing'.

Moich 'fool'.

Monticleer 'water' is claimed to be of Romany origin by Stanley Robertson who gives the form *monteclara*.

Mookie 'kiss'.

Moolie 'kill' is a form of the Scots verb *mool* 'to crumble down', 'to reduce to fragments' (both literally and figuratively); it is also related to the noun *mool* 'soil', 'earth'.

Morricans 'belly', 'body'.

Mort 'woman' is described by OED as the Cant word *mort* 'a girl or woman'.

Mush-feeker 'umbrella-mender' *Feeker* may be related to Scots *fyke* 'to work laboriously', 'to take trouble or pains (with)'.

Mutyie 'rabbit'.

Naiscoull 'father' is *coull* + prefix *nais-* 'parent'.

Naiscoull coull 'priest' *naiscoull* + *coull*, literally 'father man', to distinguish senses of 'father'.

Naismort 'mother' is *mort* + prefix *nais-* 'parent'.

Naken 'traveller' may be literally *na* 'no' + *ken* 'home' and means 'self'.

Pannie is Scots *pani* 'water', 'rain' and is acknowledged to be of gypsy origin by CSD, which lists Gipsy *pani*, Hindi *pani, panee*, and Sanskrit *paniya* 'water, liquid'. In Brightons, near Falkirk, a council housing estate erected beside the Union Canal is locally referred to as *Pannie*.

Peeve 'drink' is hard to discern. OED lists obsolete senses of *peevish as* 'silly', 'senseless', 'foolish', or 'beside oneself', 'out of one's senses', 'mad'.

Peevin kain 'pub' is *peeve* + suffix *-in* + *kain*, a variant of *ken*.

Pennam 'bread' is the accusative form of Latin *panis*; alternatively, it is *pan* + suffix *-um* or *-am*, also used elsewhere.

Persteejie 'cart' may be related to *prestige* (which may have been used in connection with a superior type of cart, just as *prestige* is used as a name for cars nowadays) + diminutive suffix.

Pluffer 'pipe' may be a Scots onomatopoeic form from Low German *pluf* (*from ploffen*), Dutch *plof* (*from pluffe[n]*) 'to puff', 'to explode' (cf. CSD).

Pooskie coull 'gamekeeper' may be related to Scots *poosk* 'a state of excitement or fidgets', 'a hurry, a confused rush or bustle' or its derivative *peeskie* 'a little spurt of speed, an ostentatious display of haste', 'a bustle' + *coull*. SND speculates that several Scandinavian words may have been confused both in form and meaning, such as Norwegian dialect *p(j)uske*, 'to pick', 'to pluck', 'to pilfer', *píska*, 'to whip', 'to whisk', 'to beat', 'to batter (of wind)', and Faeroese *piska*, 'to peck', 'to preen (of a bird), 'to pilfer'.

Poris 'pocket' may be related to Greek *poros* 'journey' or 'passage', cf. English *portage*.

Rowtler 'cow' is based on Scots *rowt* 'to bellow', 'to roar' (of cattle) (cf. CSD).

Ruffie 'Devil' is a Scots name for a 'devil' or 'fiend'. CSD lists as the third sense of *ruffie* 'cant or slang name for the Devil'. It is a reduced form of obsolete English *ruffin*.

Shan 'bad' is Scots *shan* 'of poor quality', 'bad', 'shabby' derived from Scottish Gaelic *seann* 'old' (cf. CSD).

Shannas 'badness' is a regular derivation from *shan* + Scottish Gaelic suffix *-as*.

Snottam 'hook for hanging pot over fire'.

Sprach 'beg' is Scots *spraich* 'to cry shrilly', 'to scream', 'to shriek', ultimately cognate of *sprach* from German *sprechen* (cf. CSD).

Stall 'stop', as in English.

Stardie 'prison'.

Strammel 'straw' is Scots *strammel* 'straw' and is attributed by SND to the Early Modern English cant word *strommel or strummel* 'straw', which may be from Old French **estramaille* 'straw for bedding' and ultimately Latin *stramen*, 'straw'.

Stumerer coull 'piper' combines *stumer*, which may be onomatopoeic, + agentive noun suffix + *coull*.

Stumers 'bagpipes' is clearly related to *stumerer*.

Sweetnie 'sugar' is English 'sweeten' + suffix *-ie*.

Test 'head' is Latin *testis*.

Tramplers 'feet' is Scots *trampers* 'the feet' (cf. CSD).

Trash 'afraid'.

Tuggerie 'clothes' cf. English *toggery* from *togs* + collective suffix *-ery*.

Tullum 'spoon'.

Vile 'town' is related to French *ville* and may be reinforced by a lenited form of Scottish Gaelic *baile* 'a town or village'.

Wanner 'buy', 'sell' may represent semantic extension of Scots *wanner* 'wander'.

Weed 'tea' is from English.

Whammlin cacavie 'a boiling kettle' is Scots *whummle* or *whammle* 'to roll', 'to revolve', 'to whirl', 'to toss and turn', 'to rock to and fro', a metathesised form of Middle English *quelm, w(h)elm* (> *overwhelm*) (cf. CSD and OED). *Cacavie* may be onomatopoeic or related to Latin *cavus* 'hollow' or a shortened form of English *cacophony*.

Winklers 'eyes' is based on Scots *winkers* 'the eyelids', 'eyelashes' (cf. CSD).

Yarra 'eggs' may be related to Irish *earraí* 'goods' in the sense that eggs are 'trade goods'.

Yerram 'milk'.

My Traveller Friends: A Personal Account

Sheila Douglas

Travellers, Gypsies and Cant

First of all, I have to say that, while all my Traveller friends have different ideas about their origins and history, they are all agreed on one point – they are not Gypsies, and do not like to be classed along with Gypsies. Many Scottish Travellers have been to England, and they talk of the differences they perceive between themselves and the English Gypsies, particularly with regard to literacy. English Gypsies also do not share the Celtic beliefs, customs and oral tradition of the Scottish Travellers. Nevertheless, Scottish Travellers have intermarried with Gypsies.[1]

The term *Traveller* is not a modern invention; it is a literal translation of the Gaelic *luchd siubhail*, which was used in Perthshire up to the eighteenth and nineteenth centuries. In those times, in fact, the tinkers, who were also silversmiths, had a place and a function in life in the Perthshire glens and straths. There they were not harassed and persecuted but provided the community not only with useful articles like pots and pans, baskets and hornware but also at one time made the ornaments and weapons that went with Highland dress. After the '45, they lost this latter part of their livelihood, so they came down to the farmlands to make the useful wares required by the country folk and began to do seasonal farm work for them too. When Duncan Campbell of Glenlyon writes in his memoirs in 1910 about his childhood in Perthshire, he uses the term *luchd siubhail* without any derogatory overtones. It is clear from what he tells us that the little farms in Glenlyon were visited regularly by Travellers who were native to Perthshire and were given shelter and custom by the local people, who also enjoyed their piping and storytelling. That has gone on through the twentieth century: I have many country-born friends in Perthshire who have testified to it, and who have a more tolerant and liberal attitude to the Travellers than many 'townies'. One memory I recorded from an elderly lady, Mrs. Slater, was of being on her grandparents' farm in one of the glens as a child and needing knicker elastic. The day was saved by the arrival of Martha MacGregor with her pack of useful small wares. Martha MacGregor was Belle Stewart's mother. Mrs. Slater grew up with a kindly attitude towards Travellers which she kept all through her life.

---

[1] Their lifestyle has been sympathetically depicted in *The Summer Walkers*, which was originally made as a film by Timothy Neat and Hamish Henderson in 1976–77. It was not, as some people think, a BBC documentary, but it was put onto video in the School of Scottish Studies for using with students. Cf. Timothy Neat, *The Summer Walkers* (Edinburgh: Canongate, 1996; new edition reissued Edinburgh: Birlinn Books, 2002).

Cant is not by any stretch of the imagination a fully developed language with a grammar and a vocabulary to enable articulate and creative people like the Travellers to embody the richness of their culture. I have a knowledge of Scots, English, French, German and Latin, with bits of Gaelic, Danish, Spanish and Dutch. Any of these languages would give me more scope than Cant to converse, tell stories, or express my ideas and opinions. Naturally I like Scots best. Travellers are human beings and have the same hunger as anyone else to *talk* to people. Cant may be dear to their heart, and it may satisfy their desire to be distinctive, but it is not a language like any other. Sheila Stewart is very positive that her family, who are world-renowned storytellers, *never* used Cant to do this. But her family have a fondness for their Cant, and even her minister son on the telephone from Australia was homesick enough to ask her to speak a few words of Cant to him. I know how he felt. When I was in London, I longed to hear a Scottish voice, and when I did I nearly wept for joy.

Academic Study of Travellers

Academic research is misunderstood by those who have not been trained in it. Researchers do not gather evidence to support theories they have already formed but rather do the opposite. They may try out different hypotheses, but more often, when breaking new ground, they will first gather all the information they can and draw conclusions from it. Scholars like Hamish Henderson,[2] who was born in Blairgowrie and knew Perthshire very well, and David Buchan[3] taught me to work in this way, and it distresses me to find them insulted and belittled by the criticism of people who are themselves doing the very thing for which they are criticising the scholars.

With regard to myself, and as far as the Travellers are concerned, I am not exactly an outsider. I live in an area in which there are Travellers on the road as well as settled in houses. I have been friends with the Stewarts for nearly 40 years and have shared in the life of their family, as well as in the performance of their songs and stories. I have also taught Traveller children in Perth schools.

It is true that there have been people who have come to study or collect from the Travellers with a particular political agenda and no academic background or training. For example, there is the man of the agitprop theatre, Ewan MacColl (real name Jimmy Miller). There have also been some with highly romantic ideas about the Travellers (e.g. certain Americans) or with their expectations coloured by book

---

[2] Cf. Hamish Henderson, *Alias MacAlias: Writings on Songs, Folk and Literature* (Edinburgh: Polygon, 1992) and Hamish Henderson, *Collected Poems and Songs* edited by Raymond Ross (Edinburgh: Curly Snake Publishing, 2000).

[3] Cf. David Buchan, *The Ballad and the Folk* (London, Routledge, 1972), *A Scottish Ballad Book* (London: Routledge, 1973), and *Scottish Tradition: A Collection of Scottish Folk Literature* (London: Routledge, 1984).

learned knowledge of Gypsies. MacColl, especially, has caused a lot of trouble for the Stewarts with his book *Till Doomsday in the Afternoon.*[4] With Ewan's permission, I listened to all the recordings he made, and I know that he selected from his tapes only those bits which fitted his own ideas about the Travellers. Belle may have said "There'll be Travellers till doomsday in the afternoon", but Jimmy Higgins, who married her daughter Cathy, expressed a totally different viewpoint elsewhere on the tapes. He said that, when he came out of the army, he settled down in Blairgowrie, got a job (with the cleansing department) and sent his children to school, because travelling was then a thing of the past. This view is that of many Travellers, just as some of them would agree with Belle. Ewan used Belle's words because they harmonised with his thoughts and ignored Jimmy's.

In speaking about what has been published about the Travellers, I must mention *The King o the Black Art*[5]. This is not a book based on my Ph.D. thesis, but a collection of the stories told by Belle, Alec and John Stewart and their cousin, Willie MacPhee. They were transcribed by me from field recordings, made to accompany my thesis. I thought it more important to publish the stories as close transcriptions from the tapes. Any conclusions I have come to about any aspect of the Travellers' life are based on years of listening to my friends talking, performing and telling their family history.[6]

Travellers and the Folk Revival

Hamish Henderson certainly did not label the Travellers with preconceived descriptions – he described what he observed of them and learned from them, as I have done, by being with them. He also helped to bring their talents to the notice of their community and their country, where they have been well known and well loved for many years as a consequence. That applies to many singers, both Travellers and non-Travellers. When he came upon Jeannie Robertson in the early 1950s in Aberdeen, he was not specifically researching and collecting from Travellers but from the whole population. Similarly, when he heard "The Berryfields of Blair" sung by John MacDonald of Pitgaveny, Elgin, "the singing molecatcher" and a non-Traveller,

---

[4] Ewan MacColl and Peggy Seeger, *Till Doomsday in the Afternoon: The Folklore of a Family of Scots Travellers, the Stewarts of Blairgowrie* (Manchester: Manchester University Press, 1986).

[5] Sheila Douglas, *The King o the Black Art and Other Folk Tales*, [stories told by John Stewart, Alec Stewart, Belle Stewart and Willie MacPhee] (Aberdeen: Aberdeen University Press, 1987). Cf. also Sheila Douglas, *The King o the Black*, unpublished Ph.D. thesis, University of Stirling.

[6] Incidentally, I made the publisher pay the storytellers before I got any royalties for the book.

he was told that it had been composed by "a lady in Blairgowrie", who turned out to be Belle Stewart.[7] The fact that Belle and Jeannie became regarded as source singers in the folk revival was due to the prominence Hamish gave them. What the singers of the revival realised was that tradition bearers like Belle and Jeannie, whose families had handed down the songs and stories, were giving us back our Scottish heritage which we had lost or were losing.[8]

Now, as Sheila Stewart can see clearly (see her contribution to this volume), that heritage is under threat again amongst the Travellers, since the younger generation, with a few exceptions, have given it up. Travellers have intermarried with non-Travellers, and their children and grandchildren and great-grandchildren go to school or work locally. They watch television and listen to pop music. They look on what their parents and grandparents had and passed on to them, just as other young folk do, as outdated rubbish. But there are notable exceptions. Both Sheila's elder sons are pipers, and one is also a singer and songwriter. Singer and storyteller (and fish-filleter) Stanley Robertson, in Aberdeen, who is the nephew of Jeannie Robertson and the cousin of Lizzie Higgins, has a family also, including Gabrielle and Michelle. Stanley's cousin has a daughter called Carmen Higgins, who has been dazzling us all at festivals as a fiddler since she was a child. They have both inherited the talent for singing and storytelling, and Michelle has also taken a university degree, as has Belle's granddaughter, also called Michelle. But as Betsy Williamson (daughter of Duncan), who has also been to college, has told me, "We know it means a lot to our father, but we don't relate to it now. Maybe when we're older we'll come back to it."

Travellers and Literature

As regards Traveller literature, if people *want* to write, they *will* write. It doesn't depend on education initiatives or funding or any other conventional resources. Writing is a compulsion that drives people, or it does not, and it does not matter who or what you are – old or young, educated or not, Traveller or non-Traveller, Scottish, English or Chinese – you do it because you have to. To be published – in Scotland at least – there has to be a market for you to write for, and it is the publishers, not the writers, who define this. To get a book published in Scots is a big problem, never

---

[7] Personal communication from Hamish Henderson, who told this story many times to many people. It was from "The Singing Molecatcher of Pitgaveny" – what John McDonald called himself – that Hamish Henderson first heard of Belle Stewart – "the lady in Blairgowie". Belle Stewart was originally "discovered" by Maurice Fleming while doing fieldwork for the School of Scottish Studies.

[8] For the role of travellers in the folk revival of Scotland, see Ailie Munro, *The Democratic Muse: Folk Music Revival in Scotland* (London: Kahn & Averill, 1984, re-issued Aberdeen: Scottish Cultural Press 1996).

mind anything else. Stanley Robertson[9], Duncan Williamson[10] and Betsy Whyte[11] have all had books published. Stanley is a very intelligent man and can write well. Duncan owes his books to his highly educated American second wife, Linda, who came over as a post-graduate student and married him. Without her, I doubt if his wonderful stories would ever have been in print. Peter Cook of the School of Scottish Studies and Linda Williamson helped Betsy Whyte to write about her childhood in Perthshire, but I understand from them that she did the actual writing herself. Those books are well known and loved in Scotland. A stage play was written based on Betsy's book *The Yellow on the Broom,* and two of my songs were used in it, one called "Willie MacPhee's Song" and the other called "Moving On". I went with Willie and Bella to see the play performed and introduced them to the actors afterwards, who were pleased and proud to meet them. I have also written a children's novel called *The Magic Chanter*[12] in which two of the main characters are travelling people based (with their permission) on Willie and Bella MacPhee. One of the aims of the book was to tell children about the Travellers so that they would understand their importance. This book has been used in some Scottish schools.

Travellers are masters of oral literature, and that is not the same thing as the written variety. Early ballad and song collectors made the mistake of judging material from oral tradition as if it were poetry, i.e. a literary form most of them practised themselves. They thought the ballads and songs they collected were crude and unpolished because they did not fit in with the literary tastes of their time and were in any case composed to be sung and heard rather than read from a printed page. In my experience, my Traveller friends talk much better than they write. As a graduate English teacher of 30 years' experience in Scottish schools, I am quite able to judge those matters. Few people can touch the Travellers' oral skills. Most of the older ones had minimal schooling, so it does not come from that. They are masters of spoken language, song and story (for that reason, I cannot see them being content with Cant as a language for all purposes) and can teach the rest of the population, as they have done, through the folk revival, how central they are to life.

---

[9] Stanley Robertson, *Exodus to Alford: Master Story-teller of the Traveller Folk* (Nairn: Balnain Books, 1988)

[10] Duncan and Linda Williamson, *A Thorn in the King's Foot: Stories of the Scottish Travelling People* (Harmondsworth: Penguin, 1987)

[11] Betsy Whyte, *The Yellow on the Broom: The Early Days of a Traveller Woman* (Edinburgh: Chambers, 1979; reissued Edinburgh: Birlinn 2001) and [its sequel] *Red Rowans and Wild Honey* (Edinburgh: Canongate, 1990; reissued Edinburgh: Birlinn, 2000)

[12] Sheila Douglas, *The Magic Chanter* (Perth: Scottish Children's Press, 1997)

Travellers and the Community

When I was undertaking my doctoral research on the storytelling traditions of the Stewarts, I had occasion to write to the local paper to support the proposal to build a Travellers' caravan site in Perth, in accordance with the government's policy of non-harassment. One of the responses I had to this came from a local farmer who was also a regional councillor. He rang me up and arranged to visit me "to put me right about the Travellers". His farm is only about a mile from where I live. He came and told me of all the awful things Travellers did, camping in lay-bys, letting their dogs worry his sheep, and leaving piles of rubbish behind them. I asked him what he expected them to do, when the Council did not provide a stopping place and denied the Travellers the services of the refuse department. After all, surely as a farmer he had had his neeps shawed and tatties lifted by Travellers for years. He looked at me in amazement and said, "Oh, but I'm no talkin aboot *oor traivellers*!" Of course, the Reids, Whytes, MacPhees and Townsleys were known to him, had worked for him regularly, and he had a genuine interest in their welfare. He also prized the articles they had made for him, the heather *reenges* ('brushes'), and so on, which he actually used. The Travellers he did not welcome came from "elsewhere". The late Betsy Whyte confirmed to me that this was the usual attitude of Perthshire farmers.

My experience of the Travellers' site at Doubledykes at Inveralmond on the outskirts of Perth has stretched over many years. In the 1960s, a travelling woman, Mrs. Nancy MacGregor (related to Belle), came to my door regularly for rags and anything that I could give her to pass on or sell. Over the tea that I always made for her, she told me lots about the unofficial site at Doubledykes. It was an absolute disgrace that human beings should have to camp in such a place, subject to flooding or becoming a muddy mess. She was knocked down by a car one night, at a dangerous bend on the main road and suffered a fractured leg. The shock of landing in hospital brought on a mental breakdown. She was never the same again, poor woman, physically or mentally. She got a house in the town, among the worst council tenants, of course, and I supported her attempts to get moved from it.

Later, the Council followed government recommendations and built the present site, which I know very well indeed, since our great friends Willie and Bella MacPhee, who have never lived in a house, were given a stance there. The next stance was given to another member of the family. The MacPhees were very pleased with their site and its facilities. Of course, through time, things had to be maintained by the Council, and when the area was flooded in 1993, Willie and Bella lost their trailer along with six others, when they were pulled into a neighbouring field temporarily while the Council refurbished their washing and toilet blocks. The Council at first tried to say that they were not Council tenants and not entitled to any help, but their own housing department called in a lawyer, and the next thing was the Travellers were helped to replace their trailers. Bella made a little garden beside theirs, and Willie even grew willow wands for the fine baskets he was still making a few years ago. He is now [in 2001] 91 years old, cannot walk, and is almost blind. Bella suffers from Alzheimer's. All the years we have visited them, we have never seen the warden (whom they like) and have never felt the place was being "policed" or that the folk in it are being "contained". What is more, *neither have they*. It is true that Willie asked my husband to let the bank send his letters to my home address rather than to the site, but that was for privacy from other Travellers. A few years ago, Willie, the last of the tinsmiths, was heartbroken when his *stake* ('tinsmith's anvil') was stolen from a lean-to shed on his stance, along with other stuff. It had belonged to his uncle and was irreplaceable.

If there is a Scottish equivalent to the English Criminal Justice and Public Order Act, it would be called the Criminal Justice and Public Order (Scotland) Act. The policy of the new Scottish Parliament is to aim for an "inclusive society", so this sounds a bit different. I do not think people are thrown into jail for being Travellers here, and I do not think the government has withdrawn support from Travellers. At any rate, there are plenty of them walking about the streets of Perth and Blairgowrie, and in 2001 the sites are still operating.

To say that Travellers have no sense of ownership of local authority sites prompts the question whether they should. They have no sense of ownership of the countryside they travel round either, except that it is their native soil. Council house tenants, of whom there are thousands in Scotland, also have no sense of ownership. Recently, they have been given the chance to buy their houses, but not all of them can afford to do so. As for a sense of ownership, from my knowledge of Travellers, this can have a different meaning for them: anything owned is for sharing among your family and friends. Non-Travellers tend to have a more selfish, materialistic view: "what's mine is mine alone and anyone else has to keep their hands off it!" A very clever story told by one of Sheila's uncles, entitled "Geordie MacPhee", wonderfully satirises both the Traveller and non-Traveller idea of "possession".[14]. There is no room on sites for such activities as burning scrap. But Council tenants do not have these facilities either. Nowadays, Travellers do things differently from the past and have organised their lives accordingly. Doubledykes site has water and electricity, so conditions are far from primitive.

Travellers and Ethnicity

It has sometimes been suggested that Scottish Travellers are an ethnically distinct group – a suggestion with which I always have difficulty. There are so many ethnic strands in the Scottish population, from Brythonic, to West Germanic, to Celtic, to Norse, to Norman French, perhaps with odd dashes of others thrown in, that it is

---

[14] Cf. Sheila Douglas, *The King o the Black Art*. Unpublished Ph.D. thesis, University of Stirling.

difficult to recognise any pure ethnic strain. We are, like every other country of Europe, a mongrel people! The Scottish Travellers, at least in the north, share so many Celtic beliefs and customs, music, song and story, that it is difficult not to connect them with the old clans. Their sense of kinship, their love of family and social life, their pride in hospitality and love of beautiful things make it very hard to see them ethnically as anything else but Celts. They may form a distinct *social* group, since historical change has robbed of their means of making a living so many times, but they are great survivors. They have adapted to changing circumstances over and over again. That is the reason why I made "The King o the Black Art" not only the title story of the collection, but also the title of my whole project: it is a story about survival.

The fall down the social scale is always what happens when things change (consider the miners and shipbuilders in Scotland), and different groups of people become more important or less so. In the case of the Travellers, it was because their skills became outdated and the whole social scene altered again and again. One reason I admire the Travellers is that they are so resourceful, turning their hands to anything. As Belle Stewart's eldest son John once said, "A Traveller will make a living out of the dust beneath your feet." The age of materialism arrived, and whatever the Travellers are, they are not materialistic: they retain a sense of the value of non-material things and spirituality. It is not surprising to me that one of Sheila's sons has become a minister.

My view of Scottish Travellers is not based on a garbled view of history but on what I know of the experience of past generations, mostly learnt from Travellers themselves. The conventional perception of Scottish Travellers, i.e. the most customary one held by the majority of people, is that they are a feckless, thieving, drunken lot. I do not hold that view either or anything like it. For one thing, it is invariably held by people who do not know any Travellers. I have had the privilege of learning about the Travellers from Travellers themselves, who have been my friends for many years, and for whom I have nothing but respect, admiration and affection. That does not mean that I have an idealised, romanticised picture of them. They are all human beings and have human strengths and weaknesses like everyone else.

My personal view of Travellers is of people whose ancestry goes back beyond history, but who were undoubtedly here from the earliest times, and who have kept oral culture alive through many centuries. To do so, they have gone through innumerable historical periods of change and have evinced tremendous personal qualities that have enabled them not just to survive but to survive better than many other people. Their values are those of the oldest Celtic society: kinship, hospitality, conviviality, spirituality, love of beauty. In those very far-off times, the ancient inhabitants of these islands, who were called p-Celtic people, encompassed many tribes or clans and formed part of a huge diaspora of Celtic peoples throughout Europe. The p-Celts suffered invasions by Romans, Angles, Saxons, Jutes, Vikings, q-Celts from Ireland and Norsemen from France. I see the Travellers as part of the aboriginal people. But of course, like everyone else, they have mixed and inter-married with others, particularly in recent times. They have been tried and tested to the utmost and have always won through. The social system, based on material wealth and so-called "success", that sees them as "the bottom of the pile" does not exist in my mind. If I have become a folklorist, a term which some people use quite unjustifiably as an insult, then it is because I have learned to research and find out about people and things *before* I draw a conclusion from them.

We often hear references to legislation and punishment designed to eliminate Travellers from society, but it is quite hard to cite the wording of a single law that does so. I do not think that we can jump to the conclusion that every law that was passed against undesirable elements in society was aimed at the travelling smiths, who were valued as news-carriers, storytellers and pipers and craftsmen of considerable skill. I have examined in detail the laws framed over the centuries which mention beggars and **sorners**, vagrants of all kinds and people who stravaig ('wander') about the countryside *without a trade*. I have come to the conclusion that most of them did not apply to what we now call Travellers because *they had a trade –* they were tinsmiths and before that silversmiths. I have read in local histories of places in Perthshire of such metalworkers existing in communities when those laws were in force, and they were not thrown into jail or hanged. In the times of the clans, there were many outlaws, large numbers of whom ended on the gallows, but they were not necessarily tinkers. For example, in the eighteenth century there was a tinsmith in Aberfeldy by the name of John Stewart who was regarded as a member of the community. He was most emphatically not pursued by the law, as he lived to a ripe old age, was married three times and fathered numerous children. Two brothers of the Stewart family, who were definitely forebears of my friends in Blairgowrie, were appointed by the Duke of Atholl to man the ferryboat at Logierait. John Stewart, the grandfather of Sheila, was a champion piper who won medals at the Games. He was also personal piper to Lord Ward of Dudley when he lived in Dunkeld House by grace and favour of the Duke of Atholl and was a piper in the Atholl Highlanders, the Duke of Atholl's private army. In more recent times, I am sure injustices were done to Travellers, by sending their children to industrial schools, but that was not done *only to Travellers*. As for sending boys to the army and girls into service, that was common practice in families all over rural Scotland. The Travellers are doing a good enough job of being assimilated into present-day society by *choosing* to marry non-Travellers, sending their children to school, succumbing to the attractions of the media and pop culture and turning their back on their oral culture. Like everyone else today, Travellers have been influenced by the mass media, but also like everyone else, they have *chosen* to watch television and listen to pop music. It has not been thrust upon them against their will.

Travellers as my Friends

When I claim that Travellers are my friends, I mean just that. They are people with whom I share my life, my leisure and my work. I have frequently been in their houses and trailers, and they have been often in my home: we have shared ceilidhs and birthdays and funerals, as well as ordinary days and nights. We have performed together at festivals and gone out for meals and drinks, or simply shopping. I have travelled for miles with them, and our car has carried them places too. The late Belle and Alec Stewart were close friends, and the family honoured me by asking me to speak a tribute at the graveside at Belle's funeral. She is one of the greatest women I have ever known. Her daughter Sheila and I are the best of friends, and we respect each other. Do not think because she says such flattering things about me in her contribution to this volume that she is in any way subservient to me – on the contrary, she is very much her own person. She is perfectly able to form and express her own opinions. I am also a long-time friend of Stanley Robertson, who has explained and talked about his books with me often. I knew his Aunt Jeannie and his cousin Lizzie, two of our greatest ballad singers, and I have known Stanley and his wife and family for many years. I recently told stories along with Stanley at the Aberdeen Storytelling Festival. I have since received letters from one school whose pupils were at the festival, thanking both Stanley and me for the "wonderful stories and songs". This was a school class with a Traveller boy in it, who was well liked by his class mates, many of whom commented with delight on the fact that the Festival exhibition showed photographs of his family. Some years ago, I helped to arrange an exchange visit between Scotland and Denmark, and Sheila and Stanley were two of the tradition-bearers I took to Denmark. I also know Duncan Williamson (he of the crushing handshake) and knew the late Betsy Whyte, another wise and lovable lady. I have also remained a loyal and affectionate friend of Alec Stewart's cousin, Willie MacPhee, who with his wife, Bella, has stayed on the site at Doubledykes since it was opened. I can not remember how many times I have been there in his trailer, or how many times Willie and Bella have visited my house.

I came as a child of five from Yorkshire (where my mother was born, but grew up in Ayrshire, where my father's family lived) to school in Renfrew and was also teased about my "funny accent" – in fact I was bullied to the point when I *bit* someone in retaliation. I was also picked on because I was "a swot" and "brainy", which still attracts bullying in school. My brains got me a bursary to a fee-paying school, and one lot of people started talking to me, while some others stopped, which opened my eyes at an early age to the silliness of snobbery and inverted snobbery. Travellers do not have a monopoly of being marginalised, ridiculed and bullied. It happens to other people, too.

As an English teacher for 30 years, 18 of them in Perth, I taught many Traveller children. I always kept a keen eye open to see they were not bullied. If they had been, I would have been onto it right away. They have distinctive ways of speaking that I recognise but their classmates did not. They might be aware that someone had an English voice, or even an American one, but the Travellers were never picked on for the way they spoke, which was pretty much like the other local children anyway, although their classmates knew they were Travellers (and did not apparently mind). I remember reading Joan Lingard's novel set in Belfast called *Across the Barricades*, where Sadie, the Protestant girl, says to her Catholic boyfriend, about their difficulties with their families, "I wish we could be Travellers and just go on the road." Two of my pupils felt able to say quite openly "I'm a Traveller", and no one batted an eyelid, because they already knew. They all appreciated that what Sadie desired was the freedom Travellers had to travel. Belle Stewart more than once remarked to me that, with the popularity of caravan holidays, everyone was travelling now and sites were being built everywhere. *The king may come the cadger's road some day* was the proverb she quoted by way of comment.

The Traveller way of life, with its old values and attitudes, its old customs of kinship and hospitality, its respect for traditional wisdom handed down and its spirituality *is* an anachronism in the present day, which is materialistic, money-grabbing and without respect for tradition or age-old things. That is why I admire Traveller life.

Belfast Traveller Michael Mongan

PART 2

TRAVELLERS ON TRAVELLERS' LANGUAGE
TRANSCRIPTS AND RESPONSES

At the Belfast Symposium on 15 August 2000, two Irish Travellers – Ellen McDonagh and Jimmy Power, both Cant-speakers – presented spontaneous responses to the five academic papers by Alice Binchy, Mary Burke, Sheila Douglas, Sinéad ní Shuinéar and Mícheál Ó hAodha presented there. The session was chaired by Fionnuala Carson Williams, to whom the editors are indebted.

Part 2 begins with the edited transcripts of Ellen McDonagh and Jimmy Power's presentations and the subsequent discussions.

The tape-recording of the symposium session was then played to a Gammon-speaking Irish Traveller. The Traveller's transcribed response follows. The Traveller wishes to remain anonymous.

The transcripts of Nell's, Jimmy's and the anonymous Traveller's were then sent to Richard J. Waters, a Cant-speaking Irish-American Traveller resident in New Jersey, who wrote his own response.

Meanwhile, the tape-recording of the symposium and the collected transcripts were played to and read by Sheila Stewart, a Cant-speaking Scottish Traveller, resident in Blairgowrie. The transcript of her response follows.

The set is completed by a presentation by an English Romanes speaking (Romanichal) Traveller, Len Smith, who provided his own written contribution.

The editors believe that the material presented here is unprecedented. No Travellers anywhere have ever spoken so candidly about their own language, what it means to them, when and why they use it, and how they feel about academic and other non-Traveller treatment of it.

The editors also recognise how contentious the publication of Traveller words is felt to be by Travellers. Each Traveller was consulted on the issue, and their wishes were respected. If there is a difference of opinion, that will also explain why some include the original vocabulary while others have [glosses] or Xs. Neither as editors nor as individuals have we any desire to betray their wishes; rather we seek co-operation in order for their language and culture to be better understood. Each Traveller gave the editors signed permission to publish their transcript.

The editors owe the idea for the publication of these contributions from Travellers entirely to Sinéad ní Shuinéar without whose stimulation, enthusiasm and insistence the project might never have materialised. Sinéad undertook much of the necessary work: she transcribed the Symposium tape-recording, interviewed the anonymous Gammon-speaking Traveller and transcribed the tape-recording. She brought Richard J. Waters and Len Smith into the project and provided them with transcripts and tapes. The editors are most indebted to Sinéad ní Shuinéar and to Eliza Schneider for the copies of her tape-recordings, without which material the entire project would not have been possible. We are also greatly indebted to Sheila Douglas for arranging the recording of Sheila Stewart, providing the transcript and contributing her own response ('My Traveller Friends').

Ellen McDonagh

Cant: an Irish Traveller's Perspective

I'd like to say, first of all, that I'm not here today to speak to you as a linguist, or an expert, or a professor, or an anthropologist. However, I am here to speak to you as a Traveller, and I think it's only at forums like this that people can be given an opportunity to either ask questions, or to dispel some of the myths that have been written or said about Travellers and their language.

And also: I know that this section of the conference is entirely about the language of Travellers, but I genuinely believe that all circumstances surrounding Travellers have an effect. For example, I believe that the accommodation we live in has an effect on the way we speak our language. And I'm a firm believer that the accommodation provided, such as group housing schemes or halting sites where Travellers can live within their own family groupings, has been a great advocate of learning the language and an ability to speak the language without feeling ashamed or feeling that you have anything to hide. You can be comfortable in your own environment. So accommodation and social issues that affect all of us in our everyday lives link to one another.

And I also think that today should be a forum where we can ask questions, no matter how embarrassing or difficult they may be to ask. It's only by asking and sharing the information that we can learn.

All the previous speakers were very organised and had lovely presentations. Mine isn't, right? It's Cant. Right?

A number of the previous speakers – and sometimes at forums like this I get quite angry, and quite annoyed, because – I really want to scream, and that's just putting it politely – as to what is being said about Travellers and the myths. For example, Mary was telling us all about the days gone by in literature, back in the early part of the last century, and we were all described as in "the beautiful brown faces of Travelling women". I thought that was gorgeous! But then when they came along and said, "the dark skin" and – what was it? – "uncleanly-looking men" – I thought that was nice, too! It's hard to know where we fit in.

And people have this idea that we're a displaced group of peoples that came from a line of – and I've heard loads of people trying to analyse and describe where we came from, or what part of society, where we came to be known as Travellers who speak Cant and who live in their own ethnic group. And people have described us as from the famine or pre-famine, or whatever. And fair play to people, you know, if they want to.

I don't know where we came from, but I firmly believe that we're way pre-famine, and I do believe that the language is not – definitely not – a mixture of just, *words*, because I have heard entire conversations being conducted by Travellers in Cant. And I know it's not – some people when they say "it's Irish, it's Gaelic, it's words stolen, or taken, from Gaelic". And then they will go ahead and they will describe four or five words, as in *lakeen* from *cailìn*, and X from *fuinneog* in Gaelic, and X and *doras*. And then they stop. They stop after about five words.

It reminds me of once when I was at a debate, and they were talking about Travellers, and one of the people read out the usual four or five words and says we have stolen our language from Gaelic, and then they said, "Well, need I go on?" And I wanted to say, "Well, yes, please do." But I knew that secretly they were shaking because they *couldn't* go on, because it's more than five words. It's definitely more than five words! And I have heard, as I said, entire conversations being conducted in Cant, by both young and old.

So it's not a jargon. I was pleased to hear Alice describing a number of ways our language – our language first of all was described as secret language, and then it was described as a language that was – I don't remember the exact words you used, Alice, but you gave three or four examples. And I think the danger is, that we always go for the one example. That it's a secret language, only spoken in defence, or spoken in the presence of country people when we don't want ye to know what we're saying – yes, that is true, our language, Cant, has been used in that way. But it's not the only one. As I said, I have heard Travellers, and I know that the ability is there, to converse and conduct conversations when we're in an environment when we want to. We don't always want to.

And I think one of my biggest fears is – somebody asked earlier on about a handout, and I agree that probably the only way to learn and preserve our language, is to write it down, but I do think there was a lot of wise thinking in my grannies' and grannies' before them time, of not writing it down. First of all, they probably couldn't write it down, because they didn't have the ability. But I think also that enough has been taken from us, and so much of our language and our culture and our heritage has been taken from us that our language was also – rather than us taking it, people say that we took it from the Gaelic, I think that a lot of the Irish took it from us. Our language was taken from us. I think that there's reasons for Cant not being written down – very genuine reasons.

Somebody also said here today – and I'm not sure who said it – that there was no abstract nouns. Like, it's just words. Again, that is a myth, I know there are words for 'beautiful' and words for 'almighty' and – there's other things. It's not 'just words'. And it's important to be aware that it's not 'just words' – that it's a language. I don't know how many words; I'd love to know who counted 300!

Alice Binchy: Well, I collected 300.

Ellen McDonagh: Okay. I don't know where it came from. And it angers me greatly that people who work with Travellers, or who speak on behalf of Travellers, can give such an inaccurate – and I know that's what people have been told, or what they're picking up themselves, and it's been all done, probably in the majority of cases, with respect towards Travellers – but it's not real. It's not real.

The only way that you will know anything about Cant or where it's come from, or what it is, is from Travellers themselves. And there are enough Travellers out there. I know that we're a very young population – I think 75% of the Traveller population are under the age of 15. However, I know that there are, in every town in this country, a number of Travellers who speak Cant, and who speak Cant very well. So there are enough people out there if we handled it properly, if we encouraged Travellers to do it themselves, and if we provided the support systems for Travellers to be able to learn it to their children in a constructive way – with the resources, the information is out there.

One thing was said by three or four people – it's a new one that I've been hearing now in the last couple of years: the term "settled Travellers". It's a totally contradictory term! There's no such thing as a "settled Traveller"! It's absolutely way off the board. I come from Navan, but there's a term in Meath that people use: "you're horrid nice". You know, you're horrible, but you're nice. It's a real Meath word. I think the term "settled Traveller" is totally contradictory and it's not real. It doesn't apply to any Traveller. A Traveller, whether you live in a house or whatever mode of accommodation you live in, or for however long, you're still a Traveller, and the term "settled Traveller" doesn't apply. Be aware of that – there's no such thing. Travellers will tell you, "I'm living in a house, or I'm settled in a house now, but I'm definitely not a 'settled Traveller'".

Sheila Douglas: I think it's a word used by government officials.

Sinéad ní Shuinéar: Wishful thinking is what it is.

Ellen McDonagh: Government officials have used many words to describe us which I would question. The whole danger of stereotyping people, is, again, something that we have no right to do, because it does untold damage. And that's why we're here today trying to find out where our language has come from, because people stereotyped us, they had an image of us, and they told us we stole the language; they never really took heed of what was being said, and we know ourselves that we have a language that we're very proud of, and that we're unfortunately now having to regain, and find out where it went and learn it because of the negative influence of society.

Discussion of Ellen McDonagh's Presentation

Ross Graham: I'd like to have your reaction – it's a perfectly innocent question – to the term "tinker".

Ellen McDonagh: Well, again, "tinker" was a word that was used -- it would depend on the age group of the person saying it, because my grandfather was a tinker and an excellent tinsmith. But now it's being used out of context in a derogatory way. So it's being used like the word "knacker". Some people came up with the wonderful word, glorified, of calling us "itinerants". "Tinker" is a wonderful trade, but it depends who's using the word.

Ross Graham: It passed into Hiberno-English. My mother used to say to us, when we were misbehaving, "You're a wee tinker."

Sinéad ní Shuinéar: I heard that on *Eastenders*: "Ah, you're a little tinker."

Ellen McDonagh: Well, you see, "tinker" is now used in a negative way, as in, "Ah, you tinker, you're dirty and you're ...". My Grandfather was a tinker, and he was a wonderful tinker.

Manfred Görlach: A more general question comes to mind since, on Saturday, we talked about language rights and so on: is there any provision made in the European Charter for Regional or Minority Languages for Shelta, or Travellers' language?

Alice Binchy: No. I think an attempt was made to register it as one of the lesser-used languages.

Manfred Görlach: There is some provision for continental Roma.

Alice Binchy: Yes. But I think the attempt to have it included was unsuccessful.

Sinéad ní Shuinéar: As far as I know, the premise for the European Bureau for Lesser-Used Languages is that a language must be territorially based. Therefore Yiddish and all the various Jewish languages, Romany, and any languages that have come in, no matter how large the immigrant group, are not recognised, and Traveller language as a non-territorial language is not recognised.

Manfred Görlach: Roma is mentioned somewhere. I forget the context, but it is mentioned.

Fionnuala Williams: It is officially recognised.

John Kirk: The Belfast / Good Friday Agreement talks about the minority languages of ethnic communities. Would you qualify as an ethnic community? And if so, it is covered. I just wonder – Sinéad is raising the question – where do we go now? There's a real tension here. Where we can champion equality under the human rights banner but, at the same time, as Nell was saying, we have given so much away, we're not going to give any more away. Possibly, to help you on the grounds of equality, you need more access or dialogue or information. I'm not sure. Unfortunately we didn't have a speaker from the Travelling community on Saturday,[1] so we didn't address that, but we might be able to pick up these issues when we come to the proceedings. Am I putting my finger on a potential tension here?

Sinéad ní Shuinéar: There's definitely a tension. At the moment I'm doing a doctorate and interviewing people all over the place, sometimes in person, sometimes over the telephone, and I was interviewing a Garda about completely different issues, and at the end of it he said, very conspiratorially, "They have a jargon of their own, you know!" And I said, "Really! Is that a fact?" And he said, "Ah, yes! I hear them talking it in the cells. I'd give anything to know what they're saying." And that reminded me, if I needed reminding, that I will never put one word of this language into print.

Jimmy Power: I was a youth worker for a number of years, and the Guards in Dublin, in particular areas where there's halting sites, like in Ballyfermot and Rathfarnham and Clondalkin and in the inner city, have actually picked up the Cant, so you can't talk now. Travellers who have been arrested can't talk now because the Guards are aware of the situation, and they use it against you. And it's very down-putting because, I mean, they already have the power over a prisoner in the beginning, laughing at the language and stuff like that has a very serious effect on them.

Sinéad ní Shuinéar: I know a girl who's had horrible sexual suggestions made to her by a Garda when she was in prison visiting somebody in her own language as a complete power trip. And it works.

Fionnuala Williams: That's important, and the real progress being made is that Travellers themselves are contributing to the different groups, and your opinions are being sought, and so on, whereas in the past they were not. So it's all a matter of building up trust and matters of confidentiality and so on and ensuring that no breaches are made.

---

[1] Reference to the Symposium on Language, Politics and Ethnolinguistics on Saturday 12 August 2000, the proceedings of which are published as eds. John M. Kirk and Dónall P. Ó Baoill, *Language and Politics: Northern Ireland, the Republic of Ireland, and Scotland* (Belfast: Cló Ollscoil na Banríona, 2000).

Sheila Douglas: I know of a prison officer in Perth Prison who learned Cant, but it was really to be able to comfort any Traveller prisoners.

Sinéad ní Shuinéar: Was it he who told you that? Who told you that?

Sheila Douglas: A friend who was a barman in the prison officers' club commented on what a good prison officer this older man was, and he also learned Gaelic for the same purpose, because he always felt it was more comforting for prisoners to be spoken to in their own language. And he must have got a Traveller to teach him how to do that, you know. It was done, I think, with a very good motive. That may be exceptional. I'm sure it would be. But it was nice to hear of something like that.

Fionnuala Williams: It all boils down to stereotypes again.

Maolcholaim Scott: I'm asking Siobhán about equity legislation. Travellers come under the equality legislation. Can you give a resumé of the situation?

Siobhán Molloy: I wasn't expecting that question, and we didn't put a speaker up earlier because we didn't feel that we had the expertise on the language. Today, now that more people have come and spoken, we obviously have more expertise. On the legal situation of Travellers in Northern Ireland, which is, I think, what you're asking about: under the Race Relations (Northern Ireland) Order of 1997, Travellers are now recognised in Northern Ireland as an ethnic minority – which is a slightly different status to what they have in the South of Ireland. I'm not totally familiar with what it says in the Good Friday Agreement, but I think that there is an intention in it to support the rights of all minorities and cultures, and I think there probably is room within that good intention...

Maolcholaim Scott: So it comes under the Equality Commission?

Siobhán Molloy: Yes, for support to be given. The legal rights of Travellers as an ethnic minority come under the Equality Commission now, which has incorporated the Commission for Racial Equality.

Jimmy Power

Cant: an Irish Traveller's Perspective

You must bear with me, because my education is very bad. I left school at the age of eleven, and I haven't been in a classroom since.

I just want to start off by reinforcing what Nell was saying about our lifestyle and our culture: to understand our language you have to know how we live. It's extended family, uncles, aunts, nieces and nephews living together. All the supports in that are quite important for us.

When we talk about languages, it bothers me a bit listening to people saying that it's made up and non-existent and things like that. For me, I can't understand that. Years ago, Travellers were illiterate. They couldn't read or write, and they didn't go to school. If our language, Cant, came from Irish, how can people learn it if they can't read and write?

I've a very interesting story to tell. I must say, Nell has most of the notes that I had written down between myself and Nell, and Nell has stolen them. She's a typical Traveller, stealing things! In 1995, I got the chance to go to Atlanta Georgia to visit the Irish-American Travellers there. Myself, Michael McDonagh and two other Travellers went to visit them, and there had been no contact for 150 years between Irish Travellers and American Travellers. The American Travellers left Ireland in the 1600s[1] and moved to America.

So in 1995 I got the chance to go and visit them. We went to Murphy Village. We had met the Travellers and were talking to them. We were putting on a workshop on how Irish Travellers live back home to see what we had in common with the American Travellers, with whom there had been no contact for 150 years. When we got there, a television crew had done a documentary on the American Travellers and had perceived them as very negative – as drug dealers and kidnappers and all sorts of horrible things.

We weren't aware of this, but in the camp one day, we were chatting, myself and another Traveller who came over from Ireland and speaking Cant. I was saying – I was annoyed, because the women in the camp had walked by and wouldn't speak to us or look at us. They were unfriendly and rude, and we didn't know the reasons why. I was saying to Bernie, who was the other Traveller, that the women weren't friendly since they weren't talking to us, and every time we tried to approach them to have a conversation, they ran and they wouldn't speak.

---

[1] Editorial note: in view of his other remarks, we wonder whether this was meant to be the 1800s.

Half way through the conversation in Cant, an old American Travelling Man, who was about 65, came over and joined in. I got a bit dumb-shocked. This man, who has never seen me before in his life, who has never met me, knows exactly what I'm talking about?

So it got around, and we were talking away in Cant. In the meantime, a police officer came in. One of the Travellers from Murphy Village owed a parking fine, which was around $500. They started going around collecting money to pay the fine to the police. Instead of English, they were talking Cant. They were going around looking for $5 off one fellow, $10 off another.

My point is that, though there had been no contact for 150 years, I still knew when that man mentioned $5 in Cant. When I was talking about the women and saying that they were unfriendly, he knew what I was talking about and explained to me why people were being nervous.

If it's only a made-up language, and there had been no contact for 150 years between the two groups of people, how did we understand each other?

If Travellers came from the Famine because we had no land and would be the first to move off because we were the poorest, how come there were Travellers in America from the 1600s?[2]

As I say, I'm not well up. I don't have a lot of Cant, but I have enough to have many a conversation, and maybe Nell and I might have a conversation in a while, if she's up to it. It was a brilliant experience for me in America meeting the American Travellers and speaking to them in Cant more than English.

We were coming down yesterday, myself, Sinéad and Nell, speaking about when is Cant used, and why people use it. Just a few days ago, there happened to be a Travellers' wedding, and Nell had to go and pick up her brother. He decided he was going to stay on and get a few more drinks and that someone would pick him up later on. When we got to the hotel to pick him up, there were four or five old Travellers, men in their forties, some in their fifties, and they were actually having a conversation in Cant.

Now, to say that it's only used when settled people are around is probably 40%, or maybe 50%, true. But it's not 100% true, because it is also used with other Travellers themselves. I would use it with my children, in the house if they want something done, I talk to them in Cant.

The language is very important. There had been a while when it slumped, and no one wanted to learn it or use it. But it has been revived now, and I think young people are starting to take it up again.

The introduction of mobile phones – you'll probably find this funny – has greatly improved Travellers' language. I know people will say that mobile phones are bad for you and cause this and that, but for Travellers they have had a positive effect, because

---

[2] See footnote 1.

they have increased the use of Cant. People have these radio scanners that can listen in on the mobile phones. So a lot of Travellers, if they're speaking, will speak in Cant. That has improved the language quite a bit and has given back its focus. Whereas long ago people were saying, "Ah, well, Cant sort of identifies me as a Traveller", now they see a positive side to it, and it's being used very efficiently on mobile phones. When you're having conversations, it is to protect their business. It's not being negative, it is to protect the business of what they're talking about and their privacy.

Discussion of Jimmy Power's Presentation

John Kirk: You've dispelled the myth that Cant is a secret language. Cant is used as a conversational medium between Travellers. But there's conversation and conversation – is this patter or banter? Is this jocular use as a form of verbal entertainment, ephemeral in its nature? Or would you get together to discuss government measures, good or bad, for the Travelling community in order to respond in a constructive way or to implement something rather serious as a policy – how serious can it get?

Ellen McDonagh: John, Cant is in everyday use. For example, there's nothing entertaining fighting about what you get for your dinner – it might for some people! Or giving your children access to school or what you sold in the market or what went on in the markets, and in everyday general conversation, it's used. It's not used just in a situation that's funny or to get one up on somebody. I can tell Jimmy something about you or somebody else in the audience that I find hilarious without you knowing what I'm saying. But it's used in our everyday conversation – it's part of our everyday life.

John Kirk: So, for any possible topic or purpose?

Ellen McDonagh: Yes, that's it.

John Kirk: Squaring that potential with Alice's comment that there's only 300 words puzzles me.

Alice Binchy: All I said was that I personally collected 300 words from the people I have talked to. I didn't say that there weren't more.

Ellen McDonagh: Believe you me, John, I would vow there's more than 300 words in it.

Jimmy Power: In America, the first language that the Travellers speak is Cant. It's not English or American. It is Cant.

Ellen McDonagh: It is Cant.

Jimmy Power: And they do it all the time.

Sinéad ní Shuinéar: Before we go any further I want to add that, from the context of the discussion we had in the car yesterday, the reason why that pub incident was interesting was because there was no one else in the pub except the barman at the time, who was way over from the area where they were drinking in the hotel. They could not have been overheard. And yet they were having a conversation – I don't know what about. They were just talking.

Jimmy Power: Dealing.

Sinéad ní Shuinéar: Oh! You said what they were talking about! They were reminiscing about their childhood.

Jimmy Power: Childhood, yes.

Sinéad ní Shuinéar: There was Traveller-specific experience, but they chose to speak Cant. It was relevant to that.

Terence Odlin: Two questions. One: in what parts of the USA do you find Travellers? The other question: leaving aside cases when you want to use it in a private conversation, are there cases where you use Travellers' language and you feel: "Okay, I could do this without using it, but I really think that it works a lot better in Travellers' language"?

Ellen McDonagh: Yes, and it is also to do with pride. Unfortunately, I don't have a very good grasp of Gaelic, but some of my children have gone to gaelscoils. I say that with deep regret, I would love to. Therefore, when I have an opportunity, I will speak in Cant for nothing other than the sheer pride of being able to speak my own language. That's why I speak it, not to frighten or scare or impress anybody. I'm proud that I can speak another language, and that it's my language.

Terence Odlin: Yes. And saying it in another language just wouldn't be the same.

Ellen McDonagh: No. And to answer your question in relation to the States, it was South Carolina and Georgia – that's where we found the biggest group of Irish Travellers.

Jimmy Power: And there are also some in Texas.

Sinéad ní Shuinéar: And in the northern part of the United States – they are one of the older groups.

Ellen McDonagh: There are 4,000 Irish Travelling families in South Carolina.

Sinéad ní Shuinéar: There are 2,000 individuals in Murphy Village alone.

Ellen McDonagh: Yes.

Sinéad ní Shuinéar: And that's just one community.

Mícheál Ó hAodha: In relation to what you said about the Citizen Traveller – it's about building common ground between groups. I was brought up speaking Irish. Most people agree that some of the Cant or Gammon comes from Irish. I never said all of it does, by any means: I just pointed out a few similarities. And our language is under threat as well where I come from. I think people should kind of get together to support minority languages. I wasn't knocking your language. It's well known that there was a lot of contact between Irish- and Gammon-speakers through trading, etc. That's all I was saying. I was pointing out a few words that were similar or from Irish. I don't know what percentage of Gammon is from non-Irish sources.

Alice Binchy: The number of words that seem to be clearly from Irish is very small, and an awful lot are very hard to analyse.

Sinéad ní Shuinéar: "Docked and disguised".

Jimmy Power: This is not the first time, Mícheál, that we've come to a conference. I've been involved since the age of 15 going to Traveller meetings. It's not you personally, but the words people seem to be citing year in, year out, meeting in, meeting out. ...

Mícheál Ó hAodha: But there's nothing wrong with taking words from Irish, for Irish is a very rich language too.

Jimmy Power: No, for you, it may not seem wrong. There's nothing wrong, but as a Traveller coming and hearing just the same four or five words –

Mícheál Ó hAodha: Fair enough.

Jimmy Power: Not you personally, but people coming to meetings and using the four or five words think they can speak the language, or they think they know it. That's the problem! You know, as Nell has said, they say four or five and then stop. I know Cant. I can say three or four Irish words. Does that mean I can have a conversation in Irish? It's not you personally, but if you'd been going to meetings for as long as we've been going to them, day in, day out, week in, week out, and you heard the same thing over and over again ...

Mícheál Ó hAodha: No, it's just the situation: our situations are quite similar. As I said, Irish is under threat, too.

Fionnuala Williams: I think this discussion could go on for quite a long time. The important thing is that we are having it out in the open, and it's a great landmark. We've gone a long way down the road this morning, and I'd like to congratulate the organisers of the conference for bringing these speakers together, and to thank them all. Before we disperse, Jimmy did offer a conversation with Ellen in Cant: are you still on for that?

Ellen McDonagh: He can have it by himself – he's not having it with me.

John Kirk: Can I follow from this? We put a lot of effort into trying to bring a coherent session together this morning.

Sinéad ní Shuinéar: It worked.

John Kirk: I think it worked, too. Can we take this forward? I know it's been controversial, and I know there have been different views on the same material. But can you advise Dónall and I, as potential editors of proceedings: is there a case for including these papers in the general conference volume, or should there be a separate, smaller volume with the present contributions, possibly with one or two other contributions, on the theme – a much more tightly focused volume? Or would your view be "Forget it, and don't publish these papers for heaven's sake!" Dónall and I need advice.

Ellen McDonagh: My opinion on that, John, would be that the idea of getting together with the relevant people and discussing it, and sharing, is very important, and I say that with genuine interest. For example, the wealth of information about our language in America now is unbelievable. I want to know how the Americans have preserved it, and why they've done it, and how they've done it; the same with the Scottish Travellers, and the Travellers in England. I think it's very important for the relevant people to get together and do what has to be done to preserve it and gain the respect it's entitled to.

John Kirk: I think we're getting the respect, partly through legislation. We can certainly consider organising further focused symposia for bringing people together for this type of exchange, as you suggest. But I am concerned that I do the right thing in the proceedings.

Jimmy Power: Can I add to Nell's comment that Cant should not fall into the wrong hands? I'm talking particularly of where Travellers have dealings with the law and so on. As you heard, two examples were given where it was used against the Travellers. One woman was asked for sexual favours by a Guard – trying to prove that he made sexual remarks towards her would be very difficult.

Sinéad ní Shuinéar: In a prison of all places – it's a total power trip.

Jimmy Power: Travellers are very wary of the Guards and the law – and so would I, to be honest – getting hold of Cant. And other statutory bodies and agencies use it against you. If it is being collected and preserved, that's good, but be careful. To gain people's trust, you have to be careful; they'll be asking, who's going to get it? What are you going to be doing with it? You have to be able to answer those questions for people. If you have the answers, it will work, but if you're not sure, people will be suspicious, and won't really work with you.

Sinéad ní Shuinéar: Personally, I would never write one word of it, and I'll give you an example. Alice, your work hasn't been published and is very hard to get hold of. I know, because I struggled, and only managed with the help of Aileen l'Amie. Alice's work actually has the words written down. She made a point of not making a vocabulary list, but they are scattered throughout the text. She's made it quite difficult to get them. But some bright spark in the United States, an undergraduate in, I think, Philadelphia, went to the trouble – I don't know if you're aware of this, Alice.

Alice Binchy: No!

Sinéad ní Shuinéar: – of going through it, picking out all the words and giving the English translations, and now they're all on the Internet and anybody can get them. So, in this day and age, nothing is safe, and I would not write anything myself. That's my personal point of view. I just wouldn't do it. It's not mine to do.

Mary Burke: There's a lot of Cant on the Internet.

Sinéad ní Shuinéar: Yes. There's a lot of Cant.

Mícheál Ó hAodha: Some of those would be put up by Travellers, as well.

Sinéad ní Shuinéar: Yes! But it's theirs! They can do what they want with it. But I wouldn't.

Mícheál Ó hAodha: There must be different opinions amongst the Travelling people.

Sinéad ní Shuinéar: Yes. But it's an *internal* debate. It has nothing to do with me.

Sheila Douglas: Well, I wouldn't bring anything into the public sphere without the permission of the friends who gave it to me. They really looked on me as speaking for them, and that's what I've been trying to do.

Jimmy Power: Well, I think it's different for you, Sheila, because you're coming into a country where the language won't be used again. I mean, if any of us leave here, we won't be using Scottish Cant. But if it's on your home territory.

Sheila Douglas: Perhaps you could invite Sheila Stewart to come.

John Kirk: I'd be very happy to.

Sheila Douglas: She would love to be contacted, and she does go and talk about Traveller life and things to do with culture. She's done it all over the world, and so she would be very happy to come and be involved if you wanted that. What I've said is at second hand, really.

An Anonymous Traveller[1]

Who We Really Are: Language and Identity

I do not intend to apologise to settled people for what I am. I would never, as my mother says, stoop so low to pick up so little! I will not apologise for my education being very bad, because if I do, I feel I'm being confirmed into their world automatically – also into their language. The day I start apologising for my education, I think I'm letting my parents down, and particularly I think I'm letting my mother down. The reason why is that she is totally illiterate, and she's the breadwinner of the family. A lot of my brothers can't read or write or can barely spell their own name. My own husband doesn't even know what month it is or even his own date of birth. So that would be apologising for something that I am. Any time I'm talking to country people, whether at a conference or seminar or just out in a shop, I am not prepared to apologise for who I am. If my education is a bit down, it's a bit down, and if it's up, it's up. But it's up to me to get it, and it's up to me to get on with my life. So I'm not prepared to apologise. That's a thing I have to make very clear. I am who I am. When you're saying, "Excuse me for my education," you're saying, "Excuse me for being a Traveller."

I am very proud to be a Traveller. At times, I am very much ashamed to be Irish – not all the time, but there's times I feel that, when I'm badly hurt or discriminated against. It's strange that, when I go to any part of Europe, I'm treated like the Queen Mother! It's just that – it's your own country, I suppose.

I can't – I won't – speak on behalf of all Travelling People. I also can't and won't speak giving a big sob story and saying they're all perfect saints. They're not! Travellers are as much into crime, rape and robbery as settled people. But Mountjoy[2] is not full of Travellers – I'll put it that way.

But if you look at the case of *Glenroe*,[3] do you remember the time where they used to keep calling us "knackers"?[4] I remember ringing up one time and giving them

---

[1] This contributor agreed to the taping, transcription and inclusion of her responses to what Ellen McDonagh and Jimmy Powers said at the symposium on condition that identifying details were modified to preserve her anonymity. It was recorded and transcribed by Sinéad ní Shuinéar, who also supplied the notes.

[2] Dublin's main prison.

[3] Popular Irish soap opera.

[4] Derogatory term for 'Traveller'. A website of current Hiberno-English gives *scumbag* and *undesirable* among its synonyms; cf. www.local.ie/content/41127.shtml/about_ireland/society/language

all sorts over it. And one man came on from RTÉ[5] and said, "Well, we're educating the people out there, not about knackers," he said, "but about how bad the word is." I said, "Well, what if young people are watching this? A lot of young people follow TV. What if the young people watch it and then go out and say, "Oh, Mam, look, there's knackers"? Again, they've been influenced. So when RTÉ started that I eventually put a stop to it, and they started calling them "Travellers". Now at least the settled or country child can say, "Mam, look, there's Travellers pulling in on the side of the road," instead of, "There's knackers on the side of the road." I feel that things like that should be corrected.

Now, the word "itinerant" – I'd drink my blood before I'd answer to the word, "itinerant". I was on a committee and often heard members of the government using it: "the itinerant population", for instance.

Another word I've thought about a lot to myself is "Travellers". It's like "settled people" – I'd like to get on to them and ask, if they're settled *people*, and we're *Travellers*, are we also *people*? We're Travelling *people*. I'm a Travelling *person*. They're country *people*, or settled *people*. I never say "settled" or "country". I always say "settled people" or "country people". That's another thing that I'd like to throw back. If they're "settled people" and we're just "Travellers", what's our second word?

And "*my* Travellers"! – never "my Travelling people": we're not a *people*. As far as I'm concerned, I'm belonging to no one out there! My daughter is belonging to me because I had my daughter. I am belonging to my parents, and I'm also belonging to my family and to my community. But I do not belong to a settled community! I wasn't adopted. And if I was adopted at birth, I'd still be "a tinker" or a "Travelling person". I would not be a "settled or country person".

I'm a very private person in my own way, from a very private group of people. I'm going to use the word "people" a lot, because I am a person just as much as the settled community.

I heard Nell talking about some Cant words. They're the very same words as we would use. Only some of the words are different. Maybe it's the south of Ireland, or the west – or even the north of Ireland – maybe it's just different pronunciations. Some words would be different, but it's more the way they're pronounced. But whether it's called "Cant" or "Gammon" – one group says it's called "Gammon", the other group says "Cant" – is neither here nor there when all the words are the same.

I spoke before about privacy, about the language and about giving away your language and a lot of your lifestyle, whatever that may be. Who gave away that language? It wasn't settled or country people who got that language – not without the Travelling person. One thing about the Gammon group is that they're very private.

On the language, we'll say, the word *spaghetti*. The way I say it is not the same as the Italians, and in London they leave out the *t* sound altogether. There's three

---

[5] The Irish state broadcaster.

different versions. If you look at the language of the Gammon group and the Cant group, in one sense it's just the pronunciation that's different.

Some words could be different for recognising different groups. We say, *feen*. They say *sham*. We wouldn't use the word *sham* at all. *Sham* is, we'll say, a Cant group word, where *feen* is more a Gammon group word. If I was going along to a fair and heard people saying *"Ogle sham! Ogle sham!"* they're not a Gammon group – they're a Cant group. The word distinguishes in that sense.

Some of our words, they might say, are slang words, or we might say that their words are slang words. To me, *sham* is a slang word, to be honest with you. But I won't take that away from people – I give people respect if they use that, because if that's their vocabulary, that's their business. If I see *feen* in front of me, it's a [x]. If they see something else, I'm not taking it away from them.

The Cant group and the Gammon group come from different parts of Ireland, but there's also a majority within the minority, in one sense. There's different names completely. There's also different features. Completely different features! If you look at the Cant group, they're darker, whereas the Gammon group is paler, with freckles, not really dark black hair, and not really dark skin – there's very much a difference there, as well.

Some people tell me, "You don't look like a Traveller", which is good in one sense because it proves not all Travellers are the same.

There are two different groupings, and the reason why, if you go down the tales of years and years ago, is that, when one group would move in, the other group would move out of a certain area, a camp, or whatever they'd be staying in – maybe because you'd fall in love with Tommy, and Tommy would fall in love with Betty. They wanted to keep themselves apart. But it was more the Gammon group which wanted to keep apart rather than the Cant group. I have to state that as well – I've always stated that very clearly.

I've worked with both groups, and whether you're Cant or Gammon, if you try to get into a pub or disco, the two groups become the same. And whether I'm Cant or Gammon, at the end of the day, I'm a Traveller, and that's going on any record or book. Whether it's Cant or Gammon, the two of us are going to get one refusal. I'm a Traveller, and that's my full statement. If Nell is a Traveller, so am I.

If you read the books on Travelling People, it's obvious they were written by settled people – but if you read the books, there's a lot of work done on the Cant group. There's very little done on Gammon, but I also feel that the Gammon group's very private. I suppose it means getting on with your life and trying to keep your culture and language to yourself.

For many years, people kept themselves private, a very close-knit community. I feel the Cant group has opened out much more than the Gammon group. In the magazines, such as the little FÁS magazine,[6] someone might be telling a story, relating, "My name is Betty, and I'm getting married to Tommy." When it comes to real biographies, books are all on the Cant group – there's not one book that I can find or come across on the Gammon group.

Now some people say, oh yeah, because they don't know who they are, or what group they are. We do know who we are! I can identify myself as a Traveller the same as any other group can identify themself. Or a tinker. I can identify myself as both of them. And I can very proudly identify myself as well.

But again, I will not go – and cannot go – to a shop and pick out a book on the Gammon group. As I say, I can get a FÁS magazine all right, but when it comes to books you may forget about it. Or if you find a book, you might get one story, something about years ago, but that's it.

Listening to Nell, and people going on about the "settled Traveller": it's what you're born into. It's got nothing to do with the water or the toilet or the electricity. I mean, you can have that out on the side of the road as well, at times. A good old generator there, you wouldn't be long getting a shot of electricity, a sup of water and whatever. It's not got to do with what your body goes into – a house – what people call it, "a settled Traveller". Because, again, I always disagree with that.

But it's the way the family runs within the home. It's what they're taught within that home. I could go into a big, royal mansion and be months living there, two or three years living there. And I still could come out and put up on the road and back into – I suppose different kinds of conditions all right – but at the end of the day, I'm still myself. I'm still Helen. And it's what I'm going into. It's not the house, the home, the caravan. It's what I've been taught. What I've been reared up into. That kind of thing.

It's great work for them to call people "settled Travellers", because one thing about Travellers, they can never sit down! They can never settle! Whether they're in a house – they can never settle in a house! I tell you, their nerves are more at them half the time in a house than they are out of a house. Because I often heard a Travelling man saying, "The minute I come into a house, I've four or five doors to open to get the one bit of fresh air," or something like that. "But, if I'm in a caravan, I can just open the door and away I go – if you're frustrated, like." Take the example of a football in a house. Talk about settled Travellers! You can get a ball, and you can slap it against that wall, and as soon as it hits that wall, it hits you back in the face, doesn't it? If you open one door in a house and you throw a ball, it's going to hit you back in the face. If you open one door in a caravan and throw a ball, it's gone way out. I

---

[6] Foras Áireanna Saothair (FÁS): government training for employment body which runs, inter alia, Traveller-only centres, linked by the quarterly magazine referred to here, *Voice of the Traveller*, combining news, interviews and trainees' own contributions.

suppose, your bad feelings, and your depression – I'm not saying that it's a good cure, or that it'll cure you – but it might get some of it off your mind.

Whatever about the women, they might be able to manage some way along the line, but I don't think there's any such thing as a settled Travelling man, because again, there's no man will sit down. The only thing I can see them sitting down for is coming in and having something quick to eat. He's away from the table then. Either he's out the back garden smoking with the other men, chatting, or he goes up the stairs, there's some fight on, Francis Barrett is on the telly, or – you know, they're always on the move. They'll go in and watch that, and then they're out the front door. Then someone wants to go somewhere, down to collect something, whether it's milk, or – "I'll go down!" It's always the man that's usually on it. The women as well, but particularly the men. When a countryman comes home and takes off his shoes in the evening, when he takes off his shoes he's there for the evening, he's watching his TV and he's sitting around among the kids and different things. I'm not saying that Travellers aren't sitting among their kids either! They are. But what I'm saying is, in that space of time, he could be in for the night. Where you look at the Travelling man, he's out ten times in that space of time in the one evening! He's up to his son's, he's up to such a one's place, be sitting there – do you know? He's always on the move, the whole time. Look at my own family, for instance, my brothers and my father. They can't sit down for a minute. They'll get 20 minutes at the table and after that, bye-bye, good luck. Again, as I said, they're all over the place. You know, one minute you say, "Where's your father?" "He's in the sitting room." You go into the sitting room, he's not in the sitting room, he's upstairs, if you have an upstairs house. Or if you go upstairs, "Yeah, he was here two minutes ago, he's out the back." Then he's out the back of the house. So you have a chat to him for a minute, you go back in, "Oh, yeah, he told me to go in and get a cigarette or something for him." Go back to the back of the house. He's not in the back of the house! Where is he? He's out the front of the house! You know? So there's no – I don't think there's such a thing as a "settled" Traveller.

Now, in the summer, for instance, in my house, my mother – of the women's example. "Where's Mammy?" "She's in the kitchen." "No, she's not, she's out the back washing pots." You know, she'll go out the back of the house washing pots. She won't wash the pots inside in the kitchen. "Where's Mammy now?" "She's outside having her dinner." You know, she brings the table outside. My mother, in the summer, she's outside and she's having something to eat outside in the back of the house. In the summer in particular, if there's nice days like that, they're always on the move.

My parents were out travelling on the road for many years. They were on a halting site for a long time then. I suppose they're 20-something years in the house now, at this stage. So any country person would say that they were settled Travellers, but I feel we're more Travellers than the Travellers that have been out on the side of the road for all their life. Because there's no change in us! There's no difference. Again, we're the same language, the same way of going. It's nothing got to do with the house, the four walls. It's got to do with your teaching, your parental guidance, your family, your language, your culture, everything like that. Because the woman next door to my mother is a countrywoman, for instance. And she's not speaking her language. She's not doing her culture, and what to keep away from and what to do and what not to do – we're doing it! They know, we're Travellers, and that's it!

And! No matter if you're 50 years in a house! When you come along to some pubs and discos, you're still treated the same. So what's the difference then, between a "settled" Traveller and a nomadic Traveller when the two of us walk in together?

The first, the most important thing in Gammon or Cant – let me call it Traveller language – was the food department. Because sometimes – say there were two houses, and they were begging, years ago – surviving is what I would call it, years ago. Today I'd call it begging, in the year 2000, but years ago it was surviving, feeding your family. We'll say one woman got a whole lot of [eggs] and another woman got a whole lot of [meat]. The two of them would be coming to a door, they'd be talking. They'd say, "Is the [woman] [gone] in the [house] [now]?" "She's [gone] in, yeah. Well, this [woman] I'm with is after giving me an awful lot of [meat], so [ask] her for a couple of [eggs], and when you're finished with the [eggs], I'll [give] you a lump of [meat]." So when the woman come out, "Have you any eggs, love?" You know? "Ah, [get] the [eggs] now. [Milk]. [Ask] her for a sup of [milk]! I'm after [asking for] the [quantity] of [meat], and I'm after [getting] the [eggs], and no [milk], nothing to [drink] with it, no [milk]." You've all food to eat. You've nothing to drink.

Which was good, again. Maybe if the countrywoman heard you, "Ask her for a sup of milk", she might think, "She's just being selfish now." Because – you know, it was a private thing again. If the woman maybe didn't know what you were talking about, it could be different. It was just – years ago, foodwise it was very important to speak privately.

If I was to say, "You [look] [good]", it means you look good. Or if I just say [good], it means good. Say if I sent you for something, and you got it for me, '[Good]!' That means Good! That's good! But if Sinéad looked at me and said, "Look, Helen, I bought a new dress, what do you think?" "You look [good]." It means you look well, you look beautiful. It depends on what way you use it. That's the way it works. That's the way my "beautiful" would come in.

But I'd say they were practically talking everything a lot of years ago. I'd love to see it fluently spoken. The country people, in my view, will only pick up four or five words. Because also, the Travellers talk it so fast, up or down. Country people wouldn't know if you're a Traveller or a country person if you were in a chipper, for instance. They'll say, "Is that German? Is that French? Or what kind of language is it?"

But the only problem was, a lot of the time, when you spoke, "Ah! They knows what you're [saying]! They knows what [you] is [saying] now!" It was like an identity again if you tried to keep it more private.

When it comes to safety, you couldn't talk a lot. "[Stop] your [talking]: [people are] listening [now]." Means if you were having a conversation about something, or maybe Guards came up, or the woman next door, maybe in a supermarket! God knows where it is – and you were having a conversation, and all of a sudden you hear people listening and you say, "[Stop] your [talking], [people are] listening [now]." You don't talk. You just die.

The other day I was in the supermarket, and I heard a Travelling girl talking Gammon, and her mother said, "[Stop!]! You're going to let the [people] know who you are!" Because you were identifying yourself, and we were going to be put out of this place. Speaking Traveller language identifies you as a Traveller. And I think that a lot of them would be very, very well spoken, you could get into a conversation with it, particularly with the older people. The younger generation, I don't know, because there's a fear there, as well. And the fear again is: going into a pub and speaking it, and then "Well, what language are they speaking? It's not the Irish! Oh, I heard that "sham" before, I heard that "feen" word before, they're Travellers!" So, do you understand me? You're sort of caught.

My daughter is four now and I would say to her, instead of "Shut the door, Brigid" I'd say, "[Shut] the [door]! [Shut]the [door]!" You know, things like that. "[Look at] the [dog], out through the [window]! "[Look at] the [dog] Brigid!" Those kind of things I can give her, like, "[look]" – look. If I want something done, I talk to her in Gammon. I tell her to [shut] the [door], or "[look] out the [window], [dog] outside" – things like that. I try to give her as much as I can.

And even my sister Nan, now, her children. Elizabeth is two and a half, Martin is eight and William is just four. The other day Martin was in the shop and he opened up an icepop, and he said, "I'm going to eat all this now!" he said, "Before we go up to pay for it!" And Nan was just going to give out to him and William let out with "Mammy, [God!] [God!]! We're going to be [noticed] [by] the [people]! We're going to be [noticed]. He's going to get us [arrested]." You know, things like that. And all of a sudden Nan just started laughing. That child is almost four.

But the child of two and a half will say, "[Stop], William! [Look at] the [people] [looking at] [you]! We're going to be [noticed], William, [stop]! [Stop] [now], don't [talk]!!" Even at two and a half, she's at that. But she's a real clever little girl. I think the more you talk to children in English, well, fine, the more you talk to them in your own language, as well, so eventually they'll know the phrases then, and they'll know when to talk, as well – you know what I'm saying to you? And when not to talk.

The way I look at it, it is used around country people all right, for protection, but in the family it's not only the child learning how to speak, it's the child learning *who you really are*. You know, going back again to the country people calling the Travellers "settled": being in a house, again, teaching the child "[Shut] the [door]", "Get your [shoes]" and different things like that is not only teaching the child the bit of Traveller language that you have, but it's identifying the child for who the child is. Because the child is different when the child goes out into the other community. So you're starting early. To answer, "What's this language?" or "What is this?", it's who you are.

Sometimes the little girl belonging to my sister Nan, she's two and a half years of age, and Nan says, "Elizabeth, you're acting like a country person, or a settled person!" "No, no no, no. I'm a Traveller, that's it! We're chavvelling [people], Mammy. We're chavvellin [people]" – that's the way she says it – chavvellin. Means Travelling people. [People] means people. So we're Travelling People. Or Martin, he's eight, "Martin, you're acting like a country person, what's up with you?" "I'm not no country person! I'm a Traveller!" So, coming up at that young age, not only learning to [shut] the [door] and saying the few little bits and pieces there. So all of that is... the language with the child, teaching the child young, is also identifying who they really are.

It's not just language! Language is a community, language is a person, language is people, language is a group. You know, it's like the French. If four or five French people are talking in a shop, for instance, or wherever they're talking, they're not just speaking, they're not just talking, they're automatically, "Ah! They're French!" "Bonjour." "They're French!" and we can say, "They're a different group. They're French." Well my daughter, hopefully, can say, "Well, I'm different, I'm a Traveller," you know? Or "I'm a tinker." So it identifies who you are. And particularly with a young child. So I don't know where they come in with the word "settled Traveller" when you're actually acting out a Travelling family within the four walls.

It's not only the pride of speaking your own language. Again, it's going back to identifying – not identifying to the settled people out there, it's identifying to yourself, within oneself, of who *you* are. Of who you are yourself. The pride of speaking the language is – again, it's not the language, because you were born before the language – you were born first, and then you were given the language – so when you were given the language, you had a new identity of who you really were, and who you really are, and what you really stand for.

Even if a country person can speak the four or five words or speak the language, they still can't go to the example of *who we are*. Even if they speak my language, they can't identify themselves as a Travelling person. And they can't get that feeling I have; they can't get the sense of freedom. There's so many things that they can't get! They can speak the language, but big swingin Harry, they can't speak me!

I remember going in to visit a family member one time at Mountjoy, and the warden had spoken to me in very vulgar, sexual language – that he really didn't know anything about. He just knew the two or three words and they were the very bad, dirty words that he chose. It not only embarrassed me, but it angered my brother, because I was his sister, and this man had made a very sexual remark about me; it wasn't nice. Wherever he got those words from – presumably he didn't get them from a book – it was Traveller words, so it was only obvious he had to get them from Travelling people. And it was very vulgar, and it was also used in the wrong context. And educationally I thought that was bad. The way I look at that is: if that warden had been educated differently, he wouldn't have even maybe used those words. He would have used different words.

Who took the language? The question is, who got the language? And who gave the language, in the first place?

All this, saying the language is just mixed-up Irish: I'd agree with Nell on that, because in the one sense, it's the same as asking the question, "Do you think you came around the famine time?" I think we came way, way, way before it. If you look at the research that was done with the Gypsies, when they were spreading around Europe, and they came to London, and they decided to come to Ireland[7]. And when they came to Ireland there were already people doing fortune-telling and tinsmithing and begging and whatever[8] they were doing.

Going back to the question of the language: if it is back words, can we have twenty of them? Can we have 50 of them, please? And there's not. You'll only hear those four to six words. You will not hear anything else. *Laicín*, or the *fuinneog*-thing[7] – but even if you look at it: we say *com-ra*. The Irish is *mad-ra*. You know, it's – again, it's more like a pronunciation thing than anything else. Okay – if the Irish language can come to me with 30, even 20, words similar to our language, the Travelling People's language – I'm not going to go into a feud with Gammon or Cant, I will say Traveller language – and they were the same way but different, like *madra/comra* – well then, we could be talking. But until that comes, I'd agree with Nell.

It's not Irish language. To me, whether it's Gammon or Cant, it's just Traveller language and their own language. And again, if the Traveller had made up the language in putting the Irish words differently, why didn't they make up any more

---

[7] The earliest documented evidence of Romanies in Ireland dates from 1541 and is to be found in *The Irish Fiants of the Tudor Sovereigns*, vol 1, 258 (12) "Safe conduct, for 40 days, for John Naune and his company, Egyptians, driven from Scotland by stress of weather. 20 October, xxxiii." (Torn.) (Cal. P.R., p 82, art. 3) and 264 (English) "Order of the Lord Chancellor and council (on reference from the Lord Deputy upon a petition to Parliament by Powyll Fayoff, of Lytle Egypt, his captain and company, Egyptians sojourning in Dublin) discharging the said Powyll from an indictment in the King's Bench, alleging that he had stolen newe colour sarsnet, blacke satten, and blacke damaske, at Swerds, the goods of Richard Russell, of Drogheda, merchant. 11 November, xxxiii." The earliest references for Scotland, England and Wales are, respectively, 1505, 1515, and 1579.

[8] The speaker didn't remember *fuinneog* because the Gammon word for 'window', which was used as an example, is completely different from the Cant word, which is quite similar to the Irish.

than four? Settled people are saying that we stole the language. Well, what? We stole four words?!

It's nice talking about your lifestyle, and talking about your culture and talking about your language, but people interpret it wrong. Now, fine if you were doing a book on schools, to education, and put it in the right vocabulary, it's a different kettle of fish. I mean children in school wouldn't have a clue – country children – they wouldn't have a clue. When I was going to school I learned more about the North of Ireland than I did about my own people. There was nothing in the schools.

And if Appleby is announced in the class you could say, "Well, the majority of people going to Appleby is Travelling People. They park their caravans, the kids go up the corner and mind the horses and the adults come up or down. They have food there, they do this..." You know, it's part of – the fair is part of a cultural kind of thing as well, and it's also an education kind of thing as well. So I never mind them kind of books in school. School books are school books, full stop.

It's like the Glenroe thing again, you know? It's the children growing up, "Well, why can't I call them "knackers" – on TV, they call them "knackers"." When they stop calling knackers on TV, and call them "Travellers", then I can call them "Travellers". Things like that. So I don't mind books on history or geography.

Some of the stuff in books is good and other stuff is bad, and the reason why it's bad is because it's interpreted wrong. I think some country person just went on and interviewed one or two Travelling People and took it to their own interpretation then. I'd like to see the likes of Nell McDonagh and a couple of real Travelling women getting out there and doing a joint account book as well. Not just one group but the two groups, Cant and Gammon, Travellers! And getting out there and sitting down and really doing a book – not giving away your lifestyle and everything, but just – for instance, "knackers". You could put in your book, well, that's a hurtful thing, same as calling a black man or a coloured man "nigger". Talk about the unofficial sites and things like that. People say it's a romantic life. Well, a lot of the unofficial sites out there for instance – Travellers don't want them. They don't need it. Without proper facilities, it's more hospitalisation for children – rat bites, infections, pneumonia. We all know that! Little things like that. And then go on in your book about people objecting, when they do a petition, well, put in your book, if you're refusing Travelling people, this is what you cause. Put the fall back on them: you cause chest infections and all this. Travellers, if they want that lifestyle, fine – and I like that lifestyle, I love it, particularly in summer, I move around to different places. The Travellers want the lifestyle, but they don't need the conditions that's surrounding it. Can you understand me?

So books should be done a lot, not just that you have to go three fields to the toilet, and maybe you're pregant and it's raining and it's snowing – not all that! It's just a life story, kind of, on how all hardship ways is, and maybe how you got up on your feet, and maybe the reason of how sometimes your father and mother want to go into a house, because they found it so hard on the side of the road, and maybe they want to give you a chance. But a lot of my family's on the side of the road still, after being in a house, and more of them are in a house.

I really feel Travelling women should go on it. When the book is done and written out, bring it down and say, "Look I want this book done the way we've done it, put it word for word." Do you understand that kind of feeling? I'd like to see that done. Not just "Oh, isn't it great, we've a book done about Travellers" – no, that's not done about Travellers! That's doing a version and ideas of a settled person, because a settled person will take away – take out words from it or not listen to the words, just take out what they want and put it into a book. And that's no good to Travelling People. It's no good to the settled people as well.

So this is looking at you from the outside looking in, and the inside looking out, because, as a Traveller, I can have life both ways.

Richard J. Waters[1]

The Trivialization of the Cant

I would tend to agree with Nell, Jimmy and the anonymous Traveller about the generally negative effects that many academic studies of Shelta have had on Irish Travellers. I am an Irish Traveller living in America and, like them, not a linguist or any type of scholar really. Neither am I any sort of spokesman for my extended family – nor even representative of their thinking in this regard and many others. Still, I have read much of the pertinent literature about the Cant out of an almost morbid fascination with what appears to be our dying tongue, and you may well be interested in what I have to say.

I was born in 1937 of an Irish Traveller mother and a Country father who was a great friend to Travellers – a policeman in fact. Thus my brother and I grew up with a foot in both camps, though settled, with an elementary understanding of the Cant. Sorry to disappoint: it was definitely not my first language; nor do I believe it to be so for most Irish-American Travellers; it is really learned simultaneously with English. The Cant assumed less and less importance throughout adult life until I encountered a period of prolonged personal tragedy and afterward responded almost instinctively by "hitting the road" for the better parts of seven years. With the help of close cousins I refreshed my acquaintance with the Cant, motivated by emotion more than intellect. We never thought of the language very much as anything more than an Irish pig Latin, a social marker, as it were, and useful for making comments about fellow diners in a restaurant, but certainly nothing to concern ourselves with except to take it for granted.

Then, in 1994, a friend who knew a little of my background called me with some questions about an article in the *New York Times* (International Edition) about Ellen Mongan, a Traveller and accredited Montessori teacher in Ireland, who had been elected to the Tuam, Co. Galway, town commission. Some Irish Cant was quoted there along with a translation and, much to my surprise, this American Country Person was talking to me in almost perfect Cant, the same language my family still used after being in the USA for at least 125 years. It was a bit of an epiphany for me. My preconceptions were smashed, and any notion I had that the Cant was only some bit of nonsense we had all made up in the not too distant past went with them. I determined to learn more and of course inevitably came across Macalister's *The Secret Languages of Ireland* (1937).

---

[1] This contribution was written in response to the recordings of Ellen McDonagh, Jimmy Power, and the anonymous Traveller.

While I value Macalister's compilation of the available lexicons, I am loath to accept on faith his contention that a prehistoric origin for Shelta is "incredible", even after he states that the pronunciation (of certain of its sounds) apparently "is far older than the oldest manuscript in which it is indicated" (ibid.: 166).

His "simpler" explanation: "the inventors of the language worked it out from written forms of Irish". Macalister offers no support for this preposterous "blue-sky" contention. It just "is" because he says it "is". Of course, this statement is required to justify the etymological convolutions that Sampson and Meyer used to "prove" that Shelta or "Sheldrū" (as Macalister determined how Shelta "must" have been pronounced) was an encrypted construct ultimately derived from Irish. Unlike Meyer, Macalister insists that, despite appearances, it was derived from relatively modern Irish.

One might reasonably ask of me: Who are you to dispute the work of scholars in this field? A fair question. I have no expertise in linguistics or Irish history, no advanced academic degrees; I don't read or speak Irish, and I have never set foot in Ireland. That's the point, really. If such a one as myself can spot a few obvious, egregious blunders (which, however, apparently went unquestioned by "informed experts"), it should justifiably cast doubt on all the work done in the field so far, at least enough doubt to prompt a thorough re-evaluation of the utter lack of respect that has historically underlain the academic study of Irish Travellers.

Let us consider a few of the blunders Macalister accepted without question. He stated:

> ... the language is usually called 'Shelta' [by scholars]. This, however, is not quite accurate. The right name is 'Sheldrū' ... 'Shelta' being a corruption due to imperfect speech [of Tinker informants] or hearing [of collectors]. (ibid.: 137, parenthetic insertions are mine)

Shelta has never been known by that name, or any variant, to Travellers. It seems to me to come from an obvious reference to "the walking people" in Irish.[1] A bit of an aside here: I recall some amusement at reading that Shelta (that name surfaced in the 1870s) derived from the English phrase *shelter tent* around the same time "experts" were declaring that Irish Travellers hadn't used tents at all until that identical decade. Quick work, I would say. Does the maxim, "Absence of evidence is not evidence of absence", ring any bells?

Gladar[2] is obviously not derived from the Irish for 'leather' to use the English translation of 'skin' which is an English homonym of a slang synonym for *swindle*, as

---

[1] Sinéad ní Shuinéar has also reached the same conclusion independently. Editorial note: see ní Shuinéar's explication on p. 21.

[2] A *gladar box* is a trick device for apparently producing gold coins from base metal.

Macalister claims (ibid.: 183). A far more logical and less tortured derivation would be from the Middle English word *glaed* 'shiny'.

Macalister (ibid.: 139) gives a line-by-line rendition of Sampson's "collection" of the Lord's Prayer in Shelta and English. I don't know who actually composed it (perhaps Sampson himself) but it was no Irish Traveller; it's based on the Protestant version of the prayer. That version contains the extra clause that starts with "... for Thine is the Kingdom, and the Power, and the Glory ..." It was never found in the Roman Catholic liturgy, and virtually all Irish Travellers are Roman Catholic. Why has no one questioned this in the intervening 100 years or so?

Perhaps I might make a few additional comments on Macalister. Considering the fact that the component word lists which comprise his lexicon were, for the most part, hurriedly collected (by men who, using today's standards, would be called "bigots") from chance or unlikely encounters with mere handfuls of Irish Travellers, I find it surprisingly useful. Of the 900 or so Shelta words listed, I judge that about 100 are direct ancestors of Cant words still used today in the USA. By my count, there are, at least, 300 words in more or less general use among American Irish Travellers. In that Cant group, I am also including something less than a dozen words that originate in Gaelic and are essentially undisguised loanwords. There seem to be very few neologisms. There are also several ultimately borrowed from the Romany, via Scottish and Romanichal Cant loanwords. My knowledge of the Cant is hardly encyclopaedic, and it would not surprise me if a thorough survey of all Irish Traveller families here in North America (which is far beyond my own abilities and resources) might possibly double that figure of 300 words in use.

By extrapolation, as a rule, I am comfortable with the notion that, first: those sketchy collections somehow missed up to two thirds of the actual Shelta vocabulary in use toward the end of the nineteenth century (and/or Macalister pruned excessively); and, second, that American Irish Travellers have lost 80% to 90% of that flourishing Cant in the last 100 years or so. I expect that those Cant words with sounds particularly foreign to the new 'host' language, English, were the first to go, perhaps even starting long before emigration from Ireland.

I cannot stress too strongly my belief that the Cant words I know tend to validate enough of Macalister's lexicon for me to take the rest of it on faith as regards the general accuracy of its inclusions, despite probable transcription errors. At the same time, regarding its comprehensiveness, the absence or exclusion of traceable connections to the vast majority of current Cant words (which have been used here for at least 100 years to my certain knowledge) leads me to conclude that Shelta, as actually spoken in the nineteenth century, had a vocabulary far more extensive than that listed in *The Secret Languages of Ireland*.

On a personal note, in the period when Macalister published his book, I know my grandmother was still able to carry on extended conversations in Cant with her sisters that were virtually incomprehensible to even the oldest of my generation of Cant speakers and, to the best of my knowledge, she could not speak Gaelic or any language, save English and Cant.

Macalister also made much of the typically English word order, inflections and the lack of articles in contemporary Cant to cast doubt on its antiquity and even its legitimacy. The best comment I can make on that is to express a thought experiment in comparison with Gaelic. I have read that Gaelic usage was very much reduced in Ireland by the eighteenth century. I am sure that, during that period, many Irish people who used English as their principal language also mixed in with it a scattering of uninflected Gaelic words in their Irish-to-Irish communications out of respect and love for Celtic roots that had been all but destroyed by time and circumstance. If there had been no preserved Gaelic writings, if there had not been a reservoir of Gaelic speakers still spared the pervasive influence of the overlords' language, that scattering of Gaelic might have been all that remained today of the living tongue so involved with the legends and history of the Irish people. So let me ask you this: would Gaelic never have been an ancient and honourable language, were there little left of it now besides what scholars might term an "argot" or a "jargon"? No? You say it would have been ancient and honourable. Then tell me why Cant should not be considered in the same light and given the benefit of any and every doubt, at least long enough to study it thoroughly.

On second thought, perhaps I should not be so surprised that Macalister's list of Cant words is useful, even though his speculative etymology is dubious at best. The words themselves were provided by Irish Travellers; the ridiculously fanciful theories and "facts" came from others. Especially foolish was Macalister's complete acceptance of Professor Kuno Meyer's terribly complicated "rules" for converting Gaelic to Shelta. There were enough uniquely disparate and complex "rules" to convert any language on Earth to Shelta. I have a very difficult time believing that such a system could originate among a people bereft of letters, but that difficulty pales in comparison to the sheer impossibility of disseminating it nationwide among a fully dispersed people at the speed of the human stride so well and so quickly that it would generate a common tongue. Meyer's recipe for preparing Shelta is simply beyond belief, requiring a conspiracy well beyond any ever postulated by the most preposterous tabloid newspaper.

In any event, Macalister compounded his mistakes by setting aside Leland's, Sampson's and Meyer's estimate of an ancient origin for Shelta, a decision which appears to have been based primarily on its association with English syntax over the previous 150 years. Yet the Cant words for 'death' and 'priest' are known not only to have predated Christianity but to have been preserved only by Travellers, ancient words lost to the mainstream cultures of Ireland. Alice Binchy mentioned the latter word's antiquity in *Irish Travellers: Culture and Ethnicity*. If I recall correctly about 'death' (though I cannot cite the source), some years back the almost exact equivalent was found engraved over a Pictish tomb in the British Isles from the sixth century C.E. It gave me quite a chill to read that, I can tell you.

As far as inflections in Shelta are concerned, I see no reason to believe that it was ever a particularly inflected language. I can even imagine that it must have been awkward when used within a Gaelic framework. I don't speak more than a few scraps of Gaelic, but I should think that such a highly inflected language would not share its syntax with Cant very gracefully. Simpler basic English may have been much more attractive to Cant speakers than to the Country People as the use of Gaelic was repressed almost to the point of extinction. Mícheál Ó hAodha was correct in his statement that Cant and Gaelic were both savaged by repression and neglect. Any appeal English might have held for the Cant speaker, though, must have been a double-edged sword; there is little doubt that many Cant words which used Gaelic sounds difficult for English speakers would eventually have been dropped or modified beyond recognition.

Enough of the early days; turn-of-the-century Gypsylorists had no monopoly on foolishness. What about the contemporary Cant, especially in the USA?

Jared Harper conducted research during the late 1960s. On page v of the preface to his master's thesis, "Irish Traveller Cant: An Historical, Structural, And Sociolinguistic Study of an Argot", 1969, Harper claimed that he conducted "a dozen interviews" in his fieldwork in Murphy Village, SC, but actually owns up to the fact that the bulk of his data was collected from only two of the Travellers resident there. I must state at this juncture, although I mean no disrespect to my distant kin among them, that the customs and even, to a lesser degree, the dialect of the Cant in use among the villagers are different from those of many other Irish Travellers in the USA, who far outnumber them, and therefore Harper's data and conclusions should not be extended too far beyond the borders of that small village and that particular era.

I have no argument with Harper's lexicon. It is fairly extensive and phonetically accurate. But some of his assessments and conclusions are just downright wrong. Harper claims the Cant "is a road language used only between Travelers wandering the highways and byways of the land, and it is only they who know it well. ... Some road traders simply forgot Cant when they retired from road trading, when it was no longer any great use to them. ...Whether women speak Cant as well as men has not been determined" (ibid.: ch. 3). I can honestly say that, at least among the 'Northern' Irish Travellers, those contentions are not correct. The vast majority of the Cant words that I know were taught to me by my grandmother, mother and cousin, Rosemary. Rosemary is also conversant with much of the English and Scottish Cant vocabularies and has been 'off the road' for 50 years. Occasional social gatherings, close personal intra-Traveller relationships and frequent telephone use have helped to maintain the Cant in the USA.

Nor do I have any problem with the oral history of the 'Southern' Irish Travellers collected by Harper. However, I have begun to see Harper cited for his opinions on the history, origins and uses of Cant, in Ireland as well as in the USA. To the best of my knowledge, Jared Harper mentioned no original research in Ireland, and the entire portion of his thesis, papers and articles that deal with Irish matters are derivative and evidence only superficial investigation and little understanding of their sources. For example, he states that "The misnomer 'tinker' was given to the itinerants of Ireland and Britain by Charles Leland" (ibid.: 3). Really?

In another paper, co-authored with Charles Hudson, "Irish Traveller Cant: Its Evolution and Classification",[3] Harper apparently agrees with the implied cause in: "Leland says that the cohesiveness of tinker groups and the use of Shelta declined about the time the railroads came in during the 1830s." That would be a perfect example of *post hoc* reasoning if the chronology were more suitable. The first railroad in Ireland covered only a few paltry miles by the end of that decade; hardly a force to be reckoned with in Traveller circles. Yet Harper blithely ignored the previous penal laws imposed upon all the Catholic Irish by the British, their gradual easing, the mass evictions of tenants and the effects on the immense general migrant population of the time. Therefore I would not place much credence on Harper's recipe for preparing Shelta either. It seems to be a simple copy of Meyer's, with a dollop of Macalister's recent-origin theory thrown in for good measure.

Like many writers on Shelta, Harper, I believe, allowed his judgement to be clouded by his expectations and those of his intended readership. In his paper, "'Gypsy' Research in the South,"[4] he states with great assurance that "over one-hundred and twenty, or nearly half [of Cant words and sentences he collected] are in the nature of warnings and commands." By the time he wrote "Irish Traveller Cant",[5] the fraction was "over half." In the past, I have seen U.S. news articles speculating that the percentage of the Cant specifically geared towards criminal activity is 60%, a figure that I feel almost sure was loosely based on one of Harper's articles. I say that Harper and his predecessors were betrayed by their own imaginations, thinking scenarios of a very shady nature to "illustrate" the likely situations in which they thought Cant would be used by Travellers. Harper, for example, translated the Cant for "speaking" as "swearing" in one such scenario and "eat" as "bite" in another to make his point. We may test this conjecture by listing the English translations here, as given in the lexicon from Harper's master's thesis specified above, for the first three pages, as follows:

---

[3] Jared Harper and Charles Hudson, "Irish Traveller Cant: Its Evolution and Classification," *Journal of English Linguistics* 15, 1971: 78–87

[4] Harper, Jared. 1971. "'Gypsy' Research in the South". In ed. K. Moreland. *The Not so Solid South: Anthropological Studies in Regional Subculture.* Southern Anthropological Society Proceedings No. 4. Athens, GA: University of Georgia Press Press. 16–24

[5] Harper and Hudson, "Irish Traveller Cant".

town; butter; here; to come back, return; milk; to take, give, get; small, short, little; to bargain; corn; to lose one's mind, a fool; brother; woman; fifty, half; lie [in the sense of "lie down", I believe]; *fire; to get mad; stick, wood, tree...; to be sick; clothes; to lie* [tell a fib]; *Oh! Oh!* [really more like 'wacky']; *meat; tooth; face; date; flower; lazy; laugh; soft; lame; father; mouth; shoe; to sit; negro; to ask; to be afraid; bad, rotten; card, to play cards; money; to kiss.*

The prosecution rests. The remaining pages of his lexicon are similarly comprised; there would be little sense in continuing the list. Do you agree with Jared Harper in this case, or does his own lexicon make the case for Cant as a language amply suitable for social occasions and not so much for barking at accomplices?

The foregoing papers presented at the conference and now published in this volume have pretty well covered the historic and existing relationship between Shelta (and its speakers) and academia. Of course, I personally feel somewhat constrained by the consensus of American Travellers that the Cant not be made too accessible to outsiders. Yet most of that cat is already out of the bag. We have been, however, very successful here (in the USA) at preserving our language from, but not for, our younger generations of Travellers, unfortunately. So our attitudes toward writing down our language are slowly changing. I hope they will change soon enough to save and possibly even to restore it, rather than see it disappear.

An audience member expressed some doubt during this meeting that such a restoration would be possible, given the diminished state of Shelta. I have both faith and hope that sufficient research may be able to restore a flourishing Cant and even, perhaps, to cast some light on our origins. For example, Alice Binchy brought up the Shelta word *srish* meaning 'dish'. But that translation was Macalister's substitution for Greene's 'basin', so I am imagining a dish shaped like a basin, a soup bowl perhaps. (I have substituted *sh* for Macalister's palatalized *s*.) It is also listed there as *shrish*. Yes, it is obviously a partly English construct, especially when considered alongside *shrittle*, for 'kettle', and *shrug*, for 'jug. Am I trivializing the Cant when I admit this about Shelta? Not to my mind, no! Almost certainly, to my mind, the *shr* sound had been once attached to a more Gaelic syllable or syllables that may well have been components of the Irish counterparts of 'dish', 'kettle' and 'jug'. But why *shr*? Well, it is reasonably close to the Indo-European root *sreu-* 'to flow'. And this kind of pottery is used to hold and pour liquids. Consider also *shoru*, 'a wake, funeral' and *shrugu*, 'spotted, speckled'.

Does anyone else reading these words feel the stirring winds of pre-history swirling around this ancient syllable? A thousand years or more before the Milesians, the first great traveling culture came to Ireland in the form of the Beaker Folk, traders and artisans who brought tin and bronze with them and buried their dead with characteristically patterned pottery containers. There seems to be some doubt among archaeologists and physical anthropologists about whether people already native to Ireland went to Britain or the Continent to learn their ways and return or whether Beaker Folk actually travelled to Ireland to work and trade. Either way, it was the start of a noble adventure.[6]

Will further study trivialize the Cant as it has done in the past? Not if it is done well.

Where do we go from here? I hope that the still somewhat tentative forging of bonds between the worlds of scholars and Travellers in the recent past will replace the dismal relationship that so characterized the century that followed first contact. I have corresponded with some of today's scholars who take an interest in Irish Travellers and the Cant, and read the work of others. The best of them seem to be impartial intellectually and yet still partial to Travellers emotionally. Travelling People appear no less important to them than the data we generate, and there is today among scholars a moral and professional ethic in force which should help to ensure that our trust in them will be justified.

---

[6] I am indebted to Richard J. Harrison's *The Beaker Folk* (London: Thames and Hudson, 1980) and Michael J. O'Kelly *Early Ireland* (Cambridge: Cambridge University Press, 1989) for some of the foregoing information.

Sheila Stewart[1]

Cant: A Scottish Traveller's Perspective

The terms *Tinker*, *Traveller* and *Gypsy*

The term *tinker* long ago was 'a great skilful man', but over the years, the word *tinker* got so derogatory that it was terrible. Folk would say, "Oh you're just a *tinker*." It was "dirty *tinker*" this and "dirty *tinker*" that. The Travelling People themselves objected to this, because the word got so derogatory. A good few years ago an MP from Dundee and myself took it to the House of Commons to get the wording of the Race Relations Act changed from *Tinker* to *Traveller*, since we thought in my day, when I was young, that *Traveller* was a Sunday name. But we got it changed; we got the word *Tinker* taken out. Also, the Travelling People wanted to be known as *Gypsies* in Scotland because *Gypsies* were protected by the Race Relations Act. They were recognised, as if you called a *Gypsy* a *Tinker*, it was derogatory. We got *Travellers* included with *Gypsies*, for the sake of getting legal protection. And that was through the House of Commons. But it did the Travellers a lot of harm in Scotland, because people started calling us *Gypsies* or *Gypsy Travellers*.

Traveller Sites

I worked with the Secretary of State for Scotland's Advisory Committee on Travellers for a good few years. I was in at the beginning when sites came to the fore. Now, the only way out for Travelling People, other than being thrown into jail for illegal camping, was sites. There was a lot o mistakes made tae begin wi. All local authorities were goin for *permanent* sites. Travelling People never wanted *permanent* sites. They wanted *transit* sites, so they could go from place to place. But to get money from central government for transit sites was half, sometimes a quarter, of thP money they would have got for permanent sites. So local authorities, I'm sorry to say, jumped on the band wagon, applying for £500,000 to build permanent sites. Now, the Travellers didnae want this and that's why some o the sites had to close. The Travellers wouldnae go on them. That's what happened in Millerston in Glasgow. That was the start o a lot o the controversy. The Travellers didnae like the sites that was bein built because they were bein built on a wrong concept of what the Travellers wanted. The Travellers was never ever approached to ask where they wanted the sites

---

[1] This represents a part of Sheila Stewart's immediate oral response to hearing recordings of Ellen McDonagh's, Jimmy Power's and the anonymous Traveller's presentations. It was recorded and transcribed by Sheila Douglas.

to be. The only one place that was – that was the Doubledykes [at Perth]. Because I was a member of the Secretary of State's Advisory Committee, I went to the Travellers in Perth and asked them where they wanted the site, and two out of every three Travellers that I went to said they wanted one at the Doubledykes. The Doubledykes was always a stopping place for Travellers. So I went back to the Council and identified the Doubledykes, and they said, "All right, we will build one there." Long ago, the Travellers were never asked where the sites were to be. But Perth was the only one that was. St Christopher at Montrose was a site the Travelling People always camped on, just behind the distillery. So we thought, "We'll do that, we'll build one there." It was a great thing to begin with; it could still be a great project if local authorities would give more leeway to the Travellers on what they want.

My brother got a site; he had a site in Blairgowrie. It went to the planning, and we got it through. But my brother never ever got a grant to build that site. He got to build a site for Travelling People. We had a great problem, for we had about two years goin through all the government [bureaucracy], and he finally got permission to build the site, and it was a wonderful site, a great site. But, as I say, it just got out of his hands, so anybody's allowed on the site now, not just Travelling People. The Travelling People was discriminated against for so many years. Frae the beginning of time Travelling People have been discriminated against. But when the Travelling People got sites built, people was comin in sayin, "Aw, you're discriminatin against us now." So ye couldnae win. That was the difficulty.

When the sites started up in Scotland long ago, they said the only people who could organise a site and be the warden of the site was ex-police officers. Oh yes, because they were the only ones who could keep the Travelling People in about, to show authority. And I never agreed with that. I tell ye another thing I never ever agreed wi – another Traveller running a site. We never agreed wi that either. But of course it was taken out of our hands. There was more folk than me, there was two or three other Travellers that was on the Secretary of State's Advisory Committee, and we were outvoted. But the Travellers were never consulted again. It was lack of communication between local authorities and the Travelling People that caused all this problems. But if I was on a site – and I have been on many a site – I would not like an ex-policeman to be the warden.[1] But they're causing problems for themselves wi their heavy-handed approach.

It has been said that the wardens were put in to "police" the sites, but it was a wrong, wrong word that should never have been used by local authorities. Local authorities just wanted it out of their hands – pass it on to anyone at all who would take an interest and do the job. That person was responsible to the local authorities to

---

[1] Unless it would have been Jimmy McGregor, a Perthshire police officer, now retired, who had a good understanding of and fair-minded attitude to Travellers.

put in his report of what was goin on on the site. It's true, at the beginning, it was just all the ex-policemen. Oh yes. It's changed in the way that they don't need full-time wardens now. At Doubledykes you hardly ever get a warden there. At first when the sites were built, the warden was there on call – 24 hours a day, and had to be involved. But now the warden's maybe on the site only two hours a day. The site is running itself. But there was no ex-policeman as a warden *there*.

Cant

Cant is not a fluent language. We have got to use [English] joining words like *and* and *the* and *it* and *but* and aa. It's not a fluent language. Although you use these words – the folk still doesnae understand what we are saying. It serves its purpose. It's not a fluent language. It's a language that nobody would understand, even using the joining words. But Cant was never ever used to tell stories, certainly not, in my family. They might put the odd word in, but that was all. You couldnae do any more than that. Cant is a coded language.

If you go into the Underground in London, and there is aa this different Chinese and Pakistans – they are speakin their own language in front of everybody, and that to me, that's just the way they speak, and I think the folk in Scotland looks on – we would never use the Cant in front of people that could hear it. So that is out the window. Any language that people cannae understand could be looked on as suspicious. They'll say, "Oh are they talkin about me?" That's the only context you could use that. Why single out Cant to be a suspicious language? That could be taking on all the languages of the world.

In this day and age, Travellers have got more authority in their own lives as they ever had. A hundred years ago Travellers [would say] "O ye canna mang shannas to the country hantle." We thought, because we weren't educated, that the educated man was always right. An we mustn't talk back to *them*. They *must* know cause they are educated, and we are not. An they went along with it there and then, that's 100 years ago. Then in my day, I was brought up very strict. "Ye daurna mang shannas to the country hantle," because they know, because they're educated. But see now, 2001? Travelling People are not like that. They've got a mouth now of their own. They will not stand any shit off anybody. Lots of them's got education. I've got a niece that's a lawyer. My daughter is a staff nurse. My middle son is a minister. But to me they're still just Travelling People. Their identity is as Travellers. But ye cannae say they havenae fought for this. Well, *they* didnae fight very much for it, but their forebearers fought to have a mouth. They took it up, and they have a mouth now. Travelling People are more readily accepted now.

We thought a few years ago, when the New Age Travellers came out, that they were going to jump on the bandwagon of aa the wee Acts [of Parliament] that was taken oot for Travellers, aboot ye dinnae have to go to school between April an September – well that still stands today for the Travellers – and wee things like that.

We thought they were going to jump on the bandwagon and take up residence in places that the Travellers fought so hard to keep and couldn't. So that's why the sites were built, and we thought they were going to do an awful lot of damage to the Travellers. But I've heard lots of people turn round and say, "Oh, but that's not our Travellers. Our own ethnic Travellers would never do a thing like that." So actually they've done us the world of good, because it's identified our real Travellers from the New Agers.

Traveller Song Collectors

The likes of Hamish Henderson and all the people that used to come over from America and from all the different countries of the world used to stick microphones in our faces – at the time we objected, because we were never recognised before, other than round the campfire. But if it hadnae been for the likes o Hamish Henderson and all these collectors comin round – and Sheila Douglas as well – all the stuff that we knew would have been lost. They have got stuff at the School of Scottish Studies and at Sheila Douglas's home that would have *died* if it hadn't been for these collectors coming round. Which I am so grateful for. We werenae grateful at the time because – they used to come in and put a bottle of whisky on the table and say, "Well, there's a dram for you." What they didn't realise was none of us drank! Usually it would end up with the collectors drinking all the whisky themselves. So we never benefited from the collectors coming – we never got any payment; we never got any money. But in my day and age now, at my age, I think it was the most wonderful thing that ever happened in my life – the collectors getting the songs, getting the ballads, getting the stories. I will die, but I will live on through the School of Scottish Studies and through people like Sheila Douglas, cause they'll no let me die. I think it is a culture that is dying in every aspect of life, the Travelling People's culture. But the longest, furthest back things is still going to be kept alive – the ballads, the songs, the stories, the way of life long ago. An I can only tell you from my heart of the oral tradition that it was a wonderful thing the collectors came.

Len Smith[1]

English Romani Language: Some Personal Thoughts

I speak English Romanes (pronounced like *Roman-ez* or [ro'manəz]), the language of English Gypsies. "Language" because that's what I know it as, "English" because, with slight regional variations, the same language can be found among Romani Gypsies throughout the country. Interestingly, the same dialect is still spoken by the descendants of English Gypsies who migrated to America in the mid nineteenth century. The language scholars call it *poggadi jib* – "broken talk" – but those same scholars don't own it or speak it like a natural speaker. Those of us who make ourselves understood to each other by its daily use have never known it to be incomplete or "broken". It can fill each and every verbal communication need, so why shouldn't it be "whole" in our perception? If *we* see it in that light, then it is arrogant and insulting for outsider academics to impose their definition upon it with that arbitrary name, coined by nineteenth-century Gypsylorists who, in the spirit of the age, decided that quality of language bore a close parallel to the quantity of Romani blood in the speaker, which is nonsense. Some of these Gypsylorists worked with an isolated community deep in wild Wales, whom they claimed spoke a pure dialect of Romanes,[2] akin to that spoken in the Balkans, fully grammatical and inflected. Many academics still find it compelling to use Welsh Gypsies and their language as a defining baseline by which all British Gypsies are judged. Romanies across England, however, have never been convinced.

My mother always disliked the *jib* and made that forcefully clear whenever I happened to use words picked up from the old folk, so I regret very much that I didn't

---

[1] Editorial note: Len Smith was invited to write this contribution in response to a suggestion by Sinéad ní Shuinéar that he would present an English perspective on the issue of Traveller language. Unlike Richard Waters, Sheila Stewart and the anonymous contributor, he is not writing in response to the symposium tapes.

[2] John Sampson first drew the attention of scholars of Romanes to a very small number of speakers of "original" inflected and fully grammatical Romanes in the late nineteenth century. 30 years or so later, he published a dialect dictionary on the subject: *The Dialect of the Gypsies of Wales* (1926). The revelation, surrounded by secrecy as to sources, was accepted at the time with huge enthusiasm and brought plaudits for Sampson. Since then, though often quoted, it seems that there has been little in the way of critical analysis or further verification. Sampson's subjects existed – the question is whether they spoke in the way which Sampson claimed.

acquire, through use, a really early formed vocabulary. At the age of nine, when my family made the long move from Yorkshire to rural Kent, I found that the very few words of Romanes that I knew were laughed at by local Traveller kids and those we only saw seasonally, down from the London area or other places, and I soon dropped into the local way, as kids of all cultures tend to when in a minority position, I suppose. It wasn't that words were so radically different I don't think, simply my northern accent distorting pronunciation to a degree that was comical to kids. At that age, of course, I had no idea of regional variations.

Although we kids were supposed to work at the hop- and fruit-picking and usually made a token effort for an hour or two, mostly we would skive off and go swimming in the river or looking for moorhens' eggs and all the other scallywagging that kids get up to in the countryside. I was just beginning to discover girls at that age, and I remember that the East End "Gorji"[2] girls from London were far more approachable than our own. We used to mess around at chase games in the gloomy green-lit corridors of the unpicked hop gardens, chases that ended with a bit of canoodling more often than not (well, that was the idea). We boys would spread out and listen, then shout to each other in *jib* whenever we heard one running, and that way the girls had no idea how we were narrowing the chase down so quickly. So you could say that the *jib* got me my first kisses I suppose.

When I was in my late teens I made a major move again, to the New Forest in Hampshire, southern England, where I have lived ever since, and again I had to adjust my speech slightly to fit in, though by then I had lost much of the northern overlay to my Romanes. I would guess that my vocabulary filled out much more from that time, too. Local speakers seemed to have more Romanes sounding words and less London-ish slang mixed in. Other than that, I do not lean toward the opinion of scholars who insist that regional differences are very marked.

Since then, but regrettably less so in recent years, I have used our *jib* to communicate in every possible situation, mostly at times when it was an advantage to do so: perhaps to discuss the various options or merits privately in the course of a business deal with non-Romanis or when we might be overheard by a keeper on "the right nights". Warnings muttered in Romanes that one of us had seen a light or heard a noise gave us the advantage. Although they might hear the talk, listeners were unaware that we were on to them, giving us a few precious seconds to begin slipping away.

One such comical episode when the *jib* came into good use sticks in my mind to this day. It was a year when berried holly was in very short supply. I was making Christmas wreaths that year, working as a partner of my uncle, and we had spotted a holly tree, small but well-covered with berries, standing on the open forest. The wreaths we had been making up to then hadn't been selling too well because of the

---

[2] For *gorji* 'non-Romanes', I have used the spelling as it is spoken in my region.

lack of berries, so we decided we would have this bit to help out. I guess others had seen it, as it wasn't very far from the road. Not only other Travellers, but the forest keepers too, must have known of it, but no one had dared to take it. We went for it one night, parking our little truck some way down the road out of sight and carrying a bushman saw. At Christmas, the forest keepers are on the watch for Christmas tree "rustlers" and have plenty of patrols out. One must have been watching that particular tree of holly. No sooner had we got the bush cut down, tying the branches in tight to make it easier to carry, than we nearly jumped out of our skins at the sound of someone singing very loudly out on the road. The voice was singing, in Romanes, "I'm a Romani Rai", an old song that anyone who was familiar with local pubs would have heard many times and wouldn't have thought particularly remarkable. He wasn't singing the right words, though, but telling anyone who could hear that there were keepers waiting by the road! It turned out later to be a Gypsy man who was biking home from the pub and half guessed what was going on when he saw the patrol crouching behind a hedge. His warning gave us enough time to pick up the bundle of holly and walk quietly away in a different direction, taking a much longer route back to the truck.

Like others, I have had a few words used against me – or perhaps the user *thought* they were using them against me to rile me. A policeman once told me in Romanes that my horse was a mother. (I think he meant my mother was a horse, but that wasn't what he said!) Frequently those in authority will say something like: "No good talking that *kakker rap*[3] here, we have experts who have studied it." Of course, they may have, though it's never likely, and it's a racing certainty that, even if they had, they would never understand spoken Romanes, as I found out on one rather harrowing occasion. Myself and two other men, all of us with the same name, had been arrested and were being held in police cells. Two of us were together, with the third in a different cell. My conversation with my companion (obviously in Romanes) was secretly recorded, and assessed by an "expert". I found out later, after complaining, that the police knew we two had no involvement in the serious crime that they were investigating, but hoped that we might know of it and incriminate their suspect, the third Len Smith. The tape was played back to me later at an interview, and the "expert" rendition of it was so different to what I had actually said that I had almost been incriminated on the basis of deductions that the expert made where he hadn't understood properly. (I never found out who this expert was.) I might add that the third man was also innocent, and the real culprits were caught later.

There is a vast difference between Romanes written or spoken by a non-native speaker and the 'real thing'. The non speaker will translate into Romanes by inserting a few Romanes words into an English sentence, sort of like this (square brackets

---

[3] *Kakker* is a local nickname for a Gypsy, derived from frequently hearing this used as a word for 'no'.

indicate where Romanes words would be): "There is a [man] [coming] through the [gate]" whereas a natural speaker would simply say, "[Gate]", slight pause, "[man coming]". The pause would draw attention to the focus of the sentence, the gate, and the next words would tell the story. Short sentences such as this are spoken so quickly that the words almost blur into each other, and can *only* be picked up by an ear trained over years. So by reverse inference, without the English as a guide, the non-native speaker seldom understands spoken Romanes when those using it are trying to keep their message private. Speech is free and easy at other times, when English and Romanes might freely interchange and mix at the speaker's whim. And then there is the Romanes "staged" for a researcher, or for such things as church services,[4] both of which have obvious artificialities that have to be contended with.

One *Gorji* man who really did learn to speak natural Romanes was Captain Frank Tooby, the last of the Church Army's[5] missioners to the Gypsies of the New Forest. Captain Tooby was much loved and revered. An additional duty was as a prison visitor to Winchester Prison, and that often brought him into contact with Romani men serving sentences or on remand. It was a great comfort to men locked up like that to have the Captain to talk to with a bit of Romanes, thus distracting them for a moment from their situation. I visited the old man, then in his nineties. He could still *"pukker* the *jib"* even then, and sing hymns in it too, translated by himself. I was struck by how authentically he spoke, with so little English inserted. Some *written* material that I have in his handwriting is just like speech in its form, which is extremely unusual.

I have been in a house now for about 25 years, and, although that hasn't cut me off from friends and family, it has still curtailed the amount of opportunities to speak Romanes, simply from living where I do – close to the coast, on a road that leads more or less only to the beaches, which means I get little in the way of passing casual callers. Fortunately, I have a Romani neighbour just two doors away, and we spend the summer evenings and weekends just chewing the fat and exercising little more than our *"jib* muscles" and our right arms. Romani families in this area often go

---

[4] In view of my comments above, it will be seen that to make Romanes comprehensible to the naïve ear, much English has to be inserted between Romanes words. With church services, the religious language, if it is to be translated, calls for compounding of common words to have a different overall meaning. With large numbers of English Romanies now embracing the "born again" Christian movement, partly because of an increased sense of "inclusion" when Romanes is used in services, this is becoming an increasingly significant area of development.

[5] The Church Army is a body similar to the Salvation Army but under the wing of the Church of England. In the 1890s they began horse-drawn van missions to the Gypsies of England which carried on until just before the Second World War. After the war, motor vans were used until the missions ceased. In my area this was in the late 1950s.

visiting on Sunday afternoons, and I've known as many as ten men to gather on such an afternoon, with the women gassing away together and us men talking just as fast, and just as gossipy, using Romanes for the sheer pleasure of it. It's fun, and I hope instructive, when his grandkids or mine, or the visiting kids, ask for explanations of words unknown to them, and a pleasure indeed later to hear those same words used in real communication.